P9-EKH-846

THE HUNT FOR NAZI SPIES

THE HUNT FOR NAZI SPIES

Fighting Espionage in Vichy France

SIMON KITSON

Translated by Catherine Tihanyi

The University of Chicago Press
Chicago and London

Simon Kitson is a senior lecturer of French studies at the University of Birmingham.

Catherine Tihanyi is a translator and research associate at Western Washington University.

The University of Chicago Press, Chicago 60637
The University of Chicago Press, Ltd., London

Printed in the United States of America

17 16 15 14 13 12 11 10 09 08 1 2 3 4 5

ISBN-13: 978-0-226-43893-1 (cloth)

ISBN-10: 0-226-43893-7 (cloth)

Originally published as *Vichy et la chasse aux espions nazis,* © 2005 by Éditions Autrement.
Published with the support of the National Center for the Book—French Ministry of Culture.
Ouvrage publié avec le soutien du Centre national du livre—ministère français chargé de la culture.

Library of Congress Cataloging-in-Publication Data
Kitson, Simon.
[Vichy et la chasse aux espions nazis. English]
The hunt for Nazi spies : fighting espionage in Vichy France / Simon Kitson ; Translated by Catherine Tihanyi.
p. cm.
Includes bibliographical references and index.
ISBN-13: 978-0-226-43893-1 (cloth : alk. paper)
ISBN-10: 0-226-43893-7 (cloth : alk. paper) 1. World War, 1939–1945—Collaborationists—France. 2. World War, 1939–1945—Secret service—France. 3. World War, 1939–1945—Secret service—Germany. 4. Espionage, German—France—History—20th century. 5. Spies—Germany—History—20th century. 6. France—History—German occupation, 1940–1945. I. Title.
D802.F8K5213 2007
940.54'8644—dc22

2007019790

♾ The paper used in this publication meets the minimum requirements of the American National Standard for Information Sciences—Permanence of Paper for Printed Library Materials, ANSI Z39.48-1992.

CONTENTS

PREFACE TO THE ENGLISH LANGUAGE EDITION

This book is the product of international cooperation. Originally written in French by a Briton, it was translated into English by a French woman, and is now published by an American publisher. Such an international dimension is highly appropriate given the thematic content of the book, which analyzes Franco-German and, to a much lesser extent, Franco-British and Franco-American relations.

Many modifications have been made to the French version, which came out as *Vichy et la chasse aux espions Nazis* (2005), in the process of creating this English translation, modifications inspired by a combination of several factors. Inevitably some changes occurred because of the difference of writing French history for an Anglophone public as opposed to writing it for a French public. Some points needed greater explanation, since most of the readers of this translation will be outsiders to this history—I only hope that specialists on Vichy France will be patient with me where I give explanations aimed at a wider, nonspecialist public. On the other hand, certain minor details in the original were judged superfluous in English and so have been dropped: street names in French towns that might have a local interest for a French public have generally been left out here. Given how much research went into the original book, I had the luxury of having lots of unused material. This put me in a position to bring in new examples for many of the points made. I seized on this because I wanted the English language version to be fresh and to offer something new to those who had already read the French. Other changes were imposed on the text as a response to reactions to the first version of the book. When the original manuscript came out it was widely reviewed in both popular and academic publications, and I was flattered to see how favorable these reviews generally were. There were, however, one or two remarks in a couple of the reviews that suggested to me that a few elements of my original argument had been slightly misinterpreted, and I wanted to make those points more clearly here.

After the book was published in French, I was contacted by various people who had read the text. These included former Resisters who wanted to offer me supplementary material, some of which is included in this new version. Former members of the secret services or their relatives also contacted me, generally appalled that I had presented the secret services as toeing an essentially pro-Vichy line. Historians can do one of two things when faced with such criticism: they can ignore it and claim that those offended are just being oversensitive or they can think carefully about which critical aspects to incorporate into future work. I chose the latter path, but this does not mean that I have adopted these criticisms blindly. I have eliminated a few passages that offended by being clumsily phrased in the original, and in some places I have changed various nuances where I think the criticisms were founded. I have also added new passages on the dangers faced by the secret services, since almost as soon as the original book was published, I regretted that I had not offered more on that angle. However, I have not changed my overall argumentation. In fact I have added in new material that I believe reinforces that argument, including recently released and previously unused material about the suspected involvement of counterespionage chief Paul Paillole in a plot to help Vichy head of state Marshal Pétain escape from France at the end of 1943. The decision to stick with my original argument is not just stubbornness. I did listen to the criticisms from secret service quarters, but I also looked back over my documentary material, engaged in some supplementary research on particular points, and consulted many other specialists in the field. All of this confirmed my belief that the original argument was founded—it had after all been based on a mass of archival research from various sources.

As I made clear in the original, what is offered here is just one interpretation of that mass of documentation. Others are free to offer alternative interpretations. Should the secret service community feel aggrieved, they are of course at liberty to publish their own version of these same events. I note that after initially criticizing my interpretation, the secret service veterans' association now lists my book on their Web site, without commentary, as one of the references on the subject—I hope this means that, whatever differences of interpretation we may have, they recognize that I was not setting out to attack them or to present an account that was unfavorable to them. As I said in the introduction of the original text, my intention was always to open up this new area of research for discussion. I hope other historians will rise to the challenge.

Birmingham, December 2006

ACKNOWLEDGMENTS

This book owes much to the Institut d'Histoire du Temps Present (IHTP) in Paris. During the 2000–2001 academic year, I worked there as an associate researcher. I will never forget the welcome the whole IHTP team gave me, and I wish to particularly thank Henry Rousso, Fabrice Virgili, Danièle Voldman, and Pieter Lagrou. For their excellent advice on all issues related to bibliography, Anne-Marie Pathé and Jean Astruc are to be especially praised. I am also indebted to the Arts and Humanities Research Board for providing me with financial support. At the publisher Autrement in Paris, I want to particularly mention the help of Chloé Pathé, daughter of Anne-Marie, who negotiated the English translation. At the University of Chicago Press I am very grateful to Robert Devens, who not only guided me expertly through the publication process but also gave me good tips when I visited Chicago. I am also thankful for the expert and friendly guidance provided by Mara Naselli, Megan Marz, and Elizabeth Branch Dyson. The initial English translation was done by Catherine Tihanyi.

A huge debt is owed to Sébastien Laurent and to Olivier Forcade, who went well beyond the call of duty: reading the French manuscript thoroughly, giving me the benefit of their precious advice, and defending the published text. They are in the vanguard of an excellent new group of French scholars working on related themes. Among the many researchers who helped me at various stages, in various ways and to varying degrees, I wish to acknowledge Martin Alexander, Nick Atkin, Jean-Marc Berlière, Brett Bowles, Luc Capdevilla, Jackie Clarke, Hanna Diamond, Sarah Fishman, Shannon Fogg, Robert Frank, Robert Gildea, Jean-Marie Guillon, Cécile Hochard, Julian Jackson, Colin Jones, Dominique Kalifa, Carole Lécuyer, René Lévy, Lori Maguire, Robert Mencherini, Denis Peschanski, Becky Pulju, François Rouquet, Nicolas Roussellier, Julian Swann, John F. Sweets, Barbara Trimbur, Joan Tumblety, Karine Varley, Richard Vinen, and Olivier Wieviorka. Special thanks are owed Talbot Imlay, Martin Thomas, and Peter Jackson who have been a constant source of encouragement since my beginnings as a historian. For being a first class colleague I should like to express my gratitude to Martyn Cornick. My fascination with history was fueled by the expert guidance of Rod Kedward, as well as by my thesis examiners Clive Emsley and Mark Mazower. I want also to draw attention to the early influence of Graham Gargett of the University of Ulster, since I don't think I've ever thanked him enough.

Thanks also to the late Paul Paillole and to Jean Gemähling for the interviews they granted me. Following the French publication of this book, Colette Bloch generously made me aware of the memoirs of her late husband and reference is made to these in this text.

On a personal level I also want to acknowledge my family: my late grandmother Lilian Gladys Bishop Roberts; Ann and John Salmon; Deborah and Grant Nicholas; Nicci, Saskia, William, Freya, and Timmy Tedder; Jem Kitson; Neil Kitson; my late aunt Pam Kitson; and Jennie, Sam, and Simon Borrel. For friendship and influence over the years: Mark, Helen, and Christopher Ledbury; Mark, Cathou, Jeannne, and Lucie Mehta; Dave and Fionulla Lester; Andy and Jane Lowe; Jackie Rodger; Suzie Thomas; Véronique Bouvet; Richard Parker; Arnaud Cristen; Françoise Petit; and Jacqueline Djian. In Birmingham I should like to send warm thanks to Francesca Carnevale, Helen Laville, Graeme Murdock, and Deborah Parsons. An extra special thank you is owed Kate Brookson-Morris.

This book is dedicated to my goddaughter Jeanne Mehta and my godson Timmy Tedder.

GLOSSARY AND ABBREVIATIONS

Abwehr (Defense): German military intelligence service under the command of Admiral Wilhelm Canaris.

BCC, Bureau de Coordination de Casablanca (Casablanca Coordination Bureau): Vichy French counterespionage service in Morocco.

BCRA, Bureau Central de Renseignement et d'Action (Central Bureau for Intelligence and Action): An intelligence gathering organization working for de Gaulle's Free French Resistance movement.

BMA, Bureau(x) des Menées Antinationales (Bureau for Anti-National Affairs): The name given to the army's counterespionage bureaus after the 1940 armistice. Its national chief was Lieutenant Colonel Guy d'Alès. The BMA worked for the Vichy government gathering information about the spying activities of the Germans and the Allies. Under German pressure it was scrapped in August 1942, but was secretly replaced by the SSM.

CIG, Centre d'Information Gouvernementale (Governmental Information Center): A bureau created by François Darlan in the summer of 1941 and directed by General Roux to coordinate the activities of the special services.

Cinquième Bureau (Fifth Bureau): The French counterespionage services between September 1939 and summer 1940.

After the armistice the Cinquième Bureau was divided up into the BMA and TR.

Collaborationist: Historians of wartime France generally make a distinction between the terms "collaborator" and "collaborationist." Both categories sought collaboration with Germany but varied in their degree of attachment to the German cause, with the collaborationists being more wholehearted. "Collaborationist" is used in this book to mean the radicalized, pro-Fascist groupings, such as the PPF, that were often based in Paris and prepared to engage in a full-scale collaboration with Germany. These collaborationists were rivals for power with the Vichy government, although there was some overlap in ideology and even sometimes personnel.

Deuxième Bureau (Second Bureau): Intelligence bureau of the chiefs of staff of the French armed forces. This term is often mistakenly used to describe the entire intelligence/counterespionage apparatus, but the Deuxième Bureau was just one component. It was an essentially office-bound service whose role was to centralize and analyze intelligence derived from other sources.

D Measure: French secret service euphemism for the killing of spies without trial.

Gestapo, Geheime Staatspolizei (Secret State Police): A fearsome German counterintelligence service that formed one of the bureaus of the Sipo-SD. The term "Gestapo" is sometimes wrongly used to describe all the secret police formations of the Nazi state.

IS, Intelligence Service: British espionage agency that remained active in France after the armistice of 1940.

LVF, Légion des Volontaires Français Contre le Bolchevisme (Legion of French Volunteers against Bolshevism): A collaborationist organization set up in July 1941 to recruit anti-Communist volunteers to fight alongside the Germans on the eastern front.

PPF, Parti Populaire Français: Extreme right-wing organization founded in 1936 and led by Jacques Doriot. It provided many recruits for the German secret services during the Vichy period. It was more extreme in its attachment to collaboration with the Axis than the Vichy government.

Prefect: The most senior administrator of the French state at the local level.

RSHA, Reichssicherheitshauptampt (Supreme Office for the Security of the Reich): First headed by SS Obergruppenführer Reinhard Heydrich and then, after his assassination, by SS Obergruppenführer Ernst Kaltenbrunner, the RSHA was an umbrella organization of the various parallel police agencies established by the Nazi Party.

SD, Sicherheitsdienst (Security Office): The SS intelligence service attached to the Sipo, or security police.

Sipo, Sicherheitspolizei (Security Police): A German political police under the Nazis; the infamous Gestapo was one of its bureaus.

SS, Schutzstaffeln: Initially the black-shirted militia assigned as Hitler's personal body guard, the SS expanded into a parallel army organizing elite divisions within the armed forces.

SSD, Section de Surveillance et de Documentation (Surveillance and Documentation Section): The naval counterespionage service established after the defeat.

SSM, Service de Sécurité Militaire (Military Security Service): The counterespionage organization established by Vichy in August 1942 to replace the BMA. It was entrusted to the command of Commandant Paul Paillole. The SSM broke off contact with Vichy after the German invasion of southern France in November 1942.

ST, Surveillance du Territoire (Territorial Surveillance): The counterespionage branch of the French police that organized the arrest of Axis and Allied agents. The ST was effectively abolished after the German invasion of southern France in November 1942.

TR, Travaux Ruraux (Rural Works): A secret Vichy counterespionage network set up from the remnants of the Cinquième Bureau after the 1940 defeat. Its headquarters were located in Marseille (under the code name "Cambronne"), but it also had regional branches. The service was headed by Commandant Paul Paillole and worked essentially against the Germans, although it also collected information on the Allies.

Vichy: The political regime established in France after the armistice of June 1940. It was based in the spa town of Vichy in southern France, which remained unoccupied until November 1942. Vichy's foreign policy was built on collaboration with the Germans. In terms of domestic policy it pursued a reactionary program of conservative measures known as the National Revolution. This involved a return to traditional, catholic, and rural values, a rejection of democracy and a cracking down on forces seen as the "Anti-France"—Jews, Communists, foreigners, left-wingers. Head of state under Vichy was Marshal Philippe Pétain; Pierre Laval and François Darlan acted as its premiers.

Wehrmacht: The German armed forces under the Nazis.

CHRONOLOGY OF WORLD WAR II FRANCE

3 September 1939	Britain and France declare war on Germany
10 May 1940	Germany launches offensive against France
16 May 1940	Marshal Pétain is named deputy prime minister
14 June 1940	The French government flees from Paris to Bordeaux
17 June 1940	Pétain publicly calls for an armistice
18 June 1940	De Gaulle makes a BBC broadcast calling for continued Resistance
22 June 1940	Franco-German armistice signed
25 June 1940	Franco-Italian armistice signed
2 July 1940	Pétain's government moves to Vichy
3 July 1940	The British sink part of the French fleet at Mers-el-Kébir in Algeria
10 July 1940	The National Assembly grants full powers to Pétain
2 August 1940	Vichy sentences de Gaulle to death in absentia
26 August 1940	The French colony of Chad rallies de Gaulle

27 August 1940	Cameroon rallies de Gaulle
28 August 1940	The Congo rallies de Gaulle
23–25 September 1940	Failed Gaullist attack on Vichy-held Dakar
3 October 1940	Vichy issues a Jewish statute, limiting the rights of Jews
4 October 1940	Law allows for the arrest of foreign Jews
12 October 1940	German failure in Battle of Britain
24 October 1940	Pétain meets Hitler at Montoire, near Tours
30 October 1940	Pétain declares his intention to enter the path of collaboration
16 November 1940	Germans expel 70,000 Lorrainers from north-east France
13 December 1940	Pétain sacks Pierre Laval
25 December 1940	Darlan meets with Hitler near Beauvais
29 March 1941	Vichy creates a commission for Jewish affairs
27–28 May 1941	Darlan signs Paris Protocols, designed to reinforce collaboration
2 June 1941	Vichy issues a second Jewish statute, further limiting the rights of Jews
22 June 1941	Operation Barbarossa (German invasion of Soviet Union)
July 1941	Creation of Légion des Volontaires Français contre le Bolshevisme (LVF)
12 August 1941	Pétain issues a radio broadcast admitting his government's unpopularity
4 September 1941	LVF leaves to fight Russians on eastern front
16 November 1941	Germans obtain Weygand's dismissal from North Africa
1 December 1941	Pétain meets Göring at St-Florentin
7 December 1941	Japanese attack Pearl Harbor
27 March 1942	First deportations of Jews
18 April 1942	Laval is recalled as head of government
22 June 1942	Laval publicly states his wish for a German victory
August 1942	Vichy organizes round-up of Jews for deportation in southern zone

8 November 1942	Allies invade French North Africa
11 November 1942	Germans invade previously unoccupied zone of southern France
27 November 1942	French sabotage the remains of their fleet at Toulon, and Vichy's army is abolished
30 January 1943	Vichy creates its black-shirted Milice (militia)
2 February 1943	German capitulation at Stalingrad
16 February 1943	Forced Labor Draft (STO) is introduced
13 November 1943	Pétain temporarily withdraws from his duties
1 January 1944	remodeling of Vichy government to include more overt Fascists
6 June 1944	Allied landings in Normandy
20 August 1944	Germans oblige Pétain to leave for Germany
25 August 1944	Liberation of Paris

Map 1. France's départements

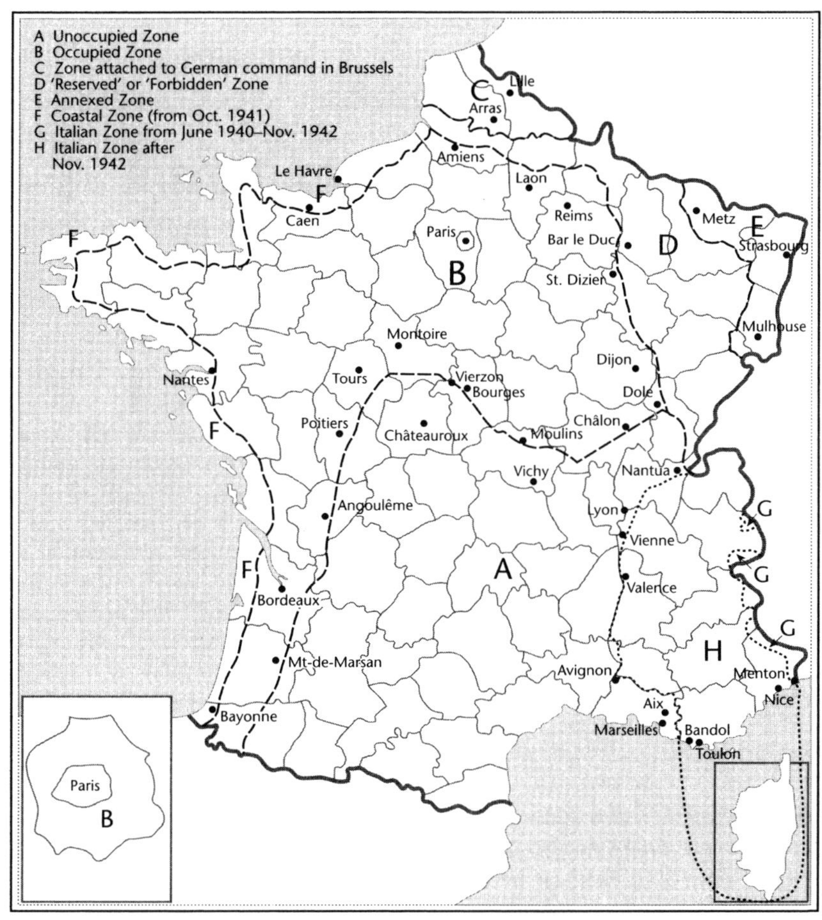

Map 2. Zones of occupation in France

INTRODUCTION

Anti-German counterespionage in France under the collaborating Vichy regime is a topic I began working on in 1997. In the course of a previous research project I stumbled on some documents concerned with police torture. Now, that in itself was not unusual. I had been researching the police long enough to be familiar with many forms of police violence. What was unusual about these particular documents was that the individuals being tortured were agents of the Abwehr or the Gestapo. In other words, the counterespionage services of the police of a collaborating state were brutalizing Nazi spies. This captured my imagination and I began to look more closely at the theme.

I discovered that this particular anti-German activity was paradoxically both well known *and* completely unknown to historians. It cannot be said that all specialists of the period of the German occupation of France are aware of the fact that the Vichy secret services continued to operate against their occupiers and to arrest Axis spies, but it is certainly the case that a number of authors, drawn from a wide range of perspectives, do make reference to this activity.[1] However, their references are seldom more than passing acknowledgements; very few authors devote more than a paragraph to this theme.[2] Even those who do have focused almost exclusively on the numerous sets of memoirs or oral testimony by former secret service personnel, in particular that of Commandant Paul Paillole, the wartime head of one of the military counterespionage services who died recently in his midnineties. Little attempt has hitherto been made to challenge the validity of these sources or to place anti-German counterespionage in its wartime political context.

Why this lack of research? Here three elements came into play, all of which were raised frequently by historians who tried to dissuade me from working on this topic, suggesting that I'd get little joy from it, or even that "it should be left to military historians." Firstly, there is an assumption among scholars that that archives would be impossible to find on this subject. The very notion of secret services obviously implies secrecy—surely there would be little written material, and what might be there would not be consultable. Secondly, many of these historians fail to comprehend and therefore dismiss the potential importance of this theme. Is it not normal that governments should arrest the spies of other nations? the skeptics ask. Why bother studying simple continuities? Thirdly, there is a factor linked to the political position of the Vichy regime. It is well known that this regime, led by Marshal Philippe Pétain, collaborated with the Germans. It organized the arrest, sometimes even the execution, of Resisters. It eventually helped the Germans round up workers for their forced-labor draft and agreed to become an active participant in the arrest of Jews to be deported for mass murder. The historian who undertakes research on anti-German aspects of Vichy policies runs the risk of being labeled an apologist for a regime capable of such atrocities. For many, Vichy's collaboration renders any sustained anti-German activity on the regime's part almost inconceivable and not worthy of investigation. Many assume, therefore, that this activity must have been carried out independently by secret services acting on their own initiative. This argument is bolstered by the memoirs of former secret service personnel, who understandably enough, have sought to distance themselves from damaging associations with a government disgraced through collaboration. There is also an instinctive feeling amongst nonspecialists that secret service activity is always somewhat maverick and divorced from the government, restricting political interest in the subject and consigning it to a more marginal institutional history of the French secret services.

It is true that at first sight, the study of secret services might appear difficult because of a lack of documentation. Most studies of this kind begin with institutionally controlled sources: memoirs and collections of archives assembled by members of the secret services. About fifteen such memoirs have been published since the war, most between 1967 and 1979.[3] The problem with such a source is that the intentions of their authors are not necessarily innocent. They seek to glorify their own role and to sing the praises of their institution. A similar problem of bias is evident in the collections of archives assembled by former members of these services such as the Fonds Paillole (Paillole collection). It is significant that these private collections are almost exclusively concerned with the anti-German aspect of their activities. They have been purged of virtually all references to secret service action against the Allies and the Resistance, thereby making it difficult to see them as a balanced source. This is not to say that these collections are not useful, but simply that they must be handled with care.

Fortunately, with the arrival of the Fonds de Moscou (Moscow collection) in the 1990s—three tons of archives recently repatriated from the former Soviet Union—historians now have a robust resource with which to reexamine espionage during the war. The 1400 boxes in this series are Vichy's military counterespionage records that were seized by the Germans at the beginning of 1943. They were transported east to be analyzed by German intelligence agencies, but by the end of the war they were commandeered by the advancing Soviet armies and sent back to Moscow. It was only in the mid-1990s that the collection was returned to France.[4] These documents are now available within the army archives known as the Service Historique de l'Armée de Terre (SHAT) at the chateau of Vincennes. The collection is something of a goldmine. In addition to individual dossiers for many of those suspected of espionage, it contains ministerial instructions as well as the training sessions of the secret services themselves. That these training sessions were so precisely recorded might appear strange, but in twentieth-century France the secret services had become obsessed with keeping a written record of their activity. Beyond the practical uses this might have, it is also sometimes hard to escape the conclusion that they were striving to be taken seriously as an administration and that the most obvious determinant of an administration's success is how much bureaucracy it creates.

My interest in this topic was actually concerned less with the institutional history of French counterespionage agencies than with the political and social aspects of the question. I wanted to know who these German spies were and how they were treated by the French once caught. I wanted to know how this fit into the political philosophy of the Vichy government—what does this tell us about the contours of collaboration and the nature of Franco-German relations? Such questions require the historian to use more imagination in the quest for documents. To find answers, I had to look beyond the archives simply generated by the secret services. It occurred to me that any arrested spies would be imprisoned and perhaps tried, so I began looking for documents relating the procedures against them. Particularly important in this regard were the files of the commissions of appeal where condemned spies would plead for clemency from either the head of state[5] or the minister of justice.[6] Surely enough, this search rapidly revealed large stocks of individual dossiers. If the government was genuinely involved in the process of counterespionage, then surely at some level correspondence between ministers must have left a trace. In the archives of Philippe Pétain, the prime minister's office, and the Ministry of the Interior, I unearthed unexpectedly rich documentation related to this question.[7] Since most Vichy ministers faced trial after the liberation of France in 1944, anti-German counterespionage may have been useful in their defense, or conversely that failures in this area may have been leveled against them by their accusers. The question was raised in all eight of the High Court of Justice trials of former Vichy ministers that I consulted.[8] Finally it occurred to me that arresting German spies in a country partially occupied by the Germans must surely have led to diplomatic incidents, and that these would be recorded in the files of the French delegation to the Armistice Commission.[9] This proved to be another rich source. Not only did it reveal large numbers of German complaints on the subject, but the French delegation files also contained another collection of individual dossiers as well as a large selection of letters written by the arrested spies themselves from their Vichy prison cells.

Surprisingly my problem with regard to archives was not that I did not have enough but rather that there were far too many. Although this allowed me to juxtapose documents from different origins on most of the key issues involved, there inevitably remained one or two gaps, where I either had to speculate from the material available or more frequently admit that I could not answer a particular question, as will be made clear in the text that follows.

So archives were not a real problem. What about the second deterrent to research on this topic—the idea that German espionage against France and French counterespionage against Germany were just simple continuities, unworthy of study? First, the idea that something should not be studied just because it is likely to be a simple continuity is in itself rather a scandalous concept of history. Changes are obviously what distinguish one historical period from another, but there is usually a backdrop of continuity behind such changes. Ignore this and you do not get the full picture by which to judge the changes. Moreover, the relativity of changed circumstance actually bestows on the continuities themselves a changed status, so that even continuities are in constant fluctuation. For instance, the arrest of German spies might have followed exactly the same process before and after the occupation of France. But the simple fact that it was then taking place in a changed context modifies its political significance: arresting German spies after occupation was certainly more difficult and hazardous than it had been before.

Having defended the study of continuities, I will now say there were important changes in German espionage against France and French counterespionage against Germany during the years 1940–42. Changes occurred in terms of the scale of operations, with a massive increase in German espionage against France *after* the French defeat of 1940 and a corresponding increase in the number of secret agents arrested by the French. The reasons for these changes of scale will become apparent in the chapters that follow. It should also be noted that the simple fact of arresting spies involved a decision-making process that cannot be attributed to simple continuities. In article 10 of the armistice, the Vichy government had signed up to a clause that explicitly forbade any part of its army from engaging in any form of anti-German activity. The Vichy government was fully aware that its counterespionage activity was in breach of the terms of the armistice it had signed in 1940 in the immediate wake of the rapid defeat of the French army by the Germans.

This suggestion that the Vichy government was aware that its secret services were active against the Germans brings us onto the third point. Anti-German counterespionage cannot be ascribed, as it always has been, to a largely autonomous activity on the part of the secret services. Although the technical day-to-day operation of the counterespionage services might have been a law unto itself, the actual process of arresting and punishing German spies was certainly not in opposition to the wishes of the Vichy government.

This poses a problem with regard to the political stance of this regime.

Not only is Vichy's collaboration now firmly established as an element of its policies, but since the work of historians such as Eberhardt Jäckel and Robert Paxton it is widely acknowledged that it was Vichy and *not* the Germans who most actively sought collaboration.[10] As Paxton has underlined for this period, "Collaboration was not a German demand. . . . collaboration was a French proposal."[11] What conclusion can we draw then from the continuation of anti-German counterespionage under Vichy? Should we throw out all the historiography of the last thirty years suggesting that Vichy collaborated sincerely, and start believing that in sponsoring this clandestine anti-German activity it was actually revealing its true colors as a government of Resistance? When the question of this policy is contextualized within the wider framework of Vichy strategy, the answer is an unequivocal no, and it becomes apparent that there is no need to challenge the idea of the sincerity of Vichy's collaboration. Rather what was happening here was that the French government was caught between the often-conflicting desires of asserting its own independence from the Germans whilst still promoting a policy of active cooperation. These conflicts explain why Vichy's behavior in the domain of counterespionage oscillated between firmness and compromise.

In this research I have attempted to reinsert this counterespionage activity into its original context by, among other things, looking at the relation between the activities of the counterespionage services and the government of the time. In spatial terms, the analysis will be concerned primarily with the nonoccupied territories, that is, the "free" zone and the French colonies (essentially North Africa) that were not immediately occupied by the Germans, since it was essentially only there that the arrest of German spies occurred. In chronological terms, it is mostly the period from the June 1940 armistice to the November 1942 German invasion of the previously "free" zone that will be dealt with because these arrests came to an abrupt stop with the total occupation. What should become apparent in the pages that follow is that counterespionage under Vichy was a complex and often surprising phenomenon.

1 ORGANIZING GERMAN ESPIONAGE

In his famous *Mein Kampf,* first published in 1925, Adolf Hitler was scathing in his comments about France. As a racist he believed the French were inferior to what he saw as the "Aryan" master race of Nordic stock. Moreover, he described France as contaminated by its colonial contacts with the peoples of Africa: "France is racially becoming more and more Negroid, so much so that now one can actually speak of the creation of an African State on European soil." He was particularly critical of French foreign policy, writing of "France's unbridled lust after hegemony." It was not just that France, as he saw it, was trying to dominate Europe. More importantly she was trying to crush Germany: "Finally we must be quite clear on the following point: France is and will remain the implacable enemy of Germany. It does not matter what Governments have ruled or will rule in France, whether Bourbon or Jacobin, Napoleonic or Bourgeois-Democratic, Clerical Republican or Red Bolshevik, their foreign policy will always be directed towards acquiring possession of the Rhine frontier and consolidating France's position on this river by disuniting and dismembering Germany."[1]

To understand the objectives of the German secret services in France, we need first to look briefly at the general framework of Nazi policy in the country, a policy that naturally shared some of Hitler's conceptions.[2]

In 1940 the Nazis were looking to erase the humiliation of their 1918 defeat. They wanted revenge for France's attitude at the 1919 Treaty of Versailles, where Prime Minister Georges Clemenceau had been the firmest in pressing for harsh terms against Germany. Of the Western powers, France was also most insistent during the interwar period on their strict application. In January 1923, after Germany had failed to meet the reparations payments it was required to make by the terms of Versailles, the French briefly invaded the Ruhr area of Germany.

In such circumstances, it might seem surprising that the Germans were initially moderate in the immediate aftermath of their crushing victory of 1940. Military leaders ordered their soldiers to behave in a "correct" manner and propaganda posters showed German soldiers caring for the abandoned population of northern France. In some respects, the Franco-German armistice signed on 22 June was lenient. The military clauses were in keeping with patterns established by previous treaties. There were no permanent territorial demands; the integrity of the French empire was respected; a part of France remained under a sovereign government; the fleet was not confiscated.

Of course, this relative moderation was a tactic. At that time the Nazis had other concerns. They were still at war with the British and wanted to see them off quickly so that Hitler could turn his war machine against his most natural ideological enemy, Soviet Russia. Knocking Britain out of the war would be easier if France was fully neutralized. This meant making sure that any French desire to continue fighting was thwarted. A relatively moderate armistice would, it was hoped, ensure that the legal government of France did not leave the mainland to pursue the war in its colonies, and would avoid giving the French fleet an incentive to join forces with the British. There was also a more diplomatic calculation at play. Hitler wanted to show the British they need not fear a brutal armistice so that he could eventually convince them to sign a similar document rather than continue in what seemed like a hopeless battle. If Britain could not be persuaded to reach terms, Hitler hoped to use France as a launching pad for Operation Sealion (the invasion of Great Britain). For this, a pacified France was required.

Despite this deliberate tactic of moderation, the Nazis could not resist the temptation of humiliating their hereditary enemy symbolically. The German victory parade followed the same route through the Arc de Triomphe and down the Champs Élysées as the French victory parade had taken after the First World War. The armistice was signed in the same railway carriage at Compiègne where the German envoys had had to sign their armistice in 1918. Along the prestigious rue de Rivoli in Paris the Nazis hung massive red, white, and black swastika flags.

Beyond the attempt to disgrace France there were also the first elements of a policy conceived to permanently weaken and reduce the country's status to that of "a large Switzerland." As a deliberate tactic to encourage division France was divided up into several zones of occupation. The main ones were the occupied zone in the north and the unoccupied or free zone in the south, but in the northeast there was also a reserved zone, a forbidden zone, an attached zone, and the Alsace-Moselle region was annexed outright, though the armistice had made no reference to the future of this province. Each zone had different administrative regimes and was separated by demarcation lines making it nigh on impossible to govern the country efficiently.

However, the Nazis were not only interested in weakening and partitioning France but also in exploiting it. As soon as they arrived in the occupied zone, Nazi services compiled an inventory of works of art. More than twenty thousand pieces of art were pillaged from France, mostly those belonging to private Jewish collections.[3] Massive exploitation of the French economy was also a feature of occupation as the Germans sought resources to bolster their war effort. The occupier made huge demands on the industrial and agricultural sectors, transporting large quantities of produce eastwards to the Reich. Each day, occupation costs ranging from 300 to 500 million francs had to be paid by the Vichy government. In addition, the occupier unilaterally imposed its own arbitrary rate of currency exchange that significantly overvalued the Deutschmark in relation to the franc.

Of course the Nazis also pursued ideological aims in France as they did in all occupied countries. In 1940, their anti-Semitic policy consisted of expelling Jews from German controlled territory and pushing them toward the free zone. Then, starting in 1942, the Nazis inaugurated a more radical phase with their deportation to the extermination camps in Eastern Europe. A brutal policy against political opponents was also applied. No opposition was tolerated. Resisters could find themselves arrested, often tortured, and sometimes executed. In carrying out these aims the Nazis relied as much as possible on the French administration and on the good will of the Vichy regime. The paradox is obvious: the Nazis aimed to permanently weaken the country, yet they needed a sufficiently strong French state to deal with any threat to public order and to resist any Allied invasion attempt. Thus, to minimize the use of German resources, Nazi leaders officially let Vichy retain a certain degree of sovereignty in the southern zone and in the colonies.

Espionage was a glaring breach of this sovereignty, but it was the only effective means of checking if Vichy deserved its relative autonomy. German intelligence agencies wanted to check that the French were loyally applying the terms of the armistice, even in the nonoccupied territories of southern France and the French colonies. The terms of the 1940 armistice charged special delegations of German officers located in the nonoccupied territories with an official mission to check the way the French were adhering to the armistice. These delegations provided a "legal" means of surveillance but they lacked spontaneity. Any official inspections they carried out had to be announced ahead of time, which gave those to be inspected the opportunity to camouflage illicit activity. Spies on the other hand could operate without passing through French bureaucratic channels and as a result were better placed to uncover breaches.

The first objective of German spying was thus to keep the French under surveillance. Joseph Barthélemy, Vichy's justice minister, complained in his memoirs that "the Germans always knew what had been said and done within minutes of each cabinet meeting."[4] He held Pierre Pucheu, minister of industrial production and then minister of the interior, responsible for these leaks, but there were many other possible sources of indiscretion around the French government. Copies of the correspondence of Pierre Laval, who served as vice-premier between July and December 1940 and then again from April 1942 to August 1944, are thought to have been communicated to the occupying authorities by the lover of his private secretary.[5] The Germans placed a spy among the police bodyguards of each of the three leading figures of the state, that is head of state Marshal Philippe Pétain, Laval, and François Darlan. The sister of the police inspector "protecting" Darlan, Vichy's vice-premier throughout 1941 and in early 1942, was the mistress of Hugo Geissler, head of the Gestapo delegation in Vichy![6] Another method of controlling the government was to exploit individuals in personal contact with it. René Bigot was arrested by the Germans in 1940 whilst trying to cross the demarcation line separating occupied and unoccupied France. Knowing that his uncle was a friend of Marcel Peyrouton, the former minister of the interior, the German secret services decided to take advantage of his contacts to gain information on the Vichy universe. In this case, the intrigue did not work for very long. Bigot, quickly overcome with remorse, confessed to a priest who put him in contact with the French counterespionage services. He was then arrested by the French police but the German attempt to use him shows clearly that even a collaborating government was to be kept under surveillance.[7]

One concern of the Germans was that the French would secretly rebuild their armed forces. To counteract a possible French military threat, they had to penetrate any organization likely to be used for such a clandestine mobilization. The police, the youth groups, the army, and any paramilitary groupings thus had to be infiltrated. Women were often used to seduce important French figures. The Marseille police was forced to transfer one of its captains, the alcoholic captain Dubois of the ST counterespionage branch, because he was sleeping with a woman known to be a German secret agent.[8]

The victors could not drop their guard. They had to keep a close watch on any possibility of rebellion. It was for this reason that spies devoted so much energy to assessing French military capabilities. They noted the position and movements of military units as well as the transport of weapons and drew up inventories of equipment, fuel stores, and ordinance. Part of their mission was to provide information on the attitude, the valor, and the general stance of French officers. Other intelligence was also sought: the fighting value of military units, their methods of recruitment, the level of the soldiers' pay. Any impulses of resistance within the army had to be eliminated. For this reason, particular attention was paid to the activities of the French intelligence services that might be in breach of article 10 of the armistice.

Indeed it would be fair to say that military espionage was the most common form of intelligence gathering activity. Albert Reymann, who was condemned to death by the French on 4 October 1941, had denounced to the Germans clandestine stocks of arms secreted in a suburb of Casablanca.[9] Guillaume Alscher was informing the Armistice Commission in Casablanca about the movement of planes and military units in French North Africa.[10] Adrien Demoulin was condemned to death in November 1941 by a court martial in Algiers for having sent on information concerning fortifications in Dakar and practical information about joining the foreign legion in Marseille.[11] Marc Dreesen was gathering intelligence on the French navy in Toulon, which he was then passing on to the German Armistice Commission of the town.[12] The charge of treason against Albert Becker was for serving as an intelligence agent for the Reich.

Between March and May 1942, he had sought information about the size and equipment of French garrisons, camouflaged military material, French troop movements, and the attitude of French troops toward the Reich.[13]

Of course it was not only the government and the army that needed to be kept under surveillance, but also the population. Lieutenant Colonel Oskar Reile of the German military intelligence network, the Abwehr, wrote, "Throughout the country we required individuals who allowed us to constantly take the pulse of the French."[14] The German secret services needed to be informed of the population's attitude toward the Pétain government to confirm that allowing France to be governed through a French government was pacifying the population in the way that Germans hoped. The risks of a revolution were also calculated. The Nazis attached great importance to public opinion, remembering how insurrection had brought to power their principal enemy, the Soviets. At the political level, certain categories such as Jews and anti-German Alsatians were the object of special scrutiny from the espionage services, leading Germans to focus on illicit departures from French ports or clandestine passages of the demarcation line.

If the accounts of former members of the Resistance are to be believed, there were few people actively opposing the Vichy regime and the Germans at the end of 1940. But the Germans were aware that the population's initial docility was likely to be brief. Any individual suspected of anti-German propaganda was to be watched. Questionnaires given to the spies asked them to note the reaction of the French authorities to the distribution of leaflets by Gaullists, supporters of the dissident General de Gaulle, who was in exile in London at the time calling for continued resistance through radio broadcasts transmitted into France on the airwaves of the BBC.[15] Agents were also expected to find the locations of illegal meetings and places that were used for Gaullist recruitment. German intelligence services used *agent-provocateurs* to infiltrate anti-German movements and networks.[16]

In addition, the secret services were responsible for ensuring the security of German administrations. Agents were sometimes sent into the southern nonoccupied territories and the colonies to investigate individuals applying for jobs in German services in the northern, occupied zone. This was a counterespionage precaution against the infiltration of their services by Allied or Gaullist agents. For two reasons it was also necessary to locate agents who had not returned from earlier missions: Firstly, if an agent had been arrested, the Germans could intervene with Vichy to try to secure their release. Secondly, some agents, paid an advance, had not been able to resist just disappearing without providing the information requested. They had to be found so they could be punished.

As has already been noted, the exploitation of France was one of the occupier's objectives. It fell to the secret services to prepare future pillaging in those areas not yet directly occupied. Locating potential war booty was amongst the tasks of the agents sent into these areas. In the files I consulted, at least three arrested agents were on missions to draw up inventories of works of art in the nonoccupied zone.[17] But the pillaging was not only cultural; it was also economic. Spies were interested in the quality of the harvest, the state of industries and maritime traffic, in food and gasoline supplies, and in stocks of coal and raw materials. This intelligence gathering had three aims. To predict potential risks of popular uprising, the Germans needed to be informed of what supplies were available to the French and colonial populations. At the same time, this intelligence could help to find business and industrial opportunities for German firms in the nonoccupied territories. Could these companies find partners or market opportunities in these regions? Could they settle there themselves? But, above all, this intelligence work made it possible to catalog the country's wealth to exploit it to the maximum.[18] In March 1942, a report from the French army's general staff estimated that each day the Germans were passing more than 100 million francs worth of merchandise from the free zone to the occupied zone.[19] From 1940 to 1944 the occupiers spent a total of almost 127 million francs buying up goods on the black market.[20] This parallel market gave them the opportunity to purchase raw materials in France without having to go through the normal channels nor bother with cumbersome bureaucracy. The intelligence services played an important role in this process. The link between the black market and the secret services was particularly evident in the case of the Abwehr, the military espionage structure. Right from the start, the Abwehr was closely associated with the biggest central procurement department for the Germans: the Otto bureaus. The Otto bureaus benefited from the Abwehr's experience in the art of camouflaging illegal transactions. For the Abwehr, the partnership brought in vast sums facilitating its administrative independence.

This is a good place to underline the role held by North Africa in the objectives of the German intelligence services.[21] At first sight, German interests there might appear limited. The armistice treaty referred only implicitly to North Africa and the immediate colonization of the region did not seem to be one of Hitler's priorities. But European countries had long coveted African territories. The Germans may have lost their own colonial possessions in Africa at the end of the First World War but they had not entirely given up their colonial designs there; these remained a long-term objective. Among the French territories in North Africa, it was Morocco that interested them most, as they had longstanding connections, including German firms that had been established there for many years. This French protectorate also had the strategic asset of a coastal line along the Atlantic. Although the German plans for territorial expansion in the immediate focused mainly on Eastern Europe, the secret services prepared the future by organizing anti-French propaganda in North Africa.[22]

A French counterespionage report of March 1941 noted a massive increase of German espionage in North Africa dating from December 1940 and January 1941.[23] This was no doubt partly a reaction to the dismissal of the pro-German vice-premier Pierre Laval from the French government on 13 December 1940. Laval's firing had irritated the Germans, who considered it, wrongly as it turned out, to signal Vichy's change in diplomatic direction. Hitler believed that it was inspired by General Maxime Weygand, who by that time was serving as Vichy's governor in North Africa.[24] Thus Weygand's North African fief was increasingly visited by numerous German agents after Laval's firing; they sought information on Weygand's activities, but also aimed to punish him.

It seems that the Abwehr was probably behind a mutiny of a regiment of Algerian soldiers within the French army. On Saturday 25 January 1941, the members of this regiment massacred their French officers and seized weapons. They advanced toward the city of Algiers where they opened fire on the European population. Investigations after the incident highlighted how the inequalities of army treatment of native soldiers compared to French soldiers had been used to stir up resentment. These investigations also mentioned that the mutiny was not spontaneous. The soldiers were thought to have been contacted by members of the Parti Populaire Algérien working for German intelligence.[25] This fact has not been checked in German archives. Was the mention of German involvement simply a sign of the paranoia of Weygand and his immediate subordinates? Probably not. Firstly, such an action would fit in with the habits of the Abwehr. Secondly, given that this action undermined public order it would fit in with the Nazi policy aimed at weakening France and taking advantage of every opportunity to divide it. Finally, there were several reports during 1941 mentioning that the Germans were trying to make use of Arab nationalism against France.[26]

Whatever the exact role of the Abwehr in this mutiny it is certain that the Germans did not trust Weygand. This was not new. As a protégé of First World War commander-in-chief Marshal Ferdinand Foch, he was associated in German minds with the signing of the 1918 armistice. Besides, Weygand's anti-German comments were well known on the German side of the Rhine. For the Germans, his appointment to North Africa increased the risk of the region's possible dissidence at a time when some French colonies had begun defecting from Vichy to support General de Gaulle. In reality Weygand was not a real threat to the Germans since he ultimately refused to disobey Marshal Pétain's instructions, but that was not how the Germans saw it. Admiral Wilhelm Canaris, Abwehr leader since 1935, was among those who thought that the French were going to use North Africa to secretly rebuild their forces. He even thought that Hitler had made an error in not occupying this area in 1940; the Abwehr sought to compensate for this oversight.

North Africa was not only dear to the French but it was also important to the Allies, and therefore to German intelligence. The British used the passage through the Mediterranean to ensure communication with their colonies. Gibraltar and the Suez Canal were of vital interest to the British, and military campaigns in Egypt and Libya were their most important theaters of operation at that point in the war. The Americans also became aware of the interest of North Africa: months before their entry into the war they had sent emissaries to Morocco in the framework of the so-called Murphy-Weygand agreements of February 1941, which allowed Americans to supply food to the French.[27] The Germans feared that these emissaries would not limit their activities to aid, and might engage military preparations in the area.[28]

Thus French North Africa gave German intelligence services reason and opportunity to spy on the Allies. One of Josef Beitelberger's missions was to inform of any Allied planes flying over Morocco or any attempt of Anglo-American forces to land in North Africa.[29] German intelligence posts in French territory kept track of the neighboring areas belonging to or occupied by the British: the post in Morocco spied on air and maritime traffic to the British territory of Gibraltar.[30] Spying missions in dissident French colonies were also launched from the German intelligence posts in Vichy's North Africa, and from spring of 1941 the activities of American envoys were also under surveillance. The specter of an Allied landing in French North Africa became more likely once the United States entered the war in December, and became increasingly so throughout 1942. From mid-October on, the Axis secret services were busy arranging their defense against a possible Allied invasion in French North Africa, and preparing a total occupation in the free zone of mainland France as a response.[31] It's probable Operation Torch, the Anglo-American landing in French North Africa, did not come entirely as a surprise. German intelligence seemed to have at least partially foreseen this landing. But the German army was no longer able to intervene effectively: although North Africa was important to the German secret services in France, it was considered secondary by the high command in Berlin, which focused primarily on the struggle between German forces and the Russians in the Soviet Union.

German secret services thus had multiple missions. The surveillance of the French was not the only objective of German intelligence—it also had to prepare future military campaigns, protect German administrations, and organize the exploitation of France. Paul Paillole, one of the leaders of the French counterespionage services, provided the following summary in April of 1942: "So, what is being spied on? What does the enemy seek among us? Everything."[32] The activities of the German secret services highlight the contradiction of Nazi policy in France. Sometimes, it sought intelligence in order to avoid insurrections. At other times, however, it seems that its priority was creating incidents or, at least, making life difficult for French authorities. In short, Germany's primary aim was the neutralization of France.

How was the German intelligence network organized in France? The development of the German secret services in France followed a similar pattern to that of the entire Nazi administrative machine, beginning with an initial domination by the military followed by the rapid rise of organizations issued directly from the Nazi Party. The structures and activities of intelligence evolved in tune with Franco-German relations, the priorities of the time, the rhythm of the war, and the political intrigues of the Nazi state.

In the military, intelligence gathering was mainly conducted by the Abwehr, which was connected to the General Staff of the German armed forces, or Wehrmacht. In addition to an administrative section, it was divided into three subsections, or Abteilungs. Abteilung 1 was the espionage service proper working for all three branches of the armed services (land, navy, and air), and also engaged in economic espionage. Technical support services were attached to it, such as those specializing in creating false documents, photography, signals, and so forth. Abteilung 2 specialized in organizing "fifth columns" through sabotage and subversive activities. It was expected to take advantage of dissident tendencies in the country and to fire up ethnic and cultural minorities (with regard to France that meant nationalists in North Africa, Brittany, and Alsace). The mission of this subsection was to spread false rumors. Abteilung 3 was in charge of counterespionage and of military security. Within this bureau a section specialized in the infiltration and misinformation of enemy networks. Such a division into specialized bureaus demonstrated the organizational changes that had occurred in the world of espionage since the end of the nineteenth century. In its modern conception, spying had become increasingly bureaucratic. Archives were essential, hence the need for an administrative section. The amount of technical equipment had also considerably increased through advances in photography and communications. Finally, another modern element: the enemy was no longer looked upon only militarily. Investigations were thus broadened to understanding public opinion and economy as well as undermining enemy capabilities through sabotage.

Prior to 1940, French territory was monitored by three posts (*Abwehrstelle* or *Ast*) of the Abwehr based in Münster, Wiesbaden, and Stuttgart. Posts in Berlin and Hamburg specialized in matters relating to aeronautics, maritime questions, and the French colonies. After the occupation of June 1940, the posts of Münster, Stuttgart, and Hamburg grew subbranches in the occupied zone. Colonel Friedrich Rudolf, the head of the Münster post, settled in Paris in the Hôtel Lutetia, a building that ironically had served as base for anti-Nazi German émigrés during the 1930s.[33] In 1941, Rudolf became the coordinator and the centralizer of all the Abwehr's activities in France. Lieutenant Colonel Reile, head of Abwehr 3-F (Abteilung 3–French section) in Paris, became leader of the counterespionage section. Later, there were also major posts in Angers, Biarritz, and Dijon.

In November 1942 the Germans invaded the previously unoccupied zone of southern France and this led to a shifting of posts and subbranches to the south and a shrinking of the Abwehr's network in the northern zone. An *Abwehrstelle* was established in Lyon, and smaller *Nebenstelle* were set-up in Limoges, Marseille, Nice, Perpignan, Toulon, and

Toulouse. Of course, the Abwehr had not waited for this total occupation to operate in the south and, still more intensively, in French North Africa. Immediately after the signing of the 1940 armistice, Germany attempted a massive infiltration of the nonoccupied territories and its staff grew spectacularly right up to the total occupation in 1942.

Two key elements stand out: German espionage against France expanded massively *after* the French defeat of 1940 and the Germans readily trespassed into the nonoccupied territories. These two elements can be explained by both a basic mistrust of the French but also the internal politics of the Nazi state, where rival administrations performing similar tasks vied to outdo each other.

Distrust toward France can be explained easily. Historically France and Germany had often been on opposing sides in a long series of military conflicts: most recently in the Napoleonic wars (1799–1815), the Franco-Prussian War (1870–71), the First and Second World Wars (respectively 1914–18 and 1939–45). France was thus a "hereditary enemy." France was unlikely, all of a sudden, to give up its claim of being a major power. Certain acts of the Vichy government already mentioned above also lent their weight to German suspicions, such as Philippe Pétain's organization of the dismissal of Vice-Premier Pierre Laval . In reality his elimination had little to do with diplomatic alliances; rather his unpopularity was discrediting the whole of the Vichy government. Throughout the country the dismissal of Laval had a positive effect on Pétain's image and some were prepared to wrongly credit him with playing a diplomatic "double game," publicly collaborating with the Germans, whilst privately negotiating with the British. Even some Resisters were initially prepared to entertain such ideas: for example, Henri Frenay's *Combat* movement was very slow to stop using Pétain's name as a reference in its clandestine newspapers. This cannot have escaped the notice of the Germans and was unlikely to inspire them with much confidence.[34] Possibly the deepest reason for Nazi mistrust of the French lay within their own history. After the First World War German leaders themselves had secretly rebuilt their country and remobilized for war, flouting many of the terms of the Versailles treaty. They remained acutely aware of the possibilities of freeing oneself from the yoke imposed by diplomatic agreements and thus insisted on keeping a tight rein on the vanquished.

This vigilant control was particularly true of the Abwehr, as its origins influenced its behavior toward occupied countries. To understand this, we need to go back to the Versailles treaty of 1919 that forbade all German espionage activity and thereby officially eliminated the military intelligence service. It recreated itself under the innocuous name of Statistiche Abteilung (statistical section) before adopting the title Abwehr in 1925, becoming an espionage as well as counterespionage organization. By around 1935 the Abwehr had developed into a large and powerful organization. The Abwehr's own clandestine origins informed its instinctive mistrust of Vichy France.

The massive growth in Abwehr activity in France was also fueled by the rivalries within the Nazi machine. In Germany, the army had already lost the battle for influence against new politicized structures born from the Nazi Party itself. But the occupied countries were virgin territories where the struggle for power could start again from scratch. The military wanted to take advantage of this situation to redistribute power in their favor; indeed, the army found itself in a position of strength following the invasion. It could bask in the glory of a spectacular victory in the field won with unexpected speed. Moreover, in 1940, France was to serve an essentially strategic and military purpose as a launching pad for Operation Sealion (the invasion of Great Britain). Moreover, at the beginning it was the army that had an official monopoly on policing and espionage in France, thus it sought to exploit its position with respect to competing Nazi agencies.

Military domination in espionage was not to last. Organizations performing similar tasks directly for the Nazi Party rapidly gained the upper hand. In 1938 the process of reorganization, centralization, and politicalization of police structures in Nazi Germany had culminated in the creation of the Reichssicherheitshauptamt (RSHA) under the command of the ruthlessly brutal Reinhard Heydrich, Canaris's determined adversary. This police structure operated as a pseudoministry with a mission to apply the Führer's will and to protect the Nazi state, particularly against ideological or racial enemies. Both the central umbrella organization, the RSHA, and its local policing structure, the Sipo-SD (Sicherheitspolizei-Sicherheitsdienst) or security police were dominated by members of the Nazi Party and the SS, that elite structure that had grown into an army from its origins as Hitler's bodyguard. The Sipo-SD is often referred to erroneously as the Gestapo, but in reality the Gestapo was only one of its sections.

These organizations installed themselves in France very discretely. Military supremacy in 1940 was such that the SS were not supposed to operate in this country at all. Their first appearance was thus clandestine. The young, ambitious, and career-minded Helmut Knochen arrived first, accompanied by a Sonderkommando (special commando) of about twenty SS. This thirty-year-old PhD, a protégé of Reinhard Heydrich, was to be the driving force behind the German police in France until 1944. Two other Sonderkommandos arrived before the end of July. To justify this, Heydrich took advantage of security measures taken during a visit Hitler made to Paris in the summer of 1940. Despite jealously guarding their prerogatives, the military nonetheless agreed that Knochen should be given an auxiliary role of surveilling ideological enemies. This compromise was accepted by the military because their own services were overworked in the political domain, the very domain in which the SS excelled.[35]

Initial SS implantation thus owed a lot to tactical maneuvers. Their expansion from the middle of 1941 reflected the growing influence of the SS within the rest of the Reich. This stemmed largely from the increasingly central place held by ideological questions—the SS's specialty—that is, the radicalization of anti-Communist and anti-Semitic policy within the Nazi state. Two events were both symbols and catalysts of this: Operation Barbarossa (the invasion of the Soviet Union) on 22 June 1941 and the Wannsee Conference on 20 January 1942 where the annihilation of Europe's Jews was organized.

The SS also took advantage of Hitler's increasing mistrust of the military, as the Führer saw the Wehrmacht as too ideologically lukewarm and too socially conservative. From June 1942, the Abwehr gradually began to lose its authority to the Sipo-SD. Although the two services coexisted till 1944, the Abwehr was eventually absorbed by its rival.

Two of the SS services are of particular interest: the fourth and sixth bureaus of the Sipo-SD. Operating in France from headquarters in Paris, the fourth bureau of the Sipo-SD was officially known as the Gestapo. In principle, Gestapo staff members were recruited from within the Nazi Party and the SS, but in reality it also contained many former civil servants and former police. The Gestapo's role was to address political questions, conduct counterespionage, and defend the Reich and the National Socialist Party against anti-German and anti-Nazi activities. Initially the Gestapo arrived in Paris under the pretext of ensuring the security of a military parade that was to take place in September 1940, but the parade was cancelled. The Gestapo was first led by Major (Sturmbannführer) Schmitz who was quickly replaced by Karl Beumelburg from Prague.[36] In the fall of 1940, the Gestapo set up a subsidiary bureau in Vichy under the auspices of SS captain (Hauptsturmbannführer) Hugo Geissler. This ordinary-looking thirty-seven-year-old was about 5 feet 8 tall, had an oval face, an inconspicuous pointy nose, very blue eyes, and slightly curly blond hair. Geissler, who had worked as an interpreter in the Nice casino before the war, spoke French pretty well and passed himself off as an Alsatian. Assisted by five German subordinates, he recruited French agents to organize intelligence missions in nonoccupied France. The main goal of these missions was to garner information on opponents of the Reich who had found refuge in France. Thus Geissler pressured the Vichy government into agreeing to the extradition of the German social democrats Rudolf Breitscheid and Rudolf Hilferding in February 1941.[37]

The sixth bureau of the Sipo-SD, the Sicherheitsdienst (SD, or security office), was the real intelligence organ of the Nazi Party and was responsible for collecting political and military information. Most of its German personnel lacked police experience and were recruited exclusively from the SS. Until 1942, the SD staff outside of Paris was smaller than its Parisian contingent, but gradually it began stepping up its operations in the nonoccupied territory. A clandestine service was established in Vichy, led by Dr. Reiche, a young SS Lieutenant (Unterstrumführer) operating undercover as a diplomat. Until 1942, the Sipo-SD showed little interest in French North Africa, although Reiche did spend a few weeks there. The Bordeaux suboffice of the Sipo-SD also had a few contacts with the colonies through French informants who were in North Africa for business reasons. Amongst its agents was the charismatic journalist Count Richard de Grandmaison (agent AG 311) who had already distinguished himself with his anti-Communist activity during the Spanish Civil War in the late 1930s. It was only from the spring of 1942 that the SD began to expand its operations in French North Africa, including the establishment of a specialized service for North African affairs.[38]

I have already mentioned the rivalries between the military and the police but there were also rivalries within the Sipo-SD itself. There were professional rivalries between the fourth and sixth bureaus leading to interference in each other's missions, and there were also personal rivalries. Beumelburg, the head of the Gestapo, often broke the chain of command, preferring to bypass Knochen and send his reports directly to Berlin.[39]

Rivalries affected the evolution of the structures, but we need to be careful not to exaggerate them. While rivalries often stimulated the administrative zeal of the different bureaus as they strove to compete with one another, there also was some overlap of ideals and even occasional cooperation. Even though the SS were more involved in the ideological struggle than the Wehrmacht, we should remember that racist, anti-Semitic, and antiliberal ideas were already common currency within the German armed forces.[40] The military's opposition to the SS was grounded more in practicality than principles: they feared the SS's methods and ambition. It should be noted, however, that despite their late opposition to the Nazi regime, the Abwehr strove for German victory and the weakening of France. Within this framework, the military at times actually worked hand in hand with its institutional rivals, the SS. Sometimes they even used the same agents and exchanged intelligence.

Axis spies in the nonoccupied territories had to use institutional or individual covers because their activities were illegal. Diplomatic missions provided the best institutional cover since they provided diplomatic immunity. Delegations of the armistice commission were established in the major cities of the southern zone and in North Africa. The American historian Robert Owen Paxton emphasizes the limited role these commissions had on the diplomatic relations between France and Germany. He is right in the sense that the most important negotiations were held through different organizations such as the Militärbefehlshaber in Frankreich (MBF, or military command in France), the German embassy and the bureaus of the Sipo-SD. Nevertheless armistice commissions did play a fundamental role in Nazi policies in France. If the colonies are taken into account, we can see that the majority of French territory was not directly occupied. Before November 1942, the Germans occupied less than 10 percent of this territory. The armistice commissions were to serve as their eyes and ears in the rest. These commissions were charged with official surveillance missions through accredited diplomats, but they also recruited unofficial agents for extraconventional activities such as black market dealings, propaganda, and espionage. How important these commissions really were was shown by Franco-German and Franco-Italian wrangles about what their exact role and staffing levels should be. Other diplomatic missions also participated in surveillance, both officially and clandestinely. The Nazis deliberately breached the neutrality of their Red Cross delegations.[41] The delegates' official role was to help German residents in France, but in fact they were often used for spying. Diplomatic consulates also organized espionage. It is thus not surprising that Theodore Auer, the general consul of Germany in French Morocco, was also the head of the Gestapo in the protectorate.

In 1942, economic espionage became increasingly important because of the growing needs of the Nazi war economy. For this type of spying, intelligence agencies were often assisted by industrial and commercial firms with branches in France or North Africa, such as the Renschauseen, Lobischlek, Mawick, and Boland companies in Morocco.[42] For the purposes of intelligence gathering in Africa, espionage services also made use of certain firms that were supplying food to the German Afrika Korps, Field Marshal Erwin Rommel's desert army. These companies, through their official mission, had a certain freedom of movement between Europe and Africa that facilitated espionage.

French surveillance of diplomatic missions encouraged the Axis to increasingly employ "independent" agents operating without direct contacts with the diplomatic institutions. Even without institutional cover, it was relatively easy to implant agents during the months following the defeat because the foreign spies could justify their presence. This was easy when so many refugees were seeking new homes after the exodus of more than six million French and Belgians who had fled in desperation in advance of the German armies in June 1940. There were also thousands of Alsatians who had been expelled from their native region when the Germans annexed it in July 1940, and thousands of Jews from Bade-Saarpfalz who had been dumped in Vichy France by the Germans that October. Some spies thus posed as refugees. French Resistance sources noted this danger in a report dated March 1942: "Often German espionage agents pass themselves off as refugees, cleverly taking advantage of the emotions of those who listen to them in order to extract a variety of information."[43] This report cited the case of a woman operating under the name of Regina Reisch, an Austrian citizen, who "passes herself off as a Jewish victim of Hitler's regime."[44] Taking advantage of circumstances is a basic tool for a spy.

Often spies pretended to be members of the Resistance. Posing as opponents of the Nazi regime was the best way to extract information from a population that generally despised Germany, and it was certainly the best way to get recruited by the Resistance organizations spies were trying to infiltrate. After their arrests, these individuals often started out by claiming they were working for the British or the Gaullists before admitting the truth.[45] Following his arrest, Edouard Buch confessed: "I was never supposed to divulge the mission I was charged with, and in the event of interrogation by the French police I was to try to convince them that my presence in the free zone was solely motivated by my desire to get away from the Germans."[46]

Certain professions also served as cover for spying activities. Journalism has traditionally been associated with espionage. The two professions are not that distant from each other because in both cases, their members have to seek information and in both cases the end justifies the means. German and French journalists freely circulated in Vichy, and their integrity was sometimes open to question. The profession of traveling salesman, whether real or fake, also provided an ideal cover because it justified the extensive travel spies often had to undertake.

For both the spies operating under diplomatic cover and the agents sent directly by the offices of the Abwehr and the SD or Gestapo, communication was an essential element for the successful completion of their task. Collecting intelligence is useless if there is no way to transmit it. Here again the Germans had recourse to institutional and individual means. Diplomatic missions made use of both official and clandestine radio networks. Intelligence sent from the nonoccupied territories through this method was centralized in Bourges in central France and in Wiesbaden in western Germany. The diplomatic pouch was also used to get around French surveillance. The "independents" also had their radio networks. A small number of agents had received radio training in spy schools in Paris, Dijon, Angers, Besançon, Stuttgart, or Barcelona.[47] In addition there were direct contacts to exchange intelligence. On 13 and 14 August 1942 there was a meeting of the principal German espionage agents in North Africa.[48] Independents often went back to their handlers in the occupied zone to give their intelligence and receive other missions. The problem with this constant to and fro was the risk of attracting the attention of French counterespionage. To remain clandestine, the intelligence networks established "mail drops" in the nonoccupied territories, that is to say addresses where agents could deposit their information. These drops had the advantage of enabling agents to extend their missions in the unoccupied zone or the French colonies whilst avoiding suspicious constant coming and going. The disadvantage was that if the drop was identified, any agent making contact with it could be caught.[49]

Axis intelligence networks worked extensively and secretly in France. Espionage is not necessarily the sign of hostility between two countries—it happens between friendly nations even in times of peace. However, the sort of spying that was carried out in France, through its nature and scope, resembled more closely the kind the Nazis carried out in enemy countries rather than in a neutral or friendly one. One might have expected the armistice to bring a reduction in German spying in France, but that was not the case. German spying took full advantage of the opportunities provided by the partial occupation of the country and expanded still further. The number of posts and sub-branches working against France doubled between June 1940 and July 1941 and kept on growing afterward, particularly in North Africa.[50] This highlighted the tensions between the French and the Germans in spite of the conciliatory stance of the Vichy government.

2 BECOMING A SPY

Who spied for Germany in the nonoccupied territories between 1940 and 1942? What were their motives? How were they recruited? We can begin to answer these questions with the interrogation reports of arrested agents, with letters written from their cells by those indicted, but also with governmental documentation produced by the military justice service and the secret services.

In June 1942, Captain Bernard of the French counterespionage service wrote the following assessment of spies in an important memo:

> Contrary to what we might read in spy novels, the secret agent does not usually appear in the shape of a hero with superior muscles, extreme intelligence and a particularly attractive physical appearance, turning on the charm in palaces and bedrooms while being the hero in a series of extraordinary adventures. Spies have always been recruited among individuals with ordinary appearance and from all social milieus. This is even more the case in the troubled times through which we are living, where many individuals suffer either from moral distress or from material difficulties which make them particularly open to offers by the foreign intelligence service.[1]

Thus spies were ordinary people who did not attract attention. Their ordinariness was all the more pronounced in that most of them were French nationals. In May of 1941, a report from the Ministry of the Interior pointed out that 80 percent of the German agents arrested since the armistice were French.[2] There were many advantages to the Germans of using French citizens. They had long-established connections and were less suspect to the native population than a foreigner speaking with an accent. Their commonness made others comfortable to speak more freely in their presence. A fundamental aim of all colonizers is to be able to occupy a territory with minimal expense, an aim that was facilitated by employing members of the occupied community. The use of French individuals also made it possible for the Germans to avoid intervening directly, thus freeing them for other theaters of operations. Finally, since the Germans wanted to permanently divide France, what better way than to encourage the French to work against each other?

It might seem surprising that so many French citizens were working for the German services. After all, public opinion reports show that from very early on, the French generally favored the Allies and were hostile toward the Reich.[3] German spies can be categorized according to their principle motives as patriots, ideologues, profiteers, the sentimental, adventurers, the vulnerable, and the reluctant.

Some secret agents worked out of patriotism. They can be divided into two groups. Firstly, there was a small core of German citizens. In the same memo cited above, Captain Bernard described their role: "They are usually used for important missions or to recruit spies of lesser status. It will thus be rare to see them wander around caserns or depots gathering trivial intelligence."[4] This explains why when an important spy network was discovered in the Marseille area in 1941 the police had to arrest around thirty individuals before capturing a German citizen, Johannes Hasse-Heyn, the recruiting agent of the group.[5]

Nationalists or regionalists made up the second subcategory of patriots. The National Breton Party sought to establish an autonomous state in Brittany, the northwestern corner of France. To achieve this, an intense collaboration with the Nazi authorities was advocated by a faction within the party.[6] The links between the Breton party and the Nazis came to light with the interception of mail coming from prisoner-of-war camps. In October of 1940, postal censors noted, "Some of the letter writers indicate that in the camps including Breton prisoners, the Germans engage in intense separatist propaganda. Some of the captives are thought to have been freed against their promise to support this movement."[7] Initially, the Germans tried to encourage Breton separatism simply as a means of dividing the French.[8] Then gradually the Germans recruited part of this nationalist movement for espionage missions. The spying activities of these Bretons outside of Brittany, however, seem to have been limited to only isolated cases.[9]

On the other side of France lay the disputed border territories of Alsace and Lorraine, which France had lost to Germany in the Franco-Prussian war of 1870; they were recuperated in 1918 only to be seized once again by the victorious Germans in 1940. As one might imagine the population of these territories was known for its strong nationalist leanings, some in favor of France, others for Germany. Alsatians and Lorrainers provided numerous recruits for the French Resistance. Nonetheless, some of the pro-German elements amongst them such as army captain Auguste Watrinet saw the occupation as an opportunity.[10] Watrinet was planning the creation of a buffer state in Lorraine that could enable the province to avoid outright annexation whilst still cutting off its ties to France, and so he wrote to the occupation authorities offering them his services.[11] Edouard Fier from the Moselle district of Lorraine was another attracted by the possibility of working for the Germans. His whole family opted for German citizenship after the invasion of France whilst twenty-three-year-old Edouard headed off to Morocco to spy for the Abwehr.[12] Emil Hanke from Neckingen was sent to southern France to buy vehicles for the SS but he combined this with collecting military intelligence.[13] A twenty-one-year-old former ski instructor Lucien Hecketsweiller from Colmar joined the French army at the end of October 1941, then deserted in November taking with him some military documents.[14]

North African nationalism was also exploited by German intelligence.[15] The French authorities interrogated North Africans coming back from the colonies after having been freed from German prisoner of war camps (or having "escaped"—there was some suspicion that these prisoners may have been released by the Nazis to carry out spy missions). These interrogations shed light on the methods used on these natives to convince them to work against France. The German lieutenant Rokka traveled to all camps holding North Africans to praise anti-French agitators and members of opposition parties, encouraging Algerians' hope of independence after the war.[16] France's most senior official in North Africa, General Weygand, pointed out how important this problem was in a letter addressed to head of state Pétain in March of 1941: "It is also clear that the Germans have pursued long-term propaganda with our North African prisoners; three thousand of them have been selected and gathered in a camp around Berlin. Apparently they were very well treated (couscous, *mechouis,* native celebrations, etc.). Propaganda is said to have been organized through films, brochures and discussions in Arabic. They were then sent off to various camps and even released to head back to North Africa."[17] Many were freed on the express condition that they would work for the Germans. In Clermont-Ferrand in central France, a special Abwehr bureau for spies of Kabyle origin was established. Commandant Paul Paillole, a senior member of the French counterespionage services, spoke of the rise of espionage in North African milieus: "Before the war, we were arresting in North Africa and the Empire a maximum of about a dozen agents of foreign intelligence agencies. Since the war, and particularly since the armistice, this number has multiplied by ten and keeps on growing."[18] The defeat highlighted France's vulnerability, and thereby fostered nationalists' hopes for liberation. German propaganda put still more oil on the fire especially by playing on an anti-Semitism that was already very present in Arab milieus.[19]

The ideologues are our second category of spies. It was mainly the ideological dimension that differentiated spying in the Second World War from spying in the first global conflict more than twenty years before. The rise of the extremist ideologies of Fascism and Communism was an essential fact of the interwar period, and these ideologies were capable of instilling an almost religious fervor in individuals. German intelligence employed a recruitment method it had found successful since Hitler had come to power in 1933: appealing to the ideological collaboration of Germanophiles.[20] These "sincere traitors" as the French Secret Services knew them were attracted to Fascism and wished for a German victory. They were also worried about the growing influence of the Resistance, particularly of the Communists within it. Some of them, even after their arrest, could be found still doing the Nazi salute and yelling "Heil Hitler!" in their prison cells.[21] According to a document written by the director of the specialist French counterespionage police, the ST, in the spring of 1941, ideology held an important place amongst the motives for espionage: "most of them were recruited under the banner of Franco-German collaboration," which gradually led them toward treason.[22] However, in the June memo noted above, Captain Bernard, suggested that these ideological spies were relatively rare among German agents.[23]

Suzanne Desseigne is an interesting example of an ideological spy. She was a member of the collaborating Fascist movement Parti Populaire Français (PPF, or French People's Party) and was arrested in March of 1941. According to her mother, Suzanne had been interested in politics since her teenage years: "[She] was a young French girl who, from the age of fifteen, while her peers were still playing without a care in the world, felt the danger of Bolshevism and of the Jewish conspiracy and never stopped fighting with all her might against these scourges of our fatherland and our civilization."[24]

In her confession, Desseigne emphasized her political and religious commitment: "And it is in perfect union with my very sincere religious convictions that I continued to be active in the antidemocratic movements. I felt that the open atheism of the leaders of the time was an obstacle to any work of proselytizing. And from that time on till my arrest I have kept on working for the Action Catholique [Catholic Action]."

She confessed her fascination with the Fascist model: "Thus how could I not feel the necessity for our country of an internal regime that would be just like the great waves of honest, healthy, orderly life that came to us from all our borders; from Italy, the inspiration of a new world, from Germany expelling Jews and Freemasons out of Europe, and from proud Catholic Spain, fighting with all its living strength against red barbarism, against the horror of the Communist revolt?"[25]

After the invasion, Desseigne found herself in the occupied zone where she got back in touch with the German milieus of Bordeaux she had frequented at the end of the 1930s. She became the mistress of a German soldier, and he recruited her for intelligence work. Betraying her country with enthusiasm and even without pay, Desseigne conducted political and military espionage missions in southern France and in French North Africa. At the time of her arrest, she claimed forcefully to be delighted with the work she had accomplished and to be ready to do it all again. In the military prison where she was locked up, she assaulted other women prisoners who did not share her political views.[26]

The ideologues were frequently recruited through political parties, and the PPF provided most of these "sincere traitors." The PPF was the party of the former Communist turned Fascist Jacques Doriot, a hulk of a man who could be seen sweating profusely in his black shirt as he delivered Mussolini-inspired rants before serried ranks of mainly lower middle-class party activists. It was probably no coincidence that in February 1941 there was an increase of the contacts between the Nazi secret services and the PPF. In the immediate aftermath of the defeat, Doriot had declared himself to be "Marshal Pétain's man." But when Pétain and his supporters organized the dismissal of the pro-German vice-premier Laval on 13 December, Doriot questioned the ideological orientation of the Vichy regime. From the beginning of 1941, the PPF moved increasingly into the German camp. In May, Doriot advocated a military alliance with the Germans in his speech at the PPF convention in Paris. In the southern zone, his right-hand man, Simon Sabiani, a charismatic Corsican who led the PPF branch in Marseille through a combination of anti-Marxism and clientelism, was mentioned several times in French counterespionage reports on account of his close relationship with Geissler, the Gestapo delegate in Vichy. From August 1941 on, the number of incidents of espionage involving the PPF increased significantly. In addition to its ideological commitment, the PPF had an economic interest in these relationships, as financial rewards were offered to the party in exchange for its espionage services.[27]

Double propaganda encouraged ideological engagement. On the one hand, according to a French counterespionage report, German propaganda "so cleverly intoxicat[ed] public opinion that some French citizens deliberately forget all dignity and the definition of the word 'traitor.'"[28] On the other hand, propaganda issued by the Vichy regime sang the virtues of Franco-German collaboration. Many of the "sincere traitors" claimed to be acting according to the government's wishes. On 2 October 1942, Henri Romain, who had been indicted for espionage, wrote to Marshal Pétain from the prison in Saint-Étienne, near Lyon. He justified his spying for the Germans, explaining, "I accepted this collaboration because I thought that I would be useful to my country, which was wounded and hurt after the war, and that I would be supporting your policy."[29] On 7 December 1943, Jean Pézard pleaded with Laval in a similar manner from his cell in the military prison of Nontron (Dordogne): "Having wished for a Franco-German entente, and guided exclusively in this by feelings of patriotism, I rallied immediately and without any second thoughts to the principles of collaboration as they had been formulated by Marshal Pétain."[30] Many other examples could be cited. We will see later on that, even though the government was itself sincerely committed to state collaborate, this uncontrolled individual collaboration was contrary to its intent.

Patriots and ideologues were valuable agents for the German intelligence services. They were strongly motivated and ready to suffer, even sometimes to die, for their cause. Their employer could trust them. The fate of the individuals they were denouncing or the rightness in helping Hitler to win the war did not seem to trouble their conscience. This kind of politicized secret agent posed a difficulty, however, in that their political or nationalist convictions were likely to undermine the objectivity of the information they provided. They tended to focus on their ideological obsessions. Rolland Nosek, from the sixth bureau of the Sicherheitsdienst (SD), complained that when he asked PPF militants to bring him information on the Vichy government in their reports, they preferred to concentrate on the internal conflicts between the different Fascist movements based in Paris.[31]

Many spies were not motivated by conviction, but rather money. The first category of these is what I will term the profiteers. Throughout history, financial incentives have probably been the spy's main motivation. After the defeat in France, economic conditions increased the number of individuals ready to spy for money. More than one million persons were out of work in October 1940, and when unemployment eased up, the population was hit by hyperinflation. It is thus not surprising that some people were ready to accept any kind of well-paid work. The report on André Bernard's activities described his motives as economic: "He was demobilized from the army in June 1940 and came back to Paris where, because of lack of jobs, his situation was close to misery. Having heard that the Germans 'paid well,' he followed a friend's advice and got in touch with a man named Braun."[32]

Demobilized soldiers were particularly targeted by the Germans because they often found themselves without work and in difficult financial straits, and their recent military experience was valuable to German intelligence. Soldiers had an intimate understanding of the French army that the Germans wanted to keep under surveillance, and they also had technical knowledge and contacts within military units—all helpful to intelligence work. Having only recently left the armed forces, they were not immediately suspected as spies, thereby making it more likely that others would unwittingly disclose information in their presence. Like other individuals in similar circumstances, they could get the money they needed from the Germans. Not all of them were able to resist temptation.

Victorious, Germany was in a particularly good position to offer financial rewards. Following the armistice it had grown rich at France's expense and it had trouble spending all the money coming into its coffers.

The terms of the 1940 armistice allowed Germany to make the defeated French pay astronomical amounts for the privilege of being occupied. "Occupation costs" were levied at between 300 and 500 million francs per day. To make matters worse, the Germans unilaterally imposed a new rate of currency exchange. Instead of being worth 12 francs as it had been before French defeat, the German mark was revalued at 20 francs, allowing the occupier to buy produce at will from the French economy. The financial means of the German secret services were thus practically unlimited.[33] French counterespionage estimated that "officers, civil servants and agents of the German secret services spend without limit and enrich themselves without scruple."[34] Journalist Philippe Aziz has uncovered the account of a meeting of the Reichssicherheitshauptamt (RSHA) in the fall of 1940 in which a reward scale was put forward: "Denunciation of a Jew: 1,000 francs; of a Gaullist or a Communist: 3,000 francs; intelligence leading to the discovery of a weapons' cache: from 5,000 to 30,000 francs, depending on the size of the cache."[35] Substantial rewards could be gained by ordinary agents, even by those of only average standing. The appropriately named Johann Dollar earned 93,000 francs in a year for information he passed on.[36] Adrien Demoulin justified his engagement as a secret agent by his financial problems and made the somewhat unlikely claim that he needed money to go to America to be able to present the plans of a helicopter he had designed.[37] The German secret services also had other resources besides money. Since the occupier had divided the country up into several zones each divided by a customs barrier or demarcation line, the Germans were in a position to limit the movements of individuals who were required to have a special pass called an *Ausweis* to cross these lines. By the same token they could offer these passes as rewards to collaborators. In some ways this was even better than a sum of money because it made it possible to visit family and friends in another zone.[38] Other rewards could take the form of freedom given to a prisoner of war, or opportunities to get food, a valuable payment for a population faced with severe rationing and shortages. Some secret agents also gained additional profits through the black market.[39] In March 1941, French counterespionage services noted that intelligence agents "take advantage of the facilities given to them by trafficking on the black market." The example of a dropout named Combatti was cited in the report. Before and during the war he had been forced to live in homeless shelters. Since the armistice, he had amassed a fortune of more that three million francs.[40]

Money facilitated the recruitment of members of the underworld. The best known was probably Henri Lafont, an escaped convict who had dropped his original surname of Chamberlin to avoid detection. Working for the Abwehr at the beginning of 1941, Lafont succeeded in infiltrating the Belgian resistance network operating in the southern zone of France and organized the arrest of one of its leaders Otto Lambrecht, which led to countless subsequent arrests.[41] The phenomenal success of this mission encouraged the Abwehr to give him free rein in organizing an unofficial police force. He was rapidly recruited by the fourth bureau of the Sipo-SD and his "French Gestapo" became infamous. Lafont was based in Paris from where he sent agents everywhere in the country. Gangsters, always enthusiastic for a quick profit, were misled into believing that if they agreed to work for the Nazis, their espionage would be protected from the French authorities and that the Germans would also guarantee their other activities against the curiosity of the French police.[42] Lafont did manage to obtain from his employers the release of twenty-seven common law prisoners on the condition that they work for the Germans.[43]

It was easy to recruit profiteers. Theodor Auer, head of the Gestapo in French Morocco confided to a double agent: "My intelligence network is achieving rapid results and that's unsurprising given that the French are trampling over each other to give us 'information.' For a bit of money, you can buy anyone in Morocco. You don't even have to seek out these informers; they come to offer their services of their own accord."[44] Profiteers often took the initiative to contact the Germans. But there was also a subcategory of profiteers: "accidental" spies who were recruited through deceptive newspaper ads, such as "conscientious traveling salesmen and sales agents sought." The initial contact with the Germans appeared innocent since the applicants probably did believe they were to be offered sales jobs. Then a private investigation agency, such as the Constant agency in Paris, would do a character check on them for the Germans. The applicants were then contacted directly, but it was only gradually that the work of spying was mentioned to them after they had been filled with visions of earning large sums of money.[45]

Another example of gradual recruitment was that of Christian Roux. A few days after his demobilization, he was sitting in a café in Montpellier. Some German soldiers, members of an armistice commission, were sitting at a nearby table. Roux used the opportunity to ask them how to correspond with some friends of his who were prisoners of war in Germany. He was told to inquire at the Hôtel Midi, the headquarters of the local armistice commission. The trap was set. In that hotel, he made the acquaintance of German officers who invited him to come back. During these conversations he told them of his precarious economic circumstances: no work and a young child. Two German officers came to visit him at his home and put an envelope containing 300 francs on his child's cot, "to buy milk." He was subsequently given other small gifts before being offered a proofreading job for the German paper *Signal*—a stable and well-paid job. But there was a condition for this golden future: he was to provide military and political intelligence. He accepted the offer. Five days later, his new job as a secret agent came to an abrupt end when he was arrested by the French police.[46]

The morality of the profiteers left much to be desired. At the beginning of 1942, a man named Rizzi was visited by his future father-in-law, Barrier, who brought him news of his fiancée. In the course of their conversation, Barrier asked Rizzi about his life as an organizer within one of Vichy's youth groups, the Chantiers de Jeunesse. Since Barrier seemed to be an honorable man, Rizzi had no qualms in giving him the information requested. However he asked him not to talk about it with anyone because the information was secret. A few days later, Barrier was arrested by the French police for military espionage and they found on him a copy of the information given to him by his future son-in-law alongside information on politicians, the army, and military movements. Barrier had been working for several months for German intelligence.[47]

The military justice report on Gabriel Le Guenne reveals another spy with financial motives. "Approached in October 1940 by a German agent, Le Guenne answered that he didn't care for whom he was working as long as he is paid."[48] But manipulating individuals with no scruples could be tricky. We can well imagine that if another intelligence service was ready to pay more, the agent would betray his original employer. Reile, the head of Abwehr counterespionage in France pointed out the drawbacks of recruiting these profiteers: "Of course none of those people were reliable. . . . They had to be used very carefully."[49]

Though the profiteers lacked both morality and patriotism, they at least had rational motivations for engagement. Other agents became German agents for less rational reasons. These were the "sentimentals," the "adventurers," and the "vulnerable."

Sentimentals were motivated by a desire for revenge or an emotional attachment. Usually, personal revenge was more often the action of an individual engaging in an occasional denunciation rather than that of a regular secret agent. For instance, Georges Besançon denounced a *passeur,* one of a breed of guides who used their local knowledge to facilitate the illegal passage across the demarcation line, generally in return for money. Besançon's motive was that this particular *passeur* had refused to help him cross the demarcation line.[50] A revenge motive also seemed to have been behind the engagement of Bourras, who infiltrated the French armistice delegation in Algiers, as it was explained by the secretary of state for war in his report: "Furious at having been dismissed by the French admiralty, he took this opportunity to get even."[51] But these isolated denunciations could sometimes lead to regular espionage work.

The second type of sentimental agent was those recruited through love affairs. Most German officers' mistresses were not secret agents even though a love relationship could lead to being recruited. Individuals having intimate relationship, usually heterosexual, with Germans were gradually encouraged to provide information. Starting with small bits of occasional information they progressed to more permanent intelligence work. That was the case of Rachel Galy, who fell in love with the recruiting agent Robert Linck. She left her husband and joined the German secret services.[52] Lucienne Delorme's engagement was inspired by both revenge and love. Her collaboration began with her affair with the interpreter-sergeant Walter Dedeck but was also inspired by her desire to get even with the police officer Binet, who had been responsible for her trial and sentencing for possession of stolen goods. She denounced him to her German lover, and denounced many others later on.[53]

Espionage is often linked to adventure.[54] The rise of the spy genre in literature and films dates from the period between the two wars, when Pierre Nord's and Robert Dumas's novels became very popular; these two authors themselves worked for the French secret services.[55] Compared to routine factory work, spying is often portrayed as romantic and full of intrigue and risk. Surprisingly in the documentation I consulted, adventure is rarely mentioned explicitly as a motive. However, it is hard to believe that the flourishing of this literary and cinematographic genre had no influence on the image of espionage and thus on the possibilities of recruitment.

The next category of spies I have chosen to call the vulnerable. Without necessarily being insane many spies are affected by psychological ailments. A recent study by the U.S. government found that, very often, they have two psychological problems. Firstly, they tend to be antisocial and this encourages the rejection of normal social rules along with an absence of remorse. Secondly, they are narcissistic, which causes them to overestimate their own abilities or importance, subsequently leading to disappointment and the feelings of being underappreciated. Being a spy reaffirms their sense of importance and helps them regain their self esteem.[56] The link between psychological disorders and espionage was already known in France during the 1940s. Arrested spies were sometimes subjected to a thorough neuropsychiatric examination.[57] The agent's history of mental health was frequently given as explanation for their work. A report written for Vice-Premier Darlan in May 1941 by Henri Rollin from the Ministry of the Interior emphasized the importance of this question. In discussing mainly pro-German activities and, to a lesser degree, pro-Allied activities, Rollin noted, "numerous cases have shown the political role that a certain number of neurotics want to play . . . In the domain of espionage as well, we can see that the stirring up of political passions can lead to the most vulgar forms of treason, as is the case with Suzanne Desseigne. Here, as for terrorism, a quasi-medical surveillance is needed to uncover and neutralize those fanatics who might become dangerous."[58]

Reluctant spies were those who claimed to have been recruited under duress because they had done something that called for the occupier's pardon. We might assume that German nationals working as spies were mainly motivated by patriotism or pro-Nazi fervor. Yet, sometimes at the root of their activities was their need to redeem themselves. During the 1930s, Hans Goepel pursued anti-Fascism to the extent of fighting on the side of the Spanish Republicans in the Spanish Civil War (1936–39), and then followed this with a stint in the French foreign legion.[59] When his compatriots invaded France, he offered them his services to buy back favor. This was just one example of a German who had been opposed to Nazi ideology seeking rehabilitation with the masters of the hour.

Some individuals who had been secret agents for the Allies or the French also felt compelled to work against their former employer after being arrested by the Germans. Joseph Christin had been working for the French intelligence services in the occupied zone until his capture by the Nazi services in May 1941. Imprisoned and feeling abandoned he went on to denounce nine of his former colleagues and agreed to change sides.[60] Harold Cole is perhaps the most famous traitor amongst British agents in France. Cole was a mechanic born in London in 1906. Working for the Pat O'Leary network, which specialized in helping Allied military personnel escape from France, Cole was arrested by the Germans near Lille in northern France on 6 December 1941. To avoid punishment he accepted to work as double agent and his subsequent denunciations led to the execution of over fifty British agents.[61]

The case of Chaplain Robert Alesch provides clues on the process that led an individual from a position of being recruited under duress to that of becoming a willing spy for the Germans. This chaplain performed humanitarian tasks for the "interallied" resistance network before being caught by the Abwehr. His entry into espionage was thus made under duress. To escape punishment for his pro-Allied activity, he agreed to provide information to the Germans. But quickly he acquired a taste for it, as he was to explain later on:

> Having no experience in the espionage domain, I had hoped to free myself after a while and return to my first convictions. But I became aware that I was caught in a spiral beyond my control. Moreover, the Germans flattered me with compliments that were not undeserved. They admired my knowledge of languages, my psychological finesse, and even my innate sense of adventure. As to myself, I felt that this new occupation took advantage of a weak spot in my soul of which I had been previously unaware, and that it ended up pleasing me.[62]

Not all the crimes of which reluctant spies were initially accused were as serious as actually working for Allied or Resistance networks. Pierre Chevrourier started working for the Germans the day a group of escaped French POWs turned up at his house in Bléré (Indre-et-Loire). They asked him to help them find a place where it would be safe to cross the demarcation line without the necessary border passes. Having accompanied them to a safe crossing point, Chevrourier then ran into a German patrol who questioned him about what he was doing. He denounced the escaped POWs who were about to cross the line. They were captured. To avoid punishment for having initially helped these escaped POWs, he agreed to establish surveillance on the demarcation line, denouncing anyone who attempted an illegal crossings. Chevrourier subsequently denounced thirty-three escaped POWs. Impressed by his work, the Germans sent Chevrourier on an intelligence mission against French troops in the neighboring commune of Ouches to find out whether they had any military equipment that had not been declared to the Germans. [63]

Usually, reluctant spies were contacted directly by the German secret services. This was for instance the case with the Austrian Josef Beitelberger. He had two things that he needed to redeem: he had served in the French foreign legion, and then, while attempting to get back to Vienna to settle an inheritance, he had passed through the demarcation line illegally. Once arrested, he was contacted in his cell by Lauer, a recruiting agent for the Germans. The prisoner was offered a deal: his freedom in exchange for information.[64] In other cases, individuals seeking to rehabilitate themselves were persuaded by friends to approach the Germans. During the 1930s, Oskar Rohr had been the prolific center-forward of Strasbourg's soccer team. His 180 goals still make him the best scorer in the history of the club. In 1939, Rohr signed up for the foreign legion. Since he was a German citizen, he found himself in a difficult position when France was invaded by his compatriots. He asked for the advice of his former coach, Rumbold, also a refugee in the southern zone, who recruited him for the German secret services. A few months before, Rumbold had found himself in the southern city of Perpignan without resources and, through the exiled Alsatian milieu in the region, had joined the German secret services.[65]

The advantage of using these reluctant agents was that they had already contacts within the movement that was to be spied upon. The drawback, and it was a major one, was that they had to be closely watched. They had already betrayed their community of origin or their first employer, so why would they not do it again? Thus the Germans had to keep them under control. We have seen in Alesch's case that in certain circumstances they kept on working for the Germans because they had acquired a taste for it. But in the meantime, the Germans threatened them with reprisals if their instructions were not followed.[66] It is probable that the obedience of the reluctant to the Nazi intelligence services was due to a fair amount of cowardice.

While various categories of motives are identifiable, it is not always possible to classify individual spies neatly in one category or another. As Alesch's case shows, one kind of motivation could easily hide another but it would seem that money was the prime motivator.

The new recruits had to prove themselves. Recruitment was usually followed by a period of testing through easy missions. The first missions involved political spying. They were not openly directed "against France," but often against Gaullist or Allied activities and could therefore be presented as helping the French government. Once these missions had been accomplished, the new recruit was told that he or she had now become too involved to be able to withdraw and that any hesitation would be met with reprisals. The new spy was asked to sign a pledge promising to faithfully serve and obey the orders of the German secret services.

Agents showing potential were provided with technical equipment and sent to training programs. There were schools for spies in Besançon, Stuttgart, Paris, and Freiburg-im-Breisgau. Here trainee spies were taught how to use clandestine transmission equipment, invisible ink, and cryptology.

Thus the Germans succeeded in creating an impressive intelligence network throughout France, including in the nonoccupied territories. On 8 July 1941, the Resistance newspaper *Les Petites Ailes de France* pessimistically commented on the spread of these networks:

> Even in the free zone the Gestapo is weaving an ever-tightening web that controls French administration a little more each day and, more generally, controls all our activities. A German civil servant charged with the surveillance of political refugees lives in Vichy. In the south east of France, the Nazi network is particularly dense. Aix-en-Provence serves as a base to two brigades of the Gestapo under the command of a member of the German Red Cross. In Marseille, the police forces of the Reich have been reinforced and are particularly busy seeking refugees and Gaullist sympathizers through *agents provocateurs.*[67]

3 THE STRUCTURES OF FRENCH COUNTERESPIONAGE

There are two points about counterespionage in Vichy France that are important to stress. Firstly, *all* the organizations described here worked against both the Axis and the Allies. This system was designed to fight against all spies, regardless of who they might be. Moreover, measures taken against one foreign intelligence service were effective against all foreign espionage agencies. Secondly, even counterespionage measures aimed primarily against the Germans were not entirely independent from the collaborating Vichy government.[1]

When referring to the French secret services, the Deuxième Bureau (second bureau) immediately comes to mind. A certain romance is attached to this institution, and its moniker has frequently appeared in movie and novel titles. However, as with the term *Gestapo,* which refers to only one bureau within the German secret service, we need to avoid oversimplifying the Deuxième Bureau. Though many laypersons, even specialists, mistakenly use the term *deuxième bureau* to refer to the whole of French espionage and counterespionage, this error obscures the actual workings of the French spy organizations.

The Deuxième Bureau was an organization attached to the Staff Headquarters of the armed forces (army, navy, and air force) both at the national level as well as at the local level within each branch. Synthesizing information from other agencies, the Deuxième Bureau collected, analyzed, and presented the intelligence that military command needed to make its decisions. Its role was therefore more bureaucratic than its public image would lead one to believe. It was primarily a leadership organ entrusted with the job of coordination and synthesis. After the invasion, the Deuxième Bureau operated clandestinely under the leadership of Lieutenant Colonel Louis Baril from both Vichy (based in the Hôtel International) and from Lyon.[2] To camouflage its activities a fake company selling construction materials was set up as a front in Lyon under the name *Technica*.[3]

However, for the present study, the Deuxième Bureau's work is less important than that of the Cinquième Bureau (fifth bureau), established in 1940 under the leadership of Colonel Louis Rivet. While the work of the Deuxième Bureau was mainly analytical, the Cinquième Bureau was assigned the more active role of actually gathering intelligence. It was divided into two sections: one gathered intelligence (the Service de Renseignements, or SR) while the other dealt with the centralization of intelligence (Section de Centralisation du Renseignement, or SCR). After the 1940 defeat, the SR was secretly reborn under the name of "Kléber network." The SR agents themselves were officially scratched off the register of army employees but continued to be paid from a secret fund.[4] The SCR was the real military counterespionage branch of the army, which Rivet sought to reorganize after the armistice.[5] On 21 June, he noted in his diary that he had given "the instruction for the dissolution of the Cinquième Bureau, including military and civilian personnel, and the selection of a reduced personnel apt to perform camouflaged operations."[6] The first employees were laid off on 27 June. In addition to reducing its numbers, the reorganization essentially divided the SCR into two subsections: the TR network and the Bureau for Anti-National Affairs (*Bureau(x) des Menées Antinationales,* or BMA). Rivet was in charge of coordinating these two organizations.

Paul Paillole, the head of *Travaux Ruraux* (rural works, or TR), is probably the best-known figure of wartime French counterespionage. Paillole was born in Rennes in northwestern France in 1905. After his father's death in combat in 1918, his mother moved to the southern city of Marseille where she worked as a schoolteacher. Paillole was a keen athlete and played soccer for the prestigious Marseille team. He was an expert at fencing and became the French youth champion and later the military champion after joining the army. His athletic abilities helped him get into the Saint-Cyr academy where he received his military education. In 1935, he was assigned to a post in the secret services, though it was not a coveted position and hardly his first choice. Paillole thought that the work would be too sedentary and he wished for something more active. Moreover, his only knowledge of the profession came from the spy novels of Pierre Nord. But he quickly developed a liking for the job and his professional skill was recognized by almost everyone.[7] Robert Terres's memoirs are interesting in this regard. Terres was an agent of the TR who was fired after his suspicious escape following his arrest by the Germans. After that, his relationship with the TR network was strained. Despite this, he described Paillole as "dynamic, intelligent, competent," and added that he "knew he [Paillole] would make a good leader of the counterespionage."[8] Jacques Soustelle, who was Paillole's institutional rival in 1943–44, considered him to be "gifted with a great capacity for work, a genuine talent for organization and unquestionable leadership abilities."[9] Paillole led the TR from 1940 to 1944.

Travaux Ruraux was called the Rural Works because the counterespionage service camouflaged itself as an agricultural organization. This was an excellent disguise in Vichy France, where the traditionalist government extolled rural values and advocated "a return to the land." The service's headquarters were located in Marseille and known under the codename Cambronne (after a French general famous for having said *merde* to the British during the Napoleonic wars). There were several reasons for establishing the headquarters in Marseille. Paillole was very familiar with the city having lived there for part of his youth. He had many friends there. The Recordier brothers, who were to become famous for their Resistance activities, were his closest childhood friends. A professional acquaintance, Jean Oswald, had just been named police commissioner of the city. Another one of Paillole's friends, the police captain Robert Blémant, had also just been transferred to Marseille. The ease of access to the city also influenced the decision to adopt Marseille as the headquarters. Its status as France's biggest port made it possible, if need be, to quickly embark for North Africa. In addition to this central office, the TR had branches throughout southern France (Annemasse, Limoges, Clermont, Lyon, Marseille, and Toulouse), and French North Africa (Algiers, Rabat-Casablanca, and Tunis). In the northern zone of France, a sub-branch operated in Paris.

In July 1941, the TR service compiled a report of its first year of activity for the armed forces command. According to this document, Paillole's service had no financial problems, unlike some other branches of the French secret services at that time.[10] The expenses of the TR till July1941 amounted to 1,383,000 francs, against receipts of 2,634,000 francs, so the service made a net profit of around 1,250,000 francs. This money was mainly recuperated from the foreign intelligence agencies against which it operated. The TR underwent rapid expansion. It went from nineteen permanent employees in July 1940 to twenty-seven in July 1941. And the number of TR agents in the field increased considerably: in July 1940, there were 60 of them and by July 1941, 429. But even this growth in recruitment was considered totally inadequate by the author of the report. The TR's intelligence gathering remained weak in other European countries, and its technical resources also fell short, according to the report.

There were other shortcomings enumerated in the report:

> Too many posts deliberately sacrifice method for action without achieving a rational equilibrium:
> —logs poorly kept or not at all kept.
> —information transmitted too slowly, with poor indication of the sources, and sometimes in a style lacking clarity;
> —agents . . . poorly directed, not followed up, at times paid irregularly;
> —poor liaison between posts, particularly with those in French North Africa;
> —excessive delays in responding to queries, particularly in the transmission of accounts.

The overall assessment of the report, however, was positive:

> Despite all manner of difficulties, TR "has overcome the defeat" and is trusted by the high command. (It is worth remembering that the posts had to be created from scratch, with personnel reduced in number, made up of young and newly appointed recruits in areas often unfamiliar to them; that they had to overcome skepticism, indifference and at times outright hostility from some quarters. Regarding TR's leadership, far from its own bosses, it had to tackle numerous material difficulties [transport of archives, etc.], it had to make do with a reduced personnel, with an ever increasing workload, a workload which testifies to the dynamism of the posts). Its various studies (summarized below) on the activities of foreign intelligence agencies, on antinational plotting, on states of mind, etc., show the immensity of the task that still needs to be accomplished.[11]

The other military counterespionage organization, the BMA, was created on 25 August 1940, but it really became operational only in November. Lieutenant Colonel Guy d'Alès, who spent most of his career as a cavalry officer, was appointed its chief. He knew practically nothing of counterespionage matters. The decision to entrust such an important service to a novice can probably be explained by the fact that he was not known to the Germans. This was important because a portion of the BMA's work was done openly. The BMA was initially tolerated by the Germans because its official role was the repression of Communist, Gaullist, and Allied activities. Because its anti-German activity had to be done in secret, it was better not to alert the Germans to this activity by entrusting the service to someone well known for an anti-German attitude.

The BMA offices were set up in each military district, but only in the territories not directly occupied by the Germans. Each BMA office was set up within the local headquarters of the military district and was made up of three or four officers and as many noncommissioned officers. The bulk of the personnel of these bureaus came from the counterespionage agencies scrapped at the time of the French defeat. Agents from these offices were then posted in all units of the army. Their status as BMA officers had to be known to their fellow soldiers so that the latter could inform them of any attempt at subversion, sabotage, or espionage.

A ministry order of November 1940 clarified the mission of the BMA.[12] Their job was to centralize and coordinate research to guide and document police investigations. They had to unmask those suspected of acts of espionage or sabotage, whether they were working for the Allies or the Axis. BMA officers were called upon to neutralize and repress foreign propaganda within the armed forces, while also fighting Communist activities in the army, navy, youth camps, as well as organizations working for national defense. More generally, the BMA was to work in concert with the police to perform surveillance of the borders, the demarcation line, and other sensitive areas. D'Alès reminded them that they also had to keep a close eye on the economic activities of the Axis in French territory. The following is an extract from his instructions of February 1942: "The information and reports on German and Italian business activities in France (the buying of movie theaters, the Todt organization, etc.) and on the means used by these companies' employees for their purchases are of particular interest to the French authorities who will probably have to reexamine the whole issue. The BMA and the TR are consequently asked to keep on collecting this information both in mainland France and in Africa."[13]

During the summer of 1942, the Germans put pressure on Vichy to abolish the BMA whose anti-German activity was known to them. On 19 August, Darlan, commander-in-chief of the armed forces, presented a proposal for the reform of their organization to Vice-Premier Laval. The personal diary of pro-German defense minister General Eugène Bridoux noted ruefully that these proposals "amount to reestablishing exactly what we had wanted to abolish."[14] The new service came into existence secretly on 24 August, under the name Service de Sécurité Militaire (SSM, Military Security Service). Its missions were similar to those of the BMA, and it reemployed a large part of its personnel.[15] Paillole was given the command of this new organization, a sure sign of the government's confidence in him.

The army was not the only institution active in counterespionage. The navy also had its own intelligence and counterespionage services.[16] The navy's Deuxième Bureau, led by Captain Sanson, worked in the same manner as that of the army: it centralized and synthesized intelligence originating from a variety of sources. As for counterespionage, intelligence centers for the navy (Centres de Renseignements de la Marine, or CRM), had been set up in 1939, and after the defeat, there were sections for surveillance and documentation added to them (Section de Surveillance et de Documentation, or SSD). These organizations were established in port cities and they contributed to the surveillance of maritime borders and the policing of navigation. They also investigated foreign infiltration and engaged in economic espionage, creating an overlap between their missions and that of other military and civilian services. The navy also had its own police for counterespionage in the form of an organization called Sûreté Navale (Naval Security).

With the exception of a handful of arrests made by Naval Security, it was the police and not the military who did the actual capturing of spies. The Surveillance du Territoire (ST, or Territorial Surveillance) branch of the police had been set up in the early years of the twentieth century but it was not until the late 1930s that it had acquired a meaningful existence. Extreme right-wing riots in Paris in February 1934 and the rise of Nazism in Germany had highlighted possible threats to France. But these threats had not always been taken seriously, and only limited specialized personnel were assigned to counterespionage within the ST. By 1938 the ST's numbers had increased but its 128 employees were still insufficient against the Fascist peril.

The defeat obviously was to have repercussions on the service. Since the armistice there were no more ST offices in the occupied zone because all its personnel had been transferred south. Even in the south, the counterespionage work of the ST was suspended following the instructions of Didkowski, the general director of the National Police.[17] Colonel Rivet, the chief of the former Cinquième Bureau, noted: "For reasons of camouflage, the ST has since 29 July stopped performing its counterespionage mission and been invited to put itself at the disposal of the Prefects and limit itself to tracking foreigners traveling in the free zone. Only a few passionate ST police captains prepared to give up their free time will continue to engage in counterespionage."[18] Following an intervention from the defense minister General Weygand, Didkowksi was replaced. His successor, Henri Chavin, asked the ST to return to its usual work, which resumed in September, after a reorganization. From then on, there were nine ST brigades spread around the southern unoccupied zone, their geographical location overlapping with the military districts (Agen, Bourg-en-Bresse, Châteauroux, Clermont-Ferrand, Limoges, Lyon, Marseille, Montpellier, and Toulouse).[19] They also had offices in the main cities of North Africa. A large staff increase in French North Africa was requested by Weygand and obtained during the first months of 1941; by then Weygand had left the defense ministry to become Vichy's delegate general in that area. Of course the aim was not limited to guarding against the German threat because the ST also worked against the supporters of De Gaulle, leader of the Resistance, and the British. Nonetheless the suggestion was put forward that a proportion of new ST personnel should come from refugees from France's northeast province of Alsace-Lorraine.[20] There were several reasons for this. There were plenty of Alsatian civil servants available in the nonoccupied zone following their exodus; they could stay aloof from the local political intrigues that were undermining the efficiency of the employees already in place; and originating from the disputed border area of Alsace might encourage them to be particularly firm against German espionage.[21] The law of 4 October 1942 further reorganized the ST. Henceforth it was to be attached to the criminal police.[22] This only entailed an administrative move as the missions and the personnel remained practically the same. After the German invasion of the southern zone in November 1942, the ST was scrapped by order of the occupation forces.

The difficulties and dangers of organizing counterespionage in France following the 1940 defeat were manifold. Following the 1940 armistice all the counterespionage services moved their headquarters to the initially unoccupied south of the country, which raised the problem of what to do with their archives. The expansion of secret services in the twentieth century had led to increasing amounts of bureaucracy. Creating folders and files had become central to the operation of all French secret services. Occupation by the Germans, however, called for the destruction of certain documents that could not be moved or hidden. On 22 of June 1940, Paillole ordered Paul Gérard-Dubot, a member of the Cinquième Bureau, to do just that. In his diary, Gérard-Dubot noted sadly that burning these documents meant watching years of hard work involving many sleepless nights and missed vacations go up in smoke.[23] They tried to save the most important documents, and Colonel Rivet noted in his diary on June 30 that these had been stored in a safe place.[24] Some were even hidden in the cellars of the Roquefort cheese factory.

Despite these precautions, some police and secret services archives fell into German hands in the summer of 1940. The archives of the National Police force were seized in its offices in number 11, rue des Saussaies. Reile, the head of Abwehr IIIF in Paris, mentioned that these were of particular interest for his bureau. The documents made it possible to find French agents working in the Reich but also provided names of potentially pro-German elements within the French population who could then be recruited for the Abwehr.[25] The archives of the navy's Cinquième Bureau were also uncovered at the same time, including the names of agents and their addresses, thereby seriously endangering them.[26]

Other archives were seized after the Germans' invasion of the southern zone in November 1942. On 3 March 1943, the Gestapo, seemingly acting on a denunciation by a policeman, discovered three tons of Deuxième Bureau archives in Lyon. Two days later, this documentation was sent to Germany to be studied.[27] Archives from the TR and BMA were also uncovered. In June 1943 the archives of the TR post in Clermont were found in their hiding place by the Abwehr. The next month, a denunciation led to the discovery of the bulk of the TR central archives in a property near Nîmes. Another portion, hidden in Dr. Recordier's home near Marseille, was preserved intact until the Liberation.[28]

Seizures and destructions of archives clearly had a very negative effect on the efficiency of French secret services. A well-organized filing system makes it possible to quickly find documents with just the slightest of reference to a given individual.[29] There were attempts to recreate this filing system after occupation, but the absence of certain files clearly had an impact on counterespionage. For instance, in a letter about an individual named Arno Donner, we can read: "Unfortunately, because of the destruction of documents resulting from the war, the Donner file is very incomplete."[30]

Alongside the difficulties linked to gaps in the archives were the usual problems of coordination of the various services involved in counterintelligence. We should not forget that specialist counterespionage organizations did not work in complete isolation. They needed the cooperation of many other institutions. This was emphasized by the Supreme Council for National Defense (Conseil Supérieur de la Défense Nationale) on 6 July 1940: "The setting up of this vast organization for gathering and using intelligence about German activities extends well beyond the Deuxième and Cinquième Bureaux of the general staff of the army because it concerns all governmental departments."[31] Thus, those senior local representatives of the French state, the prefects, and the police reported to the BMAs any suspicious activities including those of German agents. Vichy's postal and telephone censors who intercepted and noted the contents of millions of ordinary citizens' private correspondence forwarded transcripts of suspicious letters or telephone calls. Military and civilian tribunals organized the imprisonment of suspects. But in the confusion of the Vichy state, cooperation was not systematic.

The relationship with the regular police highlights the difficulties of coordination. Counterespionage had to be able to count on police cooperation, and in many cases help was given as expected. But this was not always the case. Sometimes agents of the French secret services were actually arrested by the police as a result of conflicts between the police and these services. From the start, the TR network was very aware of this problem as is shown by the measures it took to protect its headquarters from the police. At the beginning of November of 1940, d'Alès of the BMA, paid a visit to the superintendent of the Marseille police, Maurice Anne-Marie de Rodellec Du Porzic, to inform him that the TR was operating in his jurisdiction.[32] Such a precaution was necessary to prevent police raids as the suspicious activity of the TR would inevitably attract police attention in the long-run.

But for various security reasons, it was not always possible to keep the police informed of all secret services activities. Agents from the TR and Deuxième Bureau working in the northern zone sometimes fell victim to sinister intentions. There was at least one case, and probably more, of an agent denounced by a French policeman.[33] Paillole gave the following advice to new recruits: "there are members of the police who are wonderful and others who are, regrettably, horrible. When you are not totally confident in the police, even in the French police, you mustn't trust them."[34] Some individuals working for the French secret services were threatened by the police even in the southern zone. This applied particularly to German Jews recruited to work against the Nazis as the counterespionage agencies tried to take advantage of their anti-Nazi feelings and their knowledge of German. During the summer of 1942, the situation of these German-Jew agents became especially difficult. Vichy had become a zealous accomplice of the extermination campaign initiated after the Wannsee meetings of January 1942. The French police arrested Jews in large numbers and among them were agents of the French secret services, including one Leopold Hermann. At the end of July 1942, he was taken in a raid at La Ciotat, near Marseille. Captain Kessler of the Deuxième Bureau intervened at the end of September to try to help free Hermann who was one of his agents. But it was too late, Leopold Hermann had already been deported to an "unknown destination."[35]

The vast counterespionage network required coordination between different agencies, and if agencies failed, the clandestine activities of the French secret services would be vulnerable to the Axis. This raised difficulties from a very early stage. From Algiers, Weygand highlighted the problem in a letter of 7 December 1940 to Pétain. In it Vichy's chief executive officer in North Africa discussed an ongoing operation of anti-German counterespionage in Morocco: "This matter is very delicate in that it risks, if it isn't conducted with a great deal of tact, revealing the activities of the officially disbanded intelligence network to the Italian and German armistice commissions."

The operation, in which each agency acted only according to its own needs, emphasized the problem: "It is evident that the case should be the responsibility the BMA of the military high command in Morocco because it involves mostly officers of the army and some civilians having relationships with these officers. And yet, under the pretext that this case originated in Agadir and that the first person to be indicted, Pécheral, is a navy man, the navy claimed a 'right of follow up' that would allow it to take part in the prosecution."[36]

In this particular case, Weygand intervened to limit the role of the navy. But he was seeking a more permanent solution that would centralize all counterespionage services under the direction of the BMA. "I am convinced that there could be only one solution: to entrust, in each part of Africa, the struggle against antinational subversion to a sole organization—the BMA. This would include one representative from the navy and one from the air force, and would be directly in charge of the ST police force, which would in turn be reinforced, increasingly specialized and relieved of any other role—and would forbid any other organization to intervene in this domain in any other way than by conveying intelligence to the BMA or to the ST, to the exclusion of any other authority."[37]

The secretary of state, Paul Baudouin, agreed entirely with Weygand's views and sent a copy of his letter to the other ministries involved asking for their comments.[38] Writing for the interior ministry, Marcel Peyrouton saw "only benefits" from the plan.[39] The secretary of state for the air force pointed out that "such an organization had always been advocated" by the Air Ministry who had ceaselessly worked in close collaboration with his comrades in the War Ministry.[40] General Huntziger, secretary of state for war, claimed to agree completely with Weygand but he pointed out that the project should also be applied in metropolitan France, "particularly in war ports such as Toulon."[41] Does this mean there was complete harmony? The navy had yet to respond. Darlan gave his answer on 26 December 1940. Accepting the necessity of a closer collaboration between departments, he sent instructions to the SSD posts to establish their bureaus in BMA premises, or if this was not possible, for them to assign a liaison officer with these organizations. But he resisted the structural change of the navy counterespionage services under the pretext that their mission reached beyond the limits of the counterespionage framework and thus had to stay under the authority of his own ministry.[42]

The BMA still tried to centralize counterespionage as much as possible. Representatives from the navy and the air force were posted in BMA offices to minimize conflicts. Because of the importance of the Marseille port, a navy representative, Lieutenant Gardiès, was part of BMA post number 15. In the areas where air bases were located, there were representatives of the air force: for instance Lieutenant Henry at Clermont or Captain Pierrefeu in Morocco, and so forth.[43] Nevertheless, despite the many attempts to find a formula for centralization, conflicts and rivalries persisted, not only between the different branches of the armed forces, but also with the police.

Relations between the ST and the military branches were not always conflictual. In their memoirs, veterans of the military secret services wrote of some operations carried out without friction and of friendships with individual police officers. Thus we should not generalize these difficulties. But the ST often received instructions coming from various bodies: prefects, army, navy, and so on. The requests were at times conflicting and, because of its limited personnel, the ST was forced to prioritize some of the demands to the detriment of others. Nonetheless, the service was in regular contact with the military counterespionage services, and, thanks to this, conflicts could be resolved directly. Contacts with other police services were less regular and relations more distant. Furthermore, the mission of those services was broader than the single objective of counterespionage. For the regular police, intrusions into the counterespionage domain were motivated by more general policing issues, relating to crime or public order.

Marcel Jaminais' arrest is an example. He was under surveillance by the ST, which was awaiting the right moment to arrest him to reap the most benefit out of the arrest. Meanwhile, the municipal police force in Toulon arrested him for his suspicious behavior. According to a report from the TR network, "This arrest was only supposed to be carried out once Jaminais had received his radio transmitter. When checking hotels in the course of an investigation following up on a surveillance report, the local Toulon police discovered suspicious papers on Jaminais and proceeded to arrest him without prior consultation with the ST."[44]

The difficulties in coordinating the various organizations continued as occupation was spreading. They were highlighted in a letter addressed to the directorate of the armistice services (Direction des Services de l'Armistice) by Paillole, who was at that time head of the military security service (Service de Sécurité Militaire, or SSM).

> While informing the directorate of the armistice services of Dreesen's arrest, the SSM feels it is necessary to make it aware that the police, having carried out this arrest on July 25, only informed the Lyon SSM on 22 August 1942. Since the SSM does not have police powers, this sort of thing occurs fairly frequently. For instance, the apprehension of Barna (arrested at Cusset and imprisoned in Clermont) was carried out on 4 January 1942. The military au-

thority was only officially informed of it on 24 July, which caused a small incident with the control commission.[45]

The first case was particularly sensitive because Dreesen was a personal acquaintance of Adolf Hitler.

Counterespionage was not only especially difficult after the defeat; it had also become particularly dangerous. In normal circumstances counterespionage is one of the safer areas of the secret service activity.[46] During the Nazi occupation it was fraught with danger.[47] Paillole claimed that his hideouts were ransacked on at least three occasions.[48] There were constant rumors that the southern zone would be invaded by the Germans. The diary of Jacques Britsch, an officer of the Deuxième Bureau, is particularly interesting in this regard, as it reveals the anxiety of an employee of the secret services, aware that the arrival of the Germans would almost certainly mean his internment.[49] The diplomatic tensions between France and Germany following the dismissal of Vice-Premier Laval in December 1940 led to an early fear that the free zone would also be occupied. On 15 January 1941, Britsch wrote that he had been informed of the contingency plans in case of an invasion and noted sarcastically: "in the event of a German invasion, officers are to report to their place of work! In other words they should show up in a POW uniform, served on a plate!" Ten days later, however, his superiors obtained a false passport for him but said there was no immediate risk of occupation. Britsch nevertheless remained skeptical and, as a precaution, withdrew all his savings from the bank on 1 February. On 7 February he again asked himself, "Are we heading toward a total occupation?" before offering the pessimistic response: "I'll consider myself lucky if I'm not in a POW camp before the end of the month." The immediate tension died away but the officers attached to the different counterespionage services remained acutely aware of the potential danger.

The threat of total occupation did eventually materialize in November 1942. Once this invasion occurred members of these services either had to flee or go into hiding. A letter from the chief commissioner of police Jean Léonard of the ST in Marseille sent to the director of the criminal police in Vichy underlined the threat that hung over the policemen of his service. The members of the ST brigade were open to a very specific danger owing to their professional responsibilities, firstly in prewar counterespionage but later in similar activities since the armistice. Léonard singled out the position of four of his subordinates who had been in Nice before the war and had been particularly zealous in their anti-Italian activity. Leonard's own position was far from reassuring. A native of the disputed border area of Lorraine, he had joined the police as a detective in 1920 and been attached to the French army on the Rhine until his transfer to a police post in Strasbourg in 1929. In these capacities he had been heavily engaged in counterespionage activity, causing him to become the object of a violent German press campaign. But Léonard also drew attention to the fact that since January 1941, the ST branch in Marseille had carried out the arrest of over one hundred and seventy German agents. Amongst these were a number of German nationals, twelve of whom had thereafter been condemned to death by military tribunal but subsequently released by Vichy, only to complain of the brutalities they had suffered at the hands of the ST. That the ST should find itself in a delicate position in the event of a German invasion had been foreseen and precautions had been taken. Six months before the invasion of this zone members of the brigade were issued special false identity cards by the senior local police chief, the *intendant,* and were given special ration tickets in November 1942.[50] According to Colonel Rivet the counterespionage services paid a heavy price for their activity with seventy-eight deaths in the military branches alone.[51]

The secret services thus experienced many difficulties and dangers in their anti-German counterespionage work. Political pressures were added to technical difficulties as well as its personnel and coordination problems. All these hindered efficiency. But the attitude of the secret services themselves was not without its own ambiguities, which resulted in further limiting their capacity to operate successfully.

4 SECRET SERVICE AMBIGUITIES

Several foreign intelligence networks, from the Allies as well as the Axis, worked in France during the years following the military defeat. The memoirs of former members of the Vichy secret services and their veterans' association newsletter give their version of the attitude adopted toward these various threats. Several themes dominate. Firstly, the Vichy secret services had a difficult relationship with the Vichy government, although sometimes exceptions are made for Pétain and Weygand. The second is linked to the first, in that the activities of the secret services were, from the outset, defined as a form of "resistance." This brings us to the third point: the true nature of the links between Vichy's secret services and the Allies. If we are to believe the veterans of these services, there was a certain degree of harmony, perhaps not so much with the Gaullists, but at least with the British and the Americans. Because of these friendly relations, repression of the Allied and Gaullist intelligence networks was limited to the absolute minimum. Paul Paillole in particular was silent on that repression. Behind this restraint is the idea that, from the very start, anti-German feelings were the motivating factor behind the behavior of the Vichy secret service.

Even though the memoirs vary on some details, they generally concur on these main points. There is, however, one exception in Robert Terres's memoirs, which are more critical of his own activity and particularly of that of his TR network.[1] Does this stem from his strained relations with his former network, as Paillole claims, or can we see in Terres's comments an element of truth?[2] To get closer to the reality of the period we need to juxtapose these postwar memoirs with contemporaneous documents. Obviously it should be kept in mind that there were sometimes major differences between the behavior of local branches of the secret services in different regions and also between different individuals within these services. In addition it should be noted from the outset that my study of this documentation pertains mainly to the army's secret services. A lack of available archives (as well as a dearth of memoirs) prevented me from pursuing a similar line of inquiry with regard to the naval secret services.

It is easiest to begin by analyzing secret service attitudes toward the German intelligence networks because these relations are the most straightforward. If there were ambiguities in this regard it was mainly because the secret services admired the technical skills of their German colleagues. In his diary entry of 2 March 1941, Jacques Britsch of the Deuxième Bureau made the following comment: "We can't help but admire the Boche's methods."[3] In a training session for his subordinates in June 1942 Paillole compared the British and German secret services: "You might be surprised that we are studying the legendary IS (Intelligence Service) with less care than the German or Italian intelligence agencies. But we can draw lessons from the Germans, and the study of the Italians was very informative. In contrast, there's not much to learn from the English military secret services."[4] When, in this same lecture, Paillole described the harshness of the methods used by the Germans against the individuals they arrested for spying, a member of the audience interrupted him with the following question: "What are we waiting for to do the same?"

A second ambiguity of the French secret services towards the Germans was linked to the anti-Communism of this ultraconservative milieu. At times, even a preference for a German victory over the Soviet Union was expressed. Jacques Britsch from the Deuxième Bureau was resolutely anti-German, yet in his diary entry for 1 January 1941 he wrote, "The characteristic of this period is that we are oscillating between the Soviet danger and the German danger. Should we fear one over the other? This morning I am asking myself this question. If Germany and Russia were to go to war against each other, in which direction would my support go?

I think it would be for Germany, because she alone can free Europe from the Comintern." However, on the following 6 October, Britsch qualified his position, at least as pertaining to French Communists. After the German execution of Communist hostages in retaliation for Resistance attacks on the occupation forces, he wrote the following: "The Communists who died by firing squad at Châteaubriant didn't utter a single cry. They died singing the national anthem. France is under the German yoke and we are in the same boat with all those oppressed by this major enemy."[5] In Britsch's case, the heroism of Communist resisters seemed to appease his instinctive anti-Communism.

In any event, any ambiguities due to anti-Communism or technical admiration did not amount to sympathizing with the Germans. It can even be claimed, without risk of contradiction, that any study based on a thorough analysis of the archives of the Vichy secret services will inevitably lead to the conclusion that German espionage was by far their main target.

The secret services' anti-German feelings can be explained firstly by professional tradition.[6] Since 1871 and the aftermath of a rapid French defeat in the Franco-Prussian war, the secret services saw Germany as a greater enemy than Britain. From that point on, French spy activity was directed against the enemy on the other side of the Rhine. History courses given during their secret service military training reinforced this longstanding enmity. In his memoirs, Pierre Nord claims the members of the secret services "had a sense of history based on their own experience, a living and lived knowledge of history much truer than that of our leaders. This had been enough to convince them, on 25 June 1940, that the last word had not yet been spoken."[7] The frequent presence of historical references in secret service documentation of the time confirms this dimension of their hostility towards the Germans.

Secondly, the French secret services also mistrusted German intentions. On 2 December 1940 Jacques Britsch wrote in his diary: "A German victory would reduce us to the same status as Spain." Three days later he added: "I am haunted by this question: 'for whom are we defending the empire?' For Germany and Italy, if they win. It's crazy to expect that, in this eventuality, they would leave us anything else other than Algeria." Following Laval's speech of 22 June 1942 in which the Vichy premier publicly expressed his wish for a German victory, Britsch wrote in his diary "if the Axis wins France will be sliced up."[8] A report addressed to the army's high command in January 1942 by Louis Baril, head of the Deuxième Bureau, included the following assessment of German intentions: "Unfortunately for Hitler, the value of his promises is known. . . . A triumphant Germany will renege on all of its commitments. This is how the German mentality works."[9]

The anti-Germanism of the French secret services was criticized by both the Germans and the collaborationists, France's Fascist sympathizers.[10] In his diary, Vichy's war minister, the extremely pro-German general Eugène Bridoux, feared how the execution of the Abwehr agent Henri Devillers would be interpreted in Germany noting that the German ambassador Otto Abetz "sees this as the mark of the anti-German spirit in the army and he regrets it."[11] It seems that this was indeed the Germans' interpretation, since two months later, they demanded the suppression of the BMA citing its anti-German attitude. Two German reports of 1943, written after their intelligence agencies had examined captured French secret services archives, retrospectively highlighted this. In July 1943, a report from the SD (Sicherheitsdienst) claimed that "in reality, the BMA had been almost exclusively focused against agents working for Germany."[12] Another retrospective SD report concluded that, since the armistice, the French services had kept their "same anti-German attitude."[13]

The anti-German antagonism of the French secret services was also heavily criticized by the collaborationists, those ultra pro-German factions based essentially in Paris. These radicals aimed to discredit the whole of the Vichy government, which they viewed as too soft and too timid in its collaboration with Germany, and even wrongly attributed to it intentions of resistance. The collaborationists particularly hated Vichy's secret services because the agents it arrested often came from within their own extremist movements. Even bearing these reservations in mind, one cannot help but be shocked by the paranoid extremes of the collaborationist press campaign against these services. They were often, in time-honored fashion, lumped together under the all-encompassing title of Deuxième Bureau, but it seems that the whole range of French intelligence and counterintelligence agencies were targeted by these criticisms. On 26 August 1942, two days after the dissolution of the BMA, the newspaper *Nouveaux temps* led the charge. A literary review of the best-selling book *Les Décombres* (The ruins) by the Fascist Lucien Rebatet applauded its attacks on the Cinquième Bureau. Newspaper articles became increasingly aggressive after the American landing in French North Africa in November 1942 since the collaborationists saw the secret services as in cahoots with this Allied action.[14]

The collaborationist press campaign, which emphasized the secret services' anti-Germanism as much as their incompetence, irritated these services so much that the SSM (Service de Sécurité Militaire, successor to the BMA), took the unusual step of discussing with the Military Justice Department the possibility of legal action. In particular they spoke of suing the newspaper *Le Petit Parisien* for an article by Marius Larique entitled "Voyage autour de ma source" (Journey around my spring) published on 25 September 1942. In this article, Larique vigorously attacked the "officers of the Deuxième Bureau" and the Vichyites for whom "the only concern is Germany's defeat." For the Military Justice Department, four motives could justify legal proceedings. Firstly, the journalist could be accused of character defamation toward the army in violation of the 28 July 1881 law on freedom of the press. Then, the article could be found to be a breach of the decrees of 1 September 1939 and its complement of 20 January 1940, which punished information "of a nature to help the undertakings of a foreign power against France or to exert a nefarious influence on the spirit of the army and the population." Finally, according to article 76 of the penal code, the newspaper could be prosecuted for "treason" and, according to article 83, for a willful act aimed at harming national defense. But the secret services' fear of giving more publicity to the article, and particularly the wish to avoid incidents with the Germans, prevailed. In the end, no legal action was taken.[15]

The collaborationists claimed that Vichy's "softness" was inspired by the secret services' forecasts about the outcome of the war, and that these forecasts were inspired by a knee-jerk anti-Germanism. It is true that from the time of Operation Barbarossa, that is to say the German invasion of the Soviet Union in the summer of 1941, the Deuxième Bureau insisted that it was impossible for the Axis to win the war. According to an analysis of 27 June 1941 written by Baril, the Nazis were repeating history's mistakes: "We thought that Hitler, being aware of the example of his illustrious predecessor, would avoid making the same mistake that proved fatal to Napoleon." Baril foresaw that the Germans would initially win victories: "There is no doubt that there will be considerable initial successes. But Napoleon too got as far as Moscow. The conquest of the Russian territory carries within it the seeds of weakness. Victories can only be achieved at the cost of much wearing down of the German military machine." The inevitable exhaustion of the Wehrmacht caused by the conditions of battle in the East meant that even victory would leave the Germans in a very difficult situation. "If the Red Army is pushed back or beaten, the problem would remain the same because Britain would not have been beaten, and behind Britain, America is taking big steps on the path to war." Such a victory would in itself cause difficulties: "A Germany victorious over the USSR would have enormously expanded territories to occupy. Its forces would be dispersed and diluted. Not only could it not reduce its military presence, but it would have to find new administrative cadres just when it would have already used up all its resources."[16] In January 1942, one month after the Japanese attack on Pearl Harbor, Baril wrote another report on the state of the war and possible outcomes. His conclusions remained essentially unchanged since his June 1941 analysis: "When the year 1941 started, it was still possible to think that the end of the conflict could be favorable to Germany. In 1942, of the three solutions that could put an end to the war—Axis victory, a negotiated peace, Anglo-Saxon victory—the first can definitely be dismissed. No matter how long the conflict lasts, the Anglo-Americans can no longer be beaten."[17] But in Vichy the impartiality of these reports was challenged by ministers, which might explain why little account was taken of them in the formulation of foreign policy. Eugène Bridoux, Laval's defense minister, claimed that the anti-Germanism of these services blinded them to the realities of the war.[18]

Anti-Germanism also played a role in the preparation for possible future armed conflicts. In March of 1942, a document of the Deuxième Bureau dealt with the dilemma facing the French army. On the one hand, the Deuxième Bureau was faced with the need to maintain secrecy. According to September 1941 instructions, those archives of the Deuxième Bureau classified as secret "should on no account be communicated to any organization whatsoever." On the other hand, the troops needed to be prepared for the possibility of a conflict with specified weapons and named enemies. A compromise was thus preferred: information could be divulged on condition that all precautions were taken to avoid any leaks. The instruction was very explicit: "the documents thus distributed will be kept safe from the investigations of the foreign armistice control commissions," in other words, from the Germans and Italians. And for good reason! The document suggested twelve specific weapons against which the troops should be prepared. Of these, one belonged to the British army, another to the American army, and ten to the German army. It seems that the spirit of revenge still haunted the hallways of the army high command.[19]

Hostility toward the Germans also affected the counterespionage services' attitude toward the Allies and the Gaullists. This might appear paradoxical, but in some cases it seems that their arrest of Gaullist and British agents can be explained by anti-Germanism. Rightly or wrongly, the French secret services believed that some Allied or Resistance movements and networks were infiltrated by the Germans. They pointed out that German agents pretending to be Gaullists often carried out acts of provocation. In June of 1942, Captain Bernard insisted that "many German agents who want to get information on the feelings of the troops claim to be Gaullist recruiters in order to establish relationships with military personnel." This provided an extra reason to crack down on Gaullists: "Very often—or at least sometimes—the propagandist is actually a German intelligence agent. This should make us fight even more energetically against this propaganda."[20] In a report on the subject of the Allied secret services, the BMA brought up the case of the Belgian branch of the "inter-Allied" intelligence network that was "deeply infiltrated by German provocateurs who cross into the free zone, where they work not only against Gaullist milieus but also against official French organizations." The BMA explicitly noted that this German infiltration was the reason behind arrests carried out by the French within the Belgian branch of the inter-Allied network: "This situation has led the BMA to ask the police to investigate its activity in depth."[21] A TR report of January 1942 stated, "During the first trimester of 1941, the TR was able to guide police action into various branches of the inter-Allied network and of the Intelligence Service: the cases of Fuchs, Mouzillat, Potoki, Jeckiel, etc., would have been incomprehensible for the police without the preliminary explanation of the context within which these individuals were operating."[22] At first sight this suggests that the TR was encouraging the anti-Allied zeal of the police. However, as Paillole explained in his June lecture, the wider context of this affair was that of double agents working for the Germans inside the Allied network.[23]

Sometimes German agents even tried to take advantage of the anti-Germanism of Vichy's secret services. This was the case for the German agent Asoka Chand, recruited before the war in India by German intelligence from nationalist, that is, anti-British milieus. He became an agent of some standing and had carried out around twenty missions in the southern zone before his arrest near Lyon on 17 October 1941. On 14 March 1943 Chand sent a letter from his cell in Nontron prison to the German armistice delegation in Lyon asking it to intervene in his favor. In this letter, which was intercepted by the French authorities, Chand recounted his interrogation by the ST branch in Lyon, explaining that Police Captain

Triffe who interrogated him tried to turn him against the Germans, and that he pretended to accept this proposal: "I informed him that in my opinion the individuals most dangerous for the French are the British, Americans, and other foreigners who pass themselves off as agents of the Intelligence Service or as Gaullists—they are in reality 'double agents' providing important information to the occupying authorities. The police captain was duly impressed and asked me to give him the names of these individuals—it was in this way that I caused the arrests of Garrow alias Georges, Maurice, and other persons linked to the British Intelligence Service [IS]. . . . in order to create maximum disorder in the IS organization."[24] In reality, his false denunciation was not the cause of the arrest of the Scottish captain Ian Garrow, head of the IS in Marseille, who, in any case, was most definitely not a double German agent. Garrow was actually arrested a few days before Chand. The infiltration of his network by the Germans had been known since the spring of 1941. A TR report of May of that year specified that "Garrow is a recruiter for the Intelligence Service. There is an arrest warrant for him and the Germans, thanks to a provocateur that they managed to slip into his organization, are aware of his activities—what a mess!"[25] While we might doubt Chand's effectiveness, he probably was trying to create confusion in the IS by denouncing Garrow.

Another form of anti-Germanism can be seen in the struggle against the Allies. Often the decisive factor in how the French secret services treated cases involving Allied and Gaullist agents was whether their activities were really considered "anti-French" or simply directed against the Germans. The results of an October 1942 investigation by the police inspectorate typified this type of reasoning. It dealt with relations between the police, the BMA, and the Belgian intelligence network in Toulouse. In December 1941, as we have seen, the BMA asked the police to carry out an in-depth investigation of the Belgian networks so as to uncover any German infiltration in their midst. As a result, the main leaders of the Belgian network in the southwest were arrested by the ST of Montpellier. After checking their situation, the general commanding the sixteenth military district refused to prosecute these Belgians for their pro-Allied activities: "An in-depth examination of this case has not led me to make any charges against these Belgians. On the contrary, it is established that they have always worked with the French services and for France. I would underscore that some of them fought bravely in the ranks of the French army during the 1939–1940 war. I therefore suggest that, upon their release, these Belgians should not be subjected to any internment procedure."[26] This decision rested on a narrow interpretation of article 80 of the law decree of 29 July 1939, which declared guilty of breaching external state security any French person or foreigner who shared intelligence with agents of a foreign power likely to harm France. The Belgian intelligence network was not working against France but against Germany and was thus not guilty.

The follow up to this affair illustrated even more clearly the indifference of the secret services and of other French institutions toward Allied activities, as long as these were discrete and aimed against the Germans and not against Vichy. The police inspectorate discovered that in December 1941, after the French freed the leader of the Belgian intelligence network in the region, an agreement was reached enabling this network to send documents to the Belgian government in exile in London. The Belgian network first handed over these documents—mainly reports on the situation in Germany and Belgium, as well as intelligence on German installations—to police Captain Philippe of the Toulouse police, who conveyed them to the BMA to be censored. The police inspectorate explained the censorship practiced by the military authorities as follows: "The role of the BMA was to examine what in this mail was contrary to France's interests. Any information pertaining to our country was 'cut out.' These cuts were in fact fairly few in number." The BMA returned the documents twenty-four hours later to the Belgian network via Captain Philippe, and the BMA was aware that the Belgians were subsequently forwarding them to England. In this instance, Captain Philippe was certainly not acting against the wishes of his hierarchy. Before serving as intermediary, Philippe had asked advice from the Intendant Danglade, the regional police chief, who gave his approval. In fact, Phillipe was praised. The inspectorate noted that Philippe had been rewarded for his role in this affair receiving a citation from Vice-Premier Darlan on 28 March 1942 for "services rendered to national defense."[27]

How are we to explain the congratulations of Darlan and Philippe's superiors? Firstly, for reasons of national defense, the army high command was happy to receive reliable intelligence on the Germans—staying informed is important to any government. Secondly there was a certain fatalism: the police authorities of the region were convinced that the Belgian network would in any event find a way of transmitting this information to its destination. Intercepting the Belgian network's mail was thus a way of controlling it, and also a means of eliminating anti-French references. The Belgians had two reasons for going along with this: On the one hand, acting with the agreement of the police facilitated the sending of the bulk of the information. On the other hand at that moment, Belgian intelligence still trusted the armistice army: "Van Buylaere, head of Belgian intelligence, was aware of where Captain Philippe was sending these documents. He thought that the French high command might be interested in them and felt it was a duty to assist it in this way."[28] On 9 August 1942, Captain Delmas of the BMA notified Philippe that he had been ordered to put an end to the sending of such documents, which effectively did stop from that date, in other words nine months after it had started.

In a report for Premier Pierre Laval in October of 1942, the police inspectorate recommended that neither Captain Philippe nor the BMA should be punished: "In fact," the report explained, "the information was collected in Belgium and not on French territory, and it was not intended for a foreign power but for the Belgian government in London. The latter has the right to be informed by its citizens of what is happening in Belgian territory." It should be noted however that the inspectorate investigator was displaying a deliberate naivety in his conclusion since he had earlier indicated the military nature of some of the information transmitted:

> In addition to some notes regarding the general situation of Germany, the financial situation of Belgium, copies or clippings from Belgian newspapers, propaganda leaflets, there is military information. It includes, for instance, plans of targets, plans of ammunition dumps, annotated plans of a bomb cache, explanatory sketches of coastal defenses, sketches and notes pertaining to fuel processing plants, photographs of landing strips, reports on traffic in certain railway stations, the orders of the occupation authorities, documents stolen from German officers, list of targets with their coordinates (loading ramps in the Charleroi railway stations), plans of factories in the Charleroi area, plans of electric lines from Belgian electric plants, the location of the factories working for the Germans in the Louvain area, etc.[29]

Some of this information was clearly to help Allied planes find their targets. It seems that for this police inspectorate investigator transmitting information against the Germans to England was not at all objectionable, so long as this information did not include any harmful reference to Vichy. There is no record of how Laval responded to the report.

Thus far the vision presented here of the secret services has been one in which anti-Germanism was the sole determinant of their work, but these services did also work against the Allies and the Gaullists. They sought to inform Vichy's army command of the organization and activities of the British Intelligence Service. Thus, for instance, a document from the TR on the use of double agents disclosed that "On 4 August 1940, TR noted the attempts by the English Intelligence Service to enter into contact with Russian intelligence. On 12 January 1941 the TR revealed that there was total collusion between the two services."[30] A report of the first year of TR activities, compiled in July of 1941, shows that the TR network was funded by money confiscated from "enemy" intelligence agencies ("German, Italian, British, Russian, etc.").[31] The British were thus being categorized as an enemy. According to Paillole, 177 Allied and Gaullist agents were arrested in 1941 by the French secret services.[32] With regard to the secret services' anti-Allied activities, the memoirs of Robert Terres, a member of the Toulouse TR, seem credible: "In 1940, . . . since we trusted in our leaders' patriotism, we were happy to apply their directives without realizing at first how contradictory they were. I started to recruit double agents against the British, and later on, against the Americans. It's not that I really considered them enemies, but my job was to monitor them and pass the information to my chiefs. What they did with the information afterward was their own business, I trusted them. I am not sure now that I was right."[33]

It would be naive to believe that all the French secret services' actions against the Allies can be explained solely by their anti-Germanism. Other considerations came into play as well: Vichy's instructions, the risk of diplomatic incidents, and the ambiguities of the secret services themselves.

Of Vichy's instructions, Robert Terres reminds us in his memoirs, "According to Weygand's orders, we were supposed to fight not only German, Spanish and Italian infiltrations, but also all foreign intrusions. This meant not only the British (with the Intelligence Service) and the American services but also, later on, the Gaullist BCRA."[34] The Vichy regime had no sympathy for the British and looked upon Gaullism as a dissidence that made its own political situation more complicated. The regime's instructions stressed that the French secret services should crack down on these organizations' activities.[35] Thus, on 4 April 1941, to stimulate repression against the Gaullists, General Huntziger, the secretary general for war, insisted on the fact that "the promotion of national sentiment so necessary in the present circumstance to the maintenance of the unity of the empire and the absolute loyalty toward the government must be translated into merciless repression against all 'anti-French' activities, irrespective of the form they might take."[36] In fact, Vichy's justification to the Germans for the creation of a semiofficial counterespionage service, the BMA, was that it was going to work against the Allies. This became its official mission, and failure threatened to cause diplomatic incidents.

In an account written after the war, Paillole claimed that the only Allied or British agents ever arrested were those whose activities were known to the Germans.[37] It is true that the risk of diplomatic incidents encouraged the arrest of individuals whose activities were too visible. A November 1943 German SD report written from information garnered from captured French secret services archives discussed the activities of these services during the period preceding total occupation. The report noted that "the other intelligence agencies operating on French territory, such as the Belgian, Polish, Gaullist, and in its time, the inter-Allied intelligence network, were observed with the greatest mistrust by the French secret services and disabled whenever the French could not draw any immediate benefit from them. The French were worried that the activities of these organizations, which escaped their control, might attract the attention of the Germans, which would as a consequence put the French secret services in danger."[38]

Though anti-Allied and anti-Gaullist repression can be explained by pressure from above, the ambiguity of the secret services themselves has to be stressed.[39] Being hostile to the Germans did not automatically mean being for the Allies. While the attitude of these services toward the Germans was fairly straightforward, their position toward the Allies and the Gaullists was extremely complex. A report from the British secret services dating from October 1942 described the attitude toward the Allies of various figures residing in French North Africa. Among them were twenty-five security agents and members of the French secret services of whom twelve were classified in the report as being pro-Allied: four of these twelve belonged to the Deuxième Bureau of the army, one to the BMA, and seven to the police (one in the ST). The eleven considered anti-Allied included two members of the Deuxième Bureau, one BMA agent, four police officers (of whom one from the ST was described as an active member of the Fascist political movement the PPF) and four members of the navy's Deuxième Bureau. The positions of the police chief of Taroudant in Morocco and of a member of the Deuxième Bureau of the air force were not known. The sample is too small for the results to be generalized but does at least suggest a divergence of opinion among secret service personnel. It must be noted that the navy secret service members were all considered to be anti-Allied.[40] Of course anti-Allied agents were not necessarily pro-German, but this report reminds us that we must not lose sight of the fact that within the secret services, some were not entirely won over to the Allied cause.

In his memoirs, Robert Terres claims the French secret service leadership was more Anglophobic than subordinate members: "Not for a second did we see the Intelligence Service as an enemy as was the case in certain ultra-Vichyite milieus, represented in our own organization, it must be acknowledged, by certain officers of the BMA."[41] Paul Paillole typified the position of the upper echelons of Vichy secret services, declaring in his 1942 lecture, "Germany is the number one danger" and "England is the number two danger." He concluded, "Everyone is working against us. France is all alone."[42] Anglophobia was also present in Deuxième Bureau documents. To his aforementioned report explaining why a German victory had become impossible, Louis Baril added hostile comments about the Gaullists and the British: "The lack of understanding on the part of the British government, subjected to the harmful influence of some misguided Frenchmen, led us gradually to acts of hostility against the British and Imperial troops. We cannot do anything about this fact. The long-term damage is not serious and our resistance will win us the esteem of the British themselves."[43] Thus, no concessions should be made to the Anglo-Gaullists.

There were several motives for French hostility toward the Allied and Gaullist secret services. Firstly, the professional abilities of the British and Gaullist intelligence agencies were deemed inadequate. In a training lecture for his subordinates, Paillole insisted on the lack of professionalism of the British secret services. According to him, the prewar Intelligence Service had been noteworthy for its discretion, but that this discretion had been due to the fact that the IS had been virtually inactive ("up to now, security was deemed more important than results"). Since the armistice, the IS had experienced serious security problems as activity and the range of tasks exceeded the agency's capacity and capability. "I have seen many well positioned Intelligence Service agents get caught," Commander Paillole claimed, "because they had been instructed to secretly help escaped British prisoners travel to freedom."[44]

In his opinion, the various ways in which the IS maintained its contacts with France testified to its amateurism. Some IS agents arrived by boat on the shores of Brittany in northwest France whilst others were parachuted in. Laden down with heavy baggage including radio transmitters, these agents did not get very far before being arrested by the French or Germans. At the beginning of 1942, the British secret services found a radical solution to the problem of liaison. Instead of dropping men, airplanes parachuted down large numbers of boxes containing carrier pigeons. The birds carried questionnaires that French citizens were asked to fill in before sending these flying spies back in the direction of England. Obviously, this method invited false information by enemy intelligence agents who could fill in the questionnaires themselves. The Germans "responded," said Paillole, "and so did we."[45]

The great danger of British activity stemmed from its naivety, Paillole explained, which put French citizens in danger: "It is regrettable that the Intelligence Service has been so careless in its exploitation of a terrain that is potentially so generous and favorable. Currently, good French citizens, recruited to the Intelligence Service in ways which reveal an appalling degree of naivety, are being executed in large numbers. Hundreds of them."[46] According to a long-established and widespread stereotype in France, the British were thought to be selfish in political matters. They were considered to exploit others purely for their own interest. This stereotype explained the success in 1940 of the slogan "The British are going to fight till the last Frenchman." It is echoed in the Paillole quote above, and even more explicitly in a lecture given by Captain Bernard of the TR: "The British only care for their own interests and are completely indifferent to what might be France's future."[47]

The Gaullists were criticized even more for their lack of professionalism. In a training session on the subject of Gaullism, Captain Bernard emphasized, "No professional propagandist has been sent. People produce their propaganda any which way and address themselves to just anyone. Thus in nine out of ten cases, after three days of propaganda, the propagandist is denounced to the BMA officer." As a professional of counterespionage, he noted patronizingly, "They are amateurs. They don't take the precautions professionals would take." He concluded that "what is striking when these matters are studied, is the lack of organization of nine-tenths of Gaullists sympathizers. From time to time, we find a properly set-up organization for propaganda or one for clandestine departures. But this is extremely rare."[48] The French secret services probably exaggerated the scope of the German infiltration of Gaullist movements, but the risk posed by double agents was also recognized by Gaullist sources such as the newspaper *Liberté*.[49] The truth was that the Gaullist intelligence network indeed recruited amateurs; they were enthusiastic but they lacked experience and expertise.

In the view of the Vichy secret services, it was this very Gaullist amateurism that made them vulnerable to being infiltrated by the Germans. According to Captain Bernard, "As always, when one is recruiting in large numbers and hurriedly, without being able to carry out proper counterespionage checks, one gets infiltrated."[50] In another lecture Paillole took up this theme again: "I was telling you the other day that all these English, Gaullist, etc., organizations are infiltrated by Germany: it's true in the occupied zone and, unfortunately, in the free zone as well!"[51] Once an organization had been infiltrated by the Germans it became dangerous since the Germans could use their infiltration of one network as a means of penetrating any other organization which came into contact with it. Vichy's secret services were thus weary of the risk of contamination from Gaullist networks. In this same lecture, Paillole instructed his subordinates to mistrust certain Resistance organizations: "Also do not for a moment trust those ready-made organizations, where you will find people giving you information. 'I have an amazing organization, we work for the Communists, the Gaullists, etc.' This might look good and they may appear to have considerable means at their disposal. Unfortunately, these organizations are most often in the hands of provocateurs. We have seen this. All of the Gaullist groups operating in the occupied zone and which were of a certain size (you have heard of *Libération Nationale*, Heurteaux, etc.) were in the hands of the Hun."[52]

This was a dispute between amateurs who believed that their enthusiasm could overcome the limits of their training and professionals who were scathing of those newly arrived on the scene. In his postwar writings, Rivet of the Cinquième Bureau dismissed the Gaullist secret services as amateurs whose effectiveness was very limited. In an acerbic attack on Jacques Soustelle, one of the former leaders of the Gaullist secret services, Rivet was totally explicit in this sense:

> You compare the performance of your "networks" with that of the official secret services. You are very pretentious to do so. We know your "networks" very well. It's true that some of their members were good—capable of gathering intelligence. They deserve praise for their work in France. With little training and generally having to improvise, they ran risks and dangers that even our experienced agents don't take lightly. But your "networks" were not

> "pure." By that I mean . . . their missions were too diverse and they were trying to do too many things rather than just concerning themselves with the strength, the projects and the behavior of the enemy. . . . You certainly cannot claim that a few brave Frenchmen thrust into the battle of France without adequate preparation were capable of delving deeply into the whole German army on the continent. . . . That is a profession that needs to be learnt and whose organization can only develop over time.

Rivet believed that the quality individuals that the Gaullists had managed to recruit could have been better employed by his own secret services, which would have given them more focused missions:

> the place for such men was not in a heterogeneous organization that employed them willy-nilly. And this is the crime of this strange creation (your intelligence network) where political needs . . . bestowed on the same organization, and sometimes even to the same man, the missions of monitoring the opinion of the Prefect of Quimper-Corentin or the thoughts of the village policeman in Ferté Sous-Jouarre, while also working out the structure of the German organizations in France, of the Abwehr or of the Gestapo. In the realm of secret service activity there is no greater heresy and no greater fault.[53]

More political reasons also underlay French distrust of the Allies and the Gaullists.[54] In his lecture of June 1942 on Gaullism, Captain Bernard issued this criticism: "the movement has ceased to be a military movement and has become a political movement"; he deplored "the Gaullists [for] falling into the hands of politicians." Similar criticisms of politicization were aimed at the Gaullist clandestine press: "At present, in certain Gaullist newspapers, out of about twenty articles, there are at least eighteen that no longer mention Germany, military operations, etc., but write about Vichy's work charter, state oppression of the people, Vichy police tyranny, etc. You'll see when we talk of the movement in the French army, the influence of this political aspect on career soldiers' attitude toward Gaullism."[55] This criticism of Gaullist politicization appears frequently in the memoirs of former members of the French secret services. According to Henri Navarre of the Deuxième Bureau, "there were few who . . . were not worried about the presence of former politicians of the Third Republic around General de Gaulle."[56] It is in the memoirs of former TR member Michel Garder that the underlying meaning of this criticism became most explicit. Garder contrasted the politicized Gaullist secret services with the secret services Vichy had inherited from the Third Republic, claiming that the latter "were apolitical and not overly concerned about the regime that established itself in France."[57]

British and Gaullist attacks against French possessions were not exactly appreciated by the Vichy secret services. The sinking of part of the French fleet by the British at Mers el-Kébir, and Anglo-Gaullist attacks on French-held Dakar and Syria generated sharp criticisms. It was probably in the navy milieus that the Mers el-Kébir episode of 3 July 1940 produced the most resentment but it also provoked anger elsewhere. The day after the incident, the TR agent Gérard-Dubot noted in his diary: "We're going to have major difficulties. England is going to cause us all sorts of problems—it's going to get Communists, Socialists and Jews all riled up."[58] Jacques Britsch, of the Deuxième Bureau, was more philosophical. On 5 July 1940, he wrote: "While the British gesture is 'inelegant,' to put it mildly, it can be readily understood from a political point of view." The next day he added: "We are of the opinion, in spite of Mers el-Kébir, that we should not become the declared enemy of the British." But the strength of feeling about Mers el-Kébir is evident in memoirs written long after the war. In the 1970s, Robert Terres of the TR did not hide his anger: "the intolerable kick in the ass that they inflicted on us by destroying our fleet at Mers el-Kébir was the final blow to our alliance."[59]

In September 1940, after the unsuccessful attempt by Anglo-Gaullist forces to capture the strategic port of Dakar in the French colony of Senegal, the criticism was directed against both the Gaullists and the British. On 24 September, Britsch noted in his diary: "It's impossible to approve of De Gaulle who is personally leading the British attack. But who gains in this affair? Germany and only Germany."[60] In June 1942, Captain Bernard of the TR reflected retrospectively on the effects Dakar had had on the French army: "The French military became aware that the English were not behaving as Allies and were going well beyond the needs of the struggle against Germany."[61] In his memoirs, Michel Garder noted that Rivet, the head of the Cinquième Bureau, "did not approve of all the initiatives of Free France." Garder described Rivet as particularly shocked by the Dakar episode.[62]

During the summer of 1941, Britsch made several references to the British attack on the French mandated territory of Syria. On 10 June he noted that "even Anglophiles find this attack to be a very poor political move." He worried that this was likely to strike a new blow against the military prestige of the French army. In spite of this he added, "We wish nonetheless for this matter to be settled speedily and for Syria to be won by the dissidents." Three months later he noted, "the Syrian episode has in no way changed the crucial problem, that of German domination of the national territory."[63] The events of Dakar and Syria were especially sensitive issues within military intelligence circles because they opposed the Gaullists and the British against Vichy's armistice army to which the secret services belonged.

The reticence expressed respectively toward the British and the Gaullist varied between different individuals. To be hostile toward the "politicized" Gaullist did not necessarily mean being hostile toward the Allies. The resister Henri Frenay, who worked for the Deuxième Bureau for a few months in 1940, found that the members of the bureau were on the whole favorable to the British but opposed to the Gaullists. His relations with the section of the Deuxième Bureau concerned with German affairs were suddenly interrupted when it was discovered that he was working for the Gaullists and not directly for the British, "which for them was unacceptable." [64] Roger Wybot wrote a similar comment on his experience with the Marseille BMA.[65] The Gaullist Jacques Soustelle claimed that when "Saint-Jacques" an agent of the Gaullist intelligence network was arrested in February 1941 by the gendarmerie, the Deuxième Bureau officers interrogating him were lenient simply because of their loyalty to the British Intelligence Service. Saint Jacques "was rapidly discovered by the gendarmes, then questioned by Vichy's Deuxième Bureau. The tales he told them would have seemed incredible even to the most dull-witted of policemen—even more so to intelligence specialists. But they pretended to be satisfied probably because, like most officers of Vichy's secret services, they were anti-German and didn't want to be on bad terms with the Intelligence Service."[66] On the other hand there are cases in which members of the Vichy secret services showed even greater hostility toward the British than toward Gaullists. An example is Captain Bernard's lecture of June 1942. Although he was far from favorable to the Gaullists he saw them essentially as patriots who had chosen their friends unwisely: "The Gaullists are generally driven by patriotism and they are as patriotic as anyone. We thus need to show them that it is contrary to patriotism to become pawns for a power that is not favorable to us."[67]

Criticism of the Allies was mainly directed against Great Britain, while the Americans, like the Belgians, were often looked upon favorably. In the report Louis Baril of the Deuxième Bureau wrote for the high command in January 1942, he gave the following advice on the kind of policy that should be followed: "It would be unwise to upset sentimental America with harsher measures that might give the impression that France has deliberately taken Germany's side. After the war, we will need the Americans' support to reactivate economic activity in the country." According to Baril, pro-Americanism should dictate French policy: "We need to be able to preserve America's friendship. This must be the lynchpin of our policies. Everything else is just a footnote."[68] As for Paillole, he considered the United States and the American intelligence networks in a generally favorable light. In his June 1942 lecture, he explained to his subordinates that they should not be overly worried about American activities in France: "Their activity is not primarily directed against France or the empire. The Americans are mainly looking for information on the Axis."[69] He could not hide his admiration for the energy of their intelligence agencies and also noted their independence from the British, a decisive factor in his eyes: "The American intelligence network, which is new, young and whose activity has only come to our attention these past few months, gives the impression of being well motivated and dynamic and of wanting to operate independently of the Intelligence Service."[70] One of the few negative comments toward the United States or American intelligence in the sources I consulted can be found in Jacques Britsch's diary. On the evening of Pearl Harbor, he wrote: "The action against Honolulu is harsh. We are rather happy about it." Happy probably because the Japanese attack would encourage the Americans to go to war. Happy as well because Britsch saw it as a punishment against "American softness,"[71] that is, as a punishment for their previous nonengagement in the war.

Although ambivalence toward the Allies and the Gaullists was very real we should not exaggerate it. In the military and police secret services, any ambivalence felt toward the Allies or the Gaullists was eclipsed by the hatred felt toward the Germans.[72] For instance, Captain Bernard told his subordinates in a June 1942 TR training course that the danger posed by Gaullist agents was that they encouraged division amongst the French people, explaining that Gaullism "has only one quality, which is that it has preserved in certain individuals the anti-German flame and of this, of course, we have great need. . . . Gaullists have remained anti-German and amongst them we don't find the same vile attitude as amongst German spies, people who are willing to sell themselves for 2,000 francs. Regardless of the dangers posed by Gaullism, from this view point, it is very superior to the excesses of collaborationism taken to the point of espionage."[73]

I found no reference to any gesture of support from the secret services for captured German agents. In contrast, Allied or Gaullist agents under arrest frequently enjoyed a measure of kindness and at times even of help.[74] Even the anti-Gaullist Bernard did not favor the systematic incarceration of Gaullists. In his training course, he stated that efforts should be made to convince captured Gaullists of the errors of their engagement and that only the most intransigent among them should be punished: "If one notices that an individual is a true fanatic and cannot be converted . . . then prison is the only option."[75] The secret services appear to have been behind many escapes of Gaullist and Allied agents from Vichy prisons. On 25 August 1942, pro-German defense minister General Bridoux noted in his diary: "Five officers and noncommissioned officers imprisoned near Nice have escaped. There was certainly some complicity on the French side probably from agents of the secret services."[76] The British agent Bob Sheppard wrote of the kindness expressed to him by the ST and the Deuxième Bureau following his arrest by the gendarmerie. Agents from the Deuxième Bureau spoke to him about escape, but it was finally with the complicity of a policeman and some nuns that he was able to make his getaway.[77] The report on the escape of the Gaullist Pierre Fourcaud from the military hospital of Clermont-Ferrand shows that he took advantage of the negligence and the active complicity of several members of the police, in particular that of Captain Roland Sicard of the ST. That Sicard was entrusted with watching over such an important Gaullist is in itself quite revealing because at the time he was given responsibility for this prisoner, he was already suspected of having helped the escape of another Gaullist from Clermont in November 1941.[78] In her memoirs, Marie-Madeleine Fourcade of the Alliance Resistance Network related how officers from the Marseille ST organized the escape of her and her fellow prisoners. She sang the praises of these police officers: "Blessed *Marseillais!* Blessed compatriots! How lucky am I to be born here where even counterespionage has a sort of poetry."[79] Many other examples could be cited because they are so numerous. While arrests occurred for reasons discussed earlier, many secret services members were ready to help arrested Allied and Gaullist agents, either out of support for the Allies, or more often simply out of anti-Germanism.

The same logic was at play when Gaullist and Allied networks were warned of German infiltration. In his memoirs, the Scottish pastor Donald Caskie, who organized an escape network in Marseille for members of the Allied armed forces described how "Many French policemen showed kindness towards me, because they sympathized with the Allies."[80] He insisted on the fact that it was officers of the ST who informed him that the British citizen Harold Cole, who had infiltrated his network, was in fact a German agent. Any ambivalence or reticence toward the Allies tended to be overpowered by anti-German feeling when a French citizen was threatened by the Germans. It was mainly in such a defensive capacity that links occurred between Gaullist or Allied agents and Vichy's secret services.[81] It is certain that Paillole warned some Gaullists that their organizations had been infiltrated by German agents. In his June 1942 lecture, he told his subordinates of the help he had offered Colonel Alfred Heurteaux who had been one of the instigators of the Organisation Civile et Militaire (Civil and Military Organization) resistance movement: "He was arrested with all the people who worked with him, three months after we had conveyed a message to him: 'watch out, you have provocateurs in your midst.'"[82] This help was offered selectively to former officers personally known to Paillole and who were working more against the Germans than against Vichy. The best-known example is that of Henri Frenay, the head of the Combat resistance movement and a close friend of Paillole. In a report Paillole wrote in 1946 on his services' activities during the war, he claimed, "The TR service had ceased all contacts with the civil resistance groups that were forming. The sole exception was made in favor of the Combat group (Frenay)."[83] Robert Terres explained the ties with Combat as follows: "Because Combat was led by Frenay, one of Paillole's friends from the Saint-Cyr military academy, our services gave Combat a measure of support."[84] Memoirs written by both Frenay and Maurice Chevance-Bertin of Combat both confirm the reality of these ties.

Thus there were limited defensive links between the military secret services and some Gaullist organizations. In addition there was some collaboration between British secret services and their Vichy counterparts to prevent German infiltration. For instance, during interrogation, the British officer Ian Garrow, head of the Intelligence Service in Marseille, brought up his relations with Pierre d'Harcourt of the Deuxième Bureau: "I notified him about 14 days ago of the following intelligence that came to us by chance and is of greater interest to your country than to mine: In the north of France paramilitary formations called Mouvement Resurrectionnel Français. (French revivalist movement) have been organized. Their goal is to expel the invader. But I learned . . . that a man named Kraft or Krauss if I remember correctly, one of the leaders of this organization located in Paris, is in contact with the Germans." [85]

These defensive links were occasional in nature and consisted of warning an individual, a network or a movement that they were threatened by German infiltration. But what of more permanent links involving systematic exchanges of information? Links of this type are mentioned very explicitly and frequently in secret service veterans' accounts of their wartime experiences. This is not surprising since these services have a vested interest in justifying their resistance credentials. Thus, in a 1950s interview, Paul Paillole claimed that in early 1941 the technician Simonin of the TR network established a radio link with London.[86] Even Passy, former leader of the Gaullist secret service and therefore a rival of TR, claimed there were exchanges of information between the British and the Vichy secret services. He relates the following about the attitude of Paillole and Ronin (head of air force intelligence): "I knew these two officers' names and was aware that, since 1940, they had kept up a rather tenuous but nonetheless real contact with the British services. They had also (as the heads of the Intelligence Service informed me) provided some intelligence to the British, but Sir Claude Dansey informed me he considered their contribution insignificant and, given that it was only the British who were waging war, felt their demand that 'they receive an equal amount of information in exchange' was particularly unacceptable."[87]

The archives of the time confirm that exchanges did occur between Vichy's secret services and the Allied secret services. It should be noted, however, that there are several reasons why a secret service might transmit information to a foreign intelligence agency: to convey false intelligence, to exchange true information on a basis limited to the needs of the service, and to serve the personal initiative of subordinates acting independently.

A document about intelligence exchanges sheds light on the criteria involved—a note that TR branch 120, the Rabat (Morocco) branch, sent to its headquarters in October 1941. The note dealt with contacts between the TR and Robert Bouvier of the Belgian secret services who was in close relations with the Intelligence Service in London, Portugal, and Gibraltar. It was noted that he "voluntarily rendered service to [branch] 120 during his stay in Morocco during the summer of 1941" and that he was "a friend of M. Cassard, at present in London, who was in relation in the spring of 1941 with Colonel Mangès and with the Clermont-Ferrand post." Bouvier was thus entrusted in October 1941 with the mission of making contact with TR to obtain an exchange of information: "he is volunteering to pass on to us any information on the Germans and would gladly accept similar information." In its October note, TR branch 120 was thus asking advice on the answer it should give: "120 has the honor of asking the leadership if it should accept the proposed exchange of information." Two elements are of particular interest in the TR 120 note. Firstly, this post requested instructions from its leadership before accepting the proposal of the Belgian secret services. Secondly, despite this request for authorization, TR 120 proposed to bear full responsibility for the transaction: "The head of the post would give the affair an unofficial character by letting M. Bouvier believe that he is making the commitment on his own initiative." The TR 120 note was sent to Lieutenant Commandant Guy d'Alès of the BMA for his decision. It seems that in this case the proposed exchange was rejected as the information offered by Bouvier was not considered important enough.[88]

All this shows the importance for the leaders of the TR and the BMA of controlling their subordinates' contacts. This is confirmed by a note the TR had conveyed to the SSM on 2 November 1942, one week before the Allied landing in North Africa. This letter was extremely critical of the pro-Allied activities of Captain de Cervens of the Deuxième Bureau in Tunis: "In June 1942, Captain de Cervens attracted attention because he had communicated to an agent of the American secret services a copy of a letter from the Italian armistice commission of Turin to the French armistice delegation. The letter dealt with American and Gaullist activities in Tunisia. As this officer's indiscretion could paralyze the activities of the service TR would like to request his urgent transfer."[89] Uncontrolled personal actions ran the risk of endangering the whole of the secret services operation by exposing it to the Germans. This underlines what Paillole wrote in his memoirs about instructions within the secret services: "We emphasized the necessity of acting with extreme caution so as to avoid compromising our clandestine work."[90]

The TR thus wished for prudent and, above all, controlled exchanges of information. It also required that in all exchanges the information obtained should be of equal value to that given. So this was in no way a gratuitous passing on of intelligence. Also, information about the Vichy government should not be given to the Allies, thus the documents should only deal with the Germans. This probably explained Paillole's June 1942 criticism directed against "those people who are giving information to the British and claim that 'passing intelligence to the English is not treason.'"[91] This statement might seem odd coming from the mouth of someone who was himself organizing exchanges of information, but his criticism was probably aimed against the people sending information about

Vichy to London. In fact, a patriotic reflex prevented the secret services from "betraying" the national government. Two quotes from Paillole taken from an April 1942 lecture highlight this patriotic reflex that translated into the resolve to remain independent from foreign secret services: "We will not recover as long as we are in the hands of foreign intelligence agencies," and "We want to be masters in our own home."[92] Henri Navarre of the Deuxième Bureau might also be cited at this point. He recalled in his memoirs his reaction when he was contacted in June 1940 by the Intelligence Service that asked him to come to work in London: "But what the Intelligence Service expected from me was of course that I hand over to them those of our informants I could bring with me. Did I have the right to give to a foreign country what was unquestionably France's property?"[93] This exemplified many secret service professionals' reaction when it came to transmitting intelligence.

Thus there were limited but nonetheless real ties between the Vichy secret services and the Allies and the Gaullists. Veterans of these services were to claim after the war that this fact showed them to be the first Resisters. It is true that the word "Resistance" does feature in secret services documents from the period 1940 to 1942. However they only seemed to conceive of resistance within the confines of Vichy structures. An example is the report by Lieutenant Colonel Schlesser, the former head of French counterespionage, written on 28 July 1940 upon his return from a TR mission in the occupied zone. He did not hide his disgust: disgust for the propaganda means used by the Germans to demoralize French spirit, disgust for the French people who repeated the leitmotiv that the "Germans are behaving very correctly." Schlesser insisted on the seriousness of the situation: "An immediate reviving of national feeling is indispensable. There is no more serious or more urgent problem than this if the government wants to prevent a rapid colonization by the Reich." Despite this, he remained optimistic about the possibilities:

> Ferments of Resistance are not lacking. Good French people, and above all ordinary people, suffer in silence: they surely feel their hearts bleeding when they see swastika flags tarnishing the rue Rivoli, when they witness the changing of the guard ceremonies on the Place de la Concorde or in front of the statue of [the First World War commander] Marshal Joffre. A word or a gesture will suffice for them to understand they have to maintain a dignified attitude. This word must be spoken, this gesture must be learned. It is essential that, throughout the occupied provinces, members of the French elites be the

> apostles, the symbols of the soul of the resistance. It is essential that those who are returning to the occupied territory, in particular demobilized soldiers, are told how they should conduct themselves in front of the German soldiers. Only the government's energetic and immediate action can allow France in all of its territorial integrity to be worthy of its past, its greatness and its traditions.[94]

Almost one year after Schlesser's report, a TR document of July 1941 summarized the first year of Paillole's network, reflecting a combination of vague resistance impulses with Vichyite professions of faith. The fact that it was noted that the TR network got most of its money from double agents working in "enemy" secret services (German, Italian, English, Russian, etc.) suggests that the British were among these enemies. But this same report announced that attempts were being made to establish "clandestine radio communication" with London. The conclusion confirmed this strange mixture of resistance and of pro-Vichyism: "The country beaten, ruined and divided, is each day exposed to the angry blows of its numerous enemies. It is TR's mission, especially in the occupied zone, to help with objectivity and without any partisan passion those who bear the heavy burden of making France rise again. . . . TR will fight loyally, with all its power, alongside those who like it, are working towards the moral health and liberation of the country."[95]

Even in stating its wish for liberation, the leadership of the TR could not help revealing its attachment to Vichy by using expressions that were similar in tone to those used by Marshal Philippe Pétain. Pétain also liked to refer to "the heavy burden of making the country rise again," and often used expressions like "without any partisan passion." He also spoke frequently of the "moral health" of the country. It is my belief that the tone of the TR report is actually inspired by a speech that Pétain made to a military audience in Aix-en-Provence on Wednesday 23 July 1941. It is likely that senior members of the TR, based in neighboring Marseille, would have attended this meeting. Even if they did not attend in person the speech was broadcast by the radio. In it Pétain outlined the difficulties the government faced in rebuilding the country: "We fell so low last year, that we should only think of getting up, of climbing the hill again." Pétain described this procedure of rising again as "this very heavy task." He drew attention to the particular difficulties the government faced in administering the occupied zone (hence the reference in the TR report). In addition he called on the army to work for the government: "It needs you to follow its lead, to march in keeping with its thinking." Even the TR's statements about working toward French Liberation do not necessarily discount an attachment to Vichy's philosophy. Some contemporaries believed that Pétain was playing a double-game—publicly singing the praises of collaboration but privately working with the Allies. Historians have established clearly that this was not the case, but on occasion Pétain did play on this belief by making ambiguous statements. Thus in an earlier speech of 19 March 1941, he said that the government's political program, known as the National Revolution, was designed to prepare the country "for the day when France would be free again" (without however specifying how this freedom would come about). In this July speech to the army in Aix-en-Provence, he again made an ambiguous statement: "We must not abandon our military preparation. We must even be ready for all possibilities."[96] The vagueness of the statement clearly left open the interpretation that Pétain was working toward French revenge against Germany.

It would not seem unfair to summarize the position of the TR leadership as follows: a belief that France was alone with numerous enemies including Britain, which had betrayed her, accompanied by the recognition that the number one enemy was Germany, and the liberation of the country was still the priority. With this in mind, one could take advantage of contacts with the British to obtain intelligence about the Germans, even though the British were considered worthy of only very limited trust. Thus the goal was not at all to work hand in hand with the British, but rather draw the maximum benefits from contacts by giving the British the minimum information required to maintain the link. Help was at times offered to Allied or to Gaullist agents working against Germany, but there was no question of ever encouraging those who wanted to attack Vichy. Thus illusion still persisted on at least a part of the government's intentions.

The relationship of the secret services with Vichy was also full of ambiguity. It is easy to understand that after the war former members of the Vichy secret services had a vested interest in distancing themselves from a government compromised because of its policy of collaboration. Henry Navarre of the Deuxième Bureau in Algiers, gave the following interpretation of the relationship of the secret services with Vichy: "For those services that survived and adopted an attitude of resistance such as the army intelligence and counterespionage agencies and air force intelligence, these relations boiled down to a constant struggle to perform their work against Germany and Italy."[97] According to Paillole, the secret services "started in July 1940 with relationships I would dare to call 'trusting' with those at the head of the government," but he added that "our services' positions were increasingly covert and effectively opposed to the policies of the government."[98] In Rivet's unpublished memoirs we find the following evaluation: "The secret services are understood and generally approved of by only two ministers, the war minister, General Huntziger, and the air force minister, General Bergeret. Outside of these two refuges . . . Secret service officers had to avoid appearing in any ministerial office."[99]

Looking at the documentation of the time, it does indeed appear that relations with the government were tense. Some ministers never did see the usefulness of their defensive mission. This was the case notably of General Eugène Bridoux, war minister from spring 1942, and of Fernand de Brinon, Vichy's "ambassador" to the occupied territories of Northern France. Neither should we forget that Vichy's policy combined two elements that sometimes appeared in contradiction to each other: collaboration and the defense of sovereignty. When these two came into conflict, it was often collaboration that took precedence. This certainly had repercussions in the secret services, for example, Vichy's handing over of captured spies to the Germans. In the month of May 1942, for diplomatic reasons, the agent Karl Langer was handed over by the government much to the annoyance of TR who warned that serious consequences could result from this. As a result TR was forced to notify Captain Robert Blémant of the ST that the agent he had arrested was going to be set free. To make matters worse, on this occasion, the TR also lost an important informer, Fochlot, who was forced to leave Paris in a hurry: "With regard to Fochlot, TR is taking all necessary measures to get its informer to the free zone. TR is thus losing one of its best agents working in the occupied zone and against the Hamburg intelligence post."[100] The secret services' frustration at this type of event was only too evident. They often had the impression that the government did not understand their needs. The government's timidity and the diplomatic compromises were thus often criticized.

When it came to the relationship with Vichy, we have to recognize however that the conservatism of secret service circles often led them to approve of authoritarian policies. Britsch noted in his diary on 9 May 1941: "Each day I am more convinced of the necessity of scrapping all political elections for a long time. It is impossible to heal France in any other way."[101] Since the Vichy government's domestic policies were based on scrapping democracy and limiting freedoms he was thus very happy with Vichy's steps in that direction. On 13 August 1941, Britsch claimed that he totally supported the government's internal policy. He greatly admired Pétain and was particularly pleased with Pétainist slogans such as "authority comes from above!" When he heard the government announcing "parliamentary democracy is dead" he could hardly contain his pleasure: "What joy to hear this coming from a French head of state!" However, he mistrusted Vichy's foreign policy: "For this policy to triumph, we should not be simultaneously playing the game of our enemy, the occupier, of Hitlerian betrayal!"[102] Criticism of Vichy's foreign policy from the secret services was mostly aimed at vice-premiers Laval and Darlan. There was generally a greater degree of trust toward Pétain and Weygand. In spite of some reticence, the secret services chose to operate within the confines allowed by Vichy. Since the policy of arresting German spies in no way contradicted government policy, counterespionage services aimed to make use of the margin of maneuver thus offered to them.

Given their political affinities, it is easy to understand the secret services' difficulties in dissociating themselves from Vichy. After the invasion of the southern zone in November of 1942, the armistice army was abolished and the military counterespionage services could no longer work informally in the government's shadow. To continue to operate against the Germans meant joining the Resistance and going underground. So a political choice had to be made at that moment. But rather than joining the Gaullist movement, the leaders of the military services joined de Gaulle's rival, the American-sponsored General Henri Giraud, whose political platform was very conservative and reactionary bearing considerable similarity to Vichy's own philosophy. It seems that even at that juncture, they hesitated to associate themselves with the "politicized" Gaullists. Indeed a continued Pétainism was evident in this milieu highlighting how curious their own conception of being apolitical was. This is clearly demonstrated by a bizarre incident at the end of 1943. According to an investigation by the British secret services Paul Paillole was involved in a plot to help Marshal Pétain escape from France seemingly to take over the leadership of the French in exile. Predictably de Gaulle was said to be furious about the incident and, the British reported, insistent that the former Vichy secret services should be subsumed under the control of the Gaullist networks.[103] Fusion with the Gaullist secret services eventually happened in 1944 but even then only with considerable difficulty. It did not prevent the continuation of resentment between veterans of the Vichy secret services and those of de Gaulle.

In fact, tensions remained between the individuals on either side of this divide well after the war. A highly significant (and often amusing) document highlighting these continued difficulties is a pamphlet written in 1950 by General Rivet, former head of Vichy's Cinquième Bureau. The pamphlet was a reply to a book written by Jacques Soustelle of the Gaullist secret services. At times the level of the criticisms in this document (and one supposes in Soustelle's book) reaches very personal and somewhat puerile levels. Rivet wrote, "You describe me as 'small with a large cyst on my head.' But I'm 1 meter 71 tall and those that know me have difficulty detecting the 'large' cyst that, in your words, disrupts the regularity of my underdeveloped skull. Well let's imagine for a minute that my pen, becoming frivolous, describes you as 'fatty,'"[104] That they are reduced to insulting each other's physical appearance does not suggest a high level of personal respect or admiration.

The officers of the ST were presented with a similar choice after the German invasion of Southern France, but since only the ST and not the whole of the police was scrapped, there were other possibilities for them. Some, like Captain Léonard, chose to go underground but remain inactive: he abandoned his post and hid till the end of the war. Others found ways of being transferred to other police services. Thus Inspector Yves Piana of the ST was reassigned to the political affairs department (Section des Affaires Politiques), the anti-Gaullist and particularly anti-Communist section of the Marseille police. Among those who chose to join the Resistance, a minority followed the path taken by General Giraud. This was Robert Blémant's case. A large number of ST officers chose instead to align themselves with the Gaullist Resistance. The core membership of the Ajax network, one of the police resistance networks, was composed of former members of the ST, such as Captain Léon Theus, who was coleader of the network. It seems that their disagreement with the Gaullists ran less deep than that of the military secret services.

By combining contemporaneous documents with the often hagiographical memoirs written by counter-intelligence veterans a more nuanced version of Vichy's secret services' attitude emerges. In spite of their acute hatred for the Germans, their attitudes toward the Allies, particularly the British, were ambiguous. Gaullists were also criticized for their attacks against the government which, in the eyes of this ultraconservative military personnel, could aggravate the divisions within the nation. However, in spite of these considerations, whenever the chips were down, whenever the Vichy secret services had to choose a camp, they opted for the anti-German option. In this their attitude differed from the government which employed them.

5 EVERYDAY COUNTERESPIONAGE

Counterespionage does not limit itself to cracking down on enemy espionage. It also has to prevent leaks and counteract propaganda. Lieutenant Colonel Schlesser, former head of the French counterespionage, pointed out these needs in a report he wrote on 28 July 1940 upon returning from a TR mission in the northern zone. After writing of the danger of uncontrolled relations between French citizens and the occupation forces, Schlesser suggested that French people needed to be told how to behave. The document he wrote for the TR is reminiscent of *Les Conseils à l'occupé* (Advice to the occupied) written by the resister Jean Texcier around the same time, which outlined acceptable codes of behavior. In Schlesser's view, instructions to the French should be passed through a secret propaganda campaign by the Vichy government: "National propaganda against German colonization can only be whispered. An officer in charge of it should be assigned to each prefect and disguised under various labels (general secretary, assistant chief of the cabinet). He would carry out government orders, or even better, orders from French intelligence so as to avoid compromising the government. The agent's mission would be threefold: counterespionage, surveillance of antinational activities in collaboration with the police and promoting national feeling. To succeed, he would establish a network of secret contacts throughout the *département*."

Schlesser also saw the need to advise refugees who were about to return to the occupied zone after the exodus. They were instructed to adopt "a dignified attitude when faced with German propaganda." "The first people who should be contacted, and immediately, are demobilized officers and soldiers: their leaders would teach them the gestures they should adopt or avoid, the words they should or shouldn't speak." In essence Schlesser was putting forward a prototype of the model behavior later advocated in Vercors's famous Resistance novel *Le Silence de la mer*, which recommended that French people should ignore the Germans altogether: "Of course this does not involve firing on German sentries nor even stepping on their toes. But the French have the right to avoid conversations with German soldiers, to not respond to requests for information addressed to them, to not buy German newspaper (*Paris Soir* and *Le Matin* in Paris), to leave an establishment when German soldiers enter it." Finally, he gave an outline of the obligations of the French people: "They have the duty to fight against the Nazi lies, which claim that the French army did not fight, that the military and civilian leaders of France are incompetent and gave the order to flee, that the Reich had not wanted the war, that the German army is not looting, and other nonsense dreamed up by Dr. Goebbels. French citizens' attitude will remain dignified as long as it is driven by the constant thought that these German soldiers are the ones who killed their fathers, brothers, husbands and friends."[1]

It is not clear whether Schlesser's proposals were given any follow-up. However, it was not only in the occupied zone that instructions of this type were suggested. To fight against "pro-German propaganda" in North Africa, the French armistice services proposed to General Weygand a method similar to that of Schlesser. According to a memo dated 15 February 1941, pro-German propaganda should be "opposed with verbal propaganda in Moorish cafés, Moorish bathhouses, markets and other meeting places, and trustworthy and sure agents should be assigned to this delicate task."[2] Since enemy propaganda was viewed by the counterespionage services as closely linked to the recruiting of spies, the struggle against it was also supposed to ward off the danger of espionage.

Counterespionage services also advocated preventive measures to avoid leaks because they thought it was very easy for foreign intelligence to obtain information. A TR report of March 1941 stated that "the exploitation of indiscretions (and notably those of the military) is the main source of German intelligence."[3] All possible measures were to be taken to limit these leaks. According to a lecture given by Paillole in April of 1942, there were cultural reasons that made this difficult. "All that a foreign intelligence agency has to do is to read a newspaper, or listen in on a conversation, even the normal conversation of a French person who talks a lot, particularly when he is in the army."[4]

To undermine inadvertent leaks to German intelligence, training on counterespionage was intensified in the military units in the nonoccupied territories. In the spring of 1941, members of the army were instructed to sign "a statement according to which the soldier acknowledges having been given counterespionage training." This document was distributed by the BMAs who were also responsible for the training itself. The various BMA posts of the southern zone and Algeria asked for a total of 68,500 of these declaration forms.[5] Training provided by the BMA was expected to emphasize the need for discretion and also to provide specific instructions on correct behavior toward an agent of a foreign intelligence agency (these instructions were also aimed at Allied spying): "Never refuse categorically any propositions but request a new meeting by saying that the matter seems interesting. Give a report to the unit commander with a detailed description of the person in question, and of the future meeting place."[6] The troops were instructed not to give any information to German organizations, except in specific circumstances, as we can see in a letter that Colonel Schneider, commander of the Périgueux military district, sent to the units within his jurisdiction: "You need to remind all military personnel under your command that they are strictly forbidden to answer questions that might be asked of them by German civil servants or military people other than those of the armistice commissions. French military personnel questioned in this way must refer their German interlocutors to their officers, and in the first instance to their company commander. They must also report on the questions they were asked."[7]

To encourage a "counterespionage reflex" among the troops, prewar slogans were still found to be useful. In 1941 posters with the following slogans were still hanging on walls: "To be silent is to serve." "When on the indiscrete phone, don't tell your secrets." "Don't put your secret papers in the waste basket, burn them!!" "Even the smallest piece of information will interest the foreign agent." "When with a stranger, watch your mouth. Don't leave him alone in an office!!" "A discrete secretary is a perfect secretary." "The enemy spy is waiting for you and watching you everywhere." "Informing the enemy, even unconsciously, means betraying your country."[8] Obviously the use of the word "enemy" in the two last slogans was likely to be controversial. So as to not offend the Axis armistice commissions, Lieutenant Colonel Guy d'Alès, head of the BMA, insisted that these two slogans be scrapped in December 1941. The need to wage this preventive campaign discretely explains the slowness of the results. Nevertheless, a memo of July 1942 concluded that soldiers were finally becoming aware of the need for discretion.[9]

The other tactic to avoid unintended disclosures was to limit contact between civilians and the Germans. Discretion was thus also required of the population. In a letter sent to Marshal Pétain on 3 March 1941, General Weygand explained the system of warnings set up to prevent leaks of information likely to benefit the Germans in North Africa. "I drew the attention of the appropriate authorities to the disadvantages of contacts between certain persons in North Africa (civil servants, members of chambers of commerce, settlers, native leaders, etc.) and members of Axis armistice commissions, and I urged that these persons be warned against the danger resulting from individual relationships that went beyond the strict limits of the armistice framework and government instructions regarding collaboration policy."[10]

Axis armistice commissions had to be isolated if preventative counterespionage was to be successful. In July 1941, Vice-Premier Darlan emphasized the need to discourage French civil servants from directing their fellow citizens to the Germans for any administrative needs, for instance to request a special pass (*Ausweis*) needed to cross the demarcation lines between the various zones of occupation. He urged prefects to give the following instructions to their subordinates: "They should be reminded of the political disadvantages and risks posed by direct administrative contacts between the public and foreign armistice delegations, and consequently they should be absolutely forbidden to refer supplicants to these commissions."[11] This would both prevent breaches of the sovereignty of French institutions in the nonoccupied territories and limit contact between French citizens and Germans.[12] Lists of civil servants who did not follow these directives were compiled and in some cases they were suspended.[13]

To further isolate these commissions, a system of police surveillance was set up around buildings housing Axis services: the identity of individuals approaching these buildings was noted, and they were often subjected to subsequent police interrogation. Officially, this system was set up to protect the Axis organizations in the nonoccupied territories, and this protective mission was genuine, as evidenced by punishments inflicted on those who failed in their duties. In Algiers, a policeman who was not able to keep two drunks from insulting the officers of an armistice commission was suspended.[14] The French government wanted to avoid any unnecessary incidents. In Weygand's words: "Protection is indispensable. The French authorities would bear a heavy responsibility in the event of an attack, which, given the hostility of a part of the population and the presence of foreigners is always a possibility."[15] In fact, there were some incidents against members of armistice commissions in the southern zone and in North Africa. Usually, these incidents were minor, but they gave to the Germans and the Italians the feeling that they needed to be protected. Thus on 8 December 1940, in the village of La Saluce in the Hautes-Alpes, an individual approached two German officers who had come from Avignon and shouted "Hitler is a bastard!" "I hope the British win the war"; "We don't want to be oppressed."[16] Later, these officers noticed that three of the tires of their car had been slashed and were flat. On 20 July 1941 in the village of Rayol (Var) in the southeast of France, a car belonging to a German commission was also vandalized: a fifteen-year-old girl, Claude Lévy, was thought to have drawn a "V" (symbolizing an Allied victory) on the car and to have broken a mirror while the German officers were at the beach.[17] Other more serious incidents affecting Axis representatives in the nonoccupied territories were also reported. On 9 January 1941, General Boselli, the president of the Italian delegation in Algeria, was assaulted with a billy club on a street in Algiers.[18] According to the later accounts of the secret services and the French armistice delegation, this attack had been planned by French counterespionage services with the aim of convincing the Axis armistice commissions of the need for police protection.[19] After the Boselli incident, the Axis commissions gradually became persuaded of the need for such protection. Despite the protection given, incidents became more serious during the second half of 1941 as a consequence of the growth of the Resistance after the Soviet Union entered the war. In the fall of that year, the French police apprehended a "suspicious" armed individual in Oran, Algeria. He was arrested while entering the offices of a German commission, and the individual confessed that he was planning to attack one of the commission members.[20] In November 1941, a vehicle belonging to the Italian armistice commission was blown up in Marseille.[21]

Although it is clear that the French authorities were serious in their efforts to protect the Axis commissions, it was explicitly and frequently noted in letters sent between French services that this protective mission could also serve as cover for a surveillance of the commissions themselves. For instance, a letter sent by Vice-Premier Darlan on 5 July 1941 to the secretaries of state for the interior and war was entirely explicit on the means to be used to limit contact between the public and the Germans, as well as on the use of the protective mission as a cover for surveillance missions: "In each of those cities in the free zone where commissions of control or official services of the occupying power are installed, surveillance shall be undertaken with the aim of identifying persons attempting to enter into direct contact with German authorities. A certain number of them, chosen from different milieus of the population, shall be submitted to identity checks, investigation, and police summons. These measures shall be justified by the necessity to ensure the personal safety of the members of the control commission."[22]

In his memoirs, Pierre Nord, a novelist and member of the secret services during the war, described this procedure of protection-surveillance. According to him "under the most courteous pretexts, commission members were not left alone for an instant." He claimed that "the police protects the Italian and German bureaus 24 hours a day" and thus "no German can so much as buy a box of matches without a guardian angel watching over him." Nord insisted: "Any person who entered into contact with the commissions was immediately identified, catalogued and summoned to the police building and warned that a negative interpretation of his frequentations could lead to them being interned in a camp."[23] This showed the wish of the French authorities to achieve omnipresent and total surveillance. In reality however, even though the police pursued many individuals on account of their contacts with German armistice commissions, the all-encompassing power of these authorities was merely an illusion. The practice of surveillance varied considerably from one town to another, even at times from one part of the same town to another. Moreover, the shortage of police personnel made it impossible to totally isolate Axis armistice commissions.

It would be an oversimplification to say that this "protection-surveillance" was systematically considered a hostile act by the Germans and the Italians. Some Axis officials requested security measures. Sometimes German officers even encouraged French authorities to intercept individuals wanting to get in touch with their services. Thus the German delegation responsible for controlling maritime traffic in Marseille intervened with the French liaison officer to ask him to turn away some locals who had come with requests for help.[24] On the other hand, it is certain that the excessive nature of the protection-surveillance measures was the subject of frequent complaints by German services. Reichel, of the German armistice delegation in Algeria, intervened in the case of an individual called Cheron, who was arrested for his contacts with this delegation. Reichel claimed that "despite all the assurances given by the Vichy government, lower levels of the French administration continue to make life difficult for any person who shows themselves well disposed to collaboration with Germany by entering into contact with members of local armistice commissions."[25] In August 1941, General Studt, head of the German armistice commission, noted in a letter addressed to General Koeltz, his French counterpart, that "lately, I am increasingly getting reports from commission delegations informing me that the French gendarmerie and police positioned in front of the commissions' hotels hassle civilians wishing to visit commission officers, and at times even prevent them from entering."[26] In a letter dated 1 November 1941, General Max Vogl of the German armistice commission in Wiesbaden complained of these actions: "From the multitude of cases that have been drawn to my attention, I am restricting myself to drawing up a list of names of those persons who were either arrested or threatened with expulsion by the French services for the sole crime of having had personal contacts with members of the German control commission."[27] General Vogl claimed that the surveillance was so intimidating that it interfered at times with the functioning of the commissions; he pointed out that in Morocco craftsmen called in to perform urgent repairs and tradesmen selling their merchandise to the commissions found it prudent to break off contact so as not to be hassled by the authorities. Beyond the difficulties caused to the functioning of these commissions, this police vigilance was undoubtedly also a source of irritation for those members of the armistice commissions engaged in espionage.

Particularly annoying were the measures taken to prevent women from entering into contact with these commissions. From the start, intimate relationships between French women and representatives of Axis armistice commissions posed a problem for the Vichy government. The sexual independence of these women, particularly in the case of spouses of prisoners of war, went against the moralistic concepts of the Pétain's regime, which was keen to restore traditional, Catholic values of the family.[28] Supplementary reasons for disapproving of these relations were stated in various administrative documents. In August 1940, a report from the police in the town of Villeneuve-sur-Lot noted that "it won't take very long for members of the German army to enter into close relations with women" and it pointed out the damaging effects of this situation: "These 'holiday' romances have led to some criticisms and negative comments from mothers or other persons whose family or friends are prisoners of war in Germany."[29] One year later, a synthesis by the general staff of the army in French Morocco explicitly linked these "feminine intrigues" with the problem of espionage: "Leaving aside questions of pride, and despite the fact that most of these relationships are of no consequence, it is evident that some of these liaisons can offer the Germans a source of information about the evolution of public opinion, and also cause a certain scandal."[30] For reasons of pride, morality, the risk of scandal and espionage, so-called horizontal collaboration was the subject of surveillance by the authorities as early as 1940.[31] We probably also need to take into account the prejudices of the masculine dominated secret service milieu where misogynous stereotypes of the woman who "can't keep her mouth shut" were widespread.

In the southern zone, with the exception of a few internments, the authorities did not generally go beyond just surveillance of the phenomenon.[32] In North Africa, by contrast, more serious punishments were inflicted to put an end to these sexual relationships. A memo from the Algiers section of the Deuxième Bureau suggested issuing a warning to "French men and particularly French women" who have personal relationships with members of the Axis commission.

> In each town of French North Africa where there is a German or Italian commission, the suggestion put forward in agreement with the BMA is to ask the war veterans' Legion to designate a certain number of veterans (five or six) specifically chosen for their tact, education and calm. These veterans would receive from the BMA the list of persons in unauthorized contact with the German or Italian armistice commission delegations and would go to their homes to issue them with a warning. The veterans would claim to be acting on personal initiative and would accompany their warning with threats should the incriminating relations persist. It is probable that in most cases fear of scandal would be sufficient. If the relations persisted, violent punishments, organized by the BMA, would ensue. Administrative sanctions (expulsions, house arrest, internment) would be reserved for the worst cases.[33]

The exact form of this punishment was not specified here, but other documents clearly indicate that it involved head shaving. A written report by Kientz of the BCC, a special counterespionage office in Morocco, was quite explicit on this point:

> Moreover, it has been repeatedly brought to our attention that the number of women known to be guilty of carrying on intimate relations with members of the German and Italian commissions is on the rise. So as to remedy this state of affairs contrary to French morality and patriotism, the following measures could be taken: a) expulsion or house arrest; b) shaving off their hair as the Germans did in 1919 for the army of the Rhine; c) registering them as prostitutes. One thing is certain: punishment must be meted out otherwise the facts noted above will only increase to the detriment of French prestige.[34]

This report reveals that head shavings were not simply organized from below. Copies of it were sent to General Noguès, Vichy's resident general in Morocco, and to General Weygand, the governor of French North Africa. In other words the most senior Vichy officials in the region were informed of the proposed measures. Weygand is known to have complained repeatedly about acts of horizontal collaboration. In a letter dated July 1941, he expressed his anger at members of Axis commissions who were "trying to pick up women in the streets."[35] In a retrospective account, General Perier, head of Weygand's general staff, claimed that Weygand had instructed Noguès to encourage reprisals against those engaging in intimate relations, but to make them look like private initiates.[36]

It still needs to be asked whether these projected measures were actually applied. A report from the Algiers branch of the BMA discussed punishments imposed against "horizontal collaborators" during October 1941: "In the past month, eighteen European and native women who had guilty relations with members of Italian or German commissions were put under house arrest."[37] As to the extent of head shavings, it is not possible to quantify or determine the exact circumstances in which they were carried out. However one thing can be stated categorically: in the course of the months of September and October 1941, a certain number (probably limited) of head shavings occurred. This is confirmed in several accounts from former members of the secret services.[38] Another retrospective account on this topic is that of General Gross of the French delegation of the armistice commission in North Africa. In a report from April 1943 dealing with the activities of the Vichy authorities in North

Africa, he claimed that "women in contact with enemy officers were punished (heads shaved, obligation to register as prostitutes)."[39] The Germans themselves confirmed that these punishments were applied. In the middle of September 1941, the delegation of the French armistice commission received a complaint from the German commission about "the manner in which relationships with French women have been made impossible."[40] Two weeks later, the French delegation relayed another protest from General Schultheiss of the German commission: "A washerwoman from Casablanca, whom he thought was Alsatian, was insulted and mistreated by the police because she sometimes welcomed German soldiers who came to pick up their laundry from her home. She was accused of having intimate relations with German soldiers. Her husband, who has been working for twenty years in the Casablanca port, had his access to the port permit revoked."[41] From this documentation we can see that, contrary to what had been claimed by historians, the punishment of women for horizontal collaboration was first instigated by Vichy and not the Resistance, and the first head shavings took place considerably earlier than the historiography currently acknowledges.[42]

Sometimes instead of punishing women for having intimate relationships with Axis representatives, the BMA tried to transform them into agents for its own intelligence purposes.[43] Another surveillance strategy was to place agents within the German services so as to obtain intelligence on German intentions or on their espionage activities. In March 1941, General Vergez, commander of French troops in Morocco, warned Weygand that this internal surveillance of the German services was insufficient: "It doesn't seem that the present surveillance system is very efficient. In order to achieve reliable results, we would need constant internal surveillance that would be done through hotel personnel (maids, bell-hops, etc.), under the leadership of liaison officers. Precious information could be obtained in this way that would then enable us to know the activities of the armistice control commissions."[44] Counterespionage services thus tried to use every opportunity to infiltrate German organizations. In the month of December 1941, the BMA learned that the German commissions in North Africa were about to recruit French drivers so as to free German drivers for the Russian front. This was an opportunity to place agents within these services, so the BMA immediately sought confirmation of the rumor to fully take advantage of the new situation.[45]

French liaison officers attached to the armistice commissions were at the very heart of the infiltration of German services. Detachments of military personnel, carefully chosen for their tact and firmness, were placed permanently within each foreign control commission, officially to facilitate liaison with the Germans and Italians. We can divide this personnel into two categories: mobile and fixed.

Mobile personnel were normally called upon to accompany members of control commissions in their travels. In fact, the armistice commissions did not have the right to visit French installations unless accompanied by a French liaison officer, and the instructions given to military units visited were very clear: they must not give information to Axis armistice commission delegates unless they were accompanied by a liaison officer. This officer's job was to limit these commissions' activities. The French armistice services issued them with the following instructions:

> The role of the liaison officers should not be limited to a simple escorting mission. In addition, their mission calls upon them to maintain the operations of control within the objectives and limits fixed by the armistice conventions and the instructions for their application issued by the French delegation to the armistice. This essential mission may force them to intervene during a control so as to prevent answers to questions which fall beyond the framework of the instructions they were given: they will do this with all the required tact toward the Axis officer carrying out the control as well as toward the head of the controlled organization—but they should never let the Axis control commission go beyond what it has the right to do, even if this might risk provoking an incident.[46]

Liaison officers' mission also included informing French authorities on the questions asked. After each control visit, the officer wrote a report of the mission and copies were then sent to the French armistice delegation headquarters as well as to the local military command.

The second category of liaison personnel was fixed. Fixed personnel were posted in the offices of the Axis commissions to serve as intermediaries between visitors or French authorities and commission members. These officers wrote weekly reports on the activities of the foreign commission with which they were placed. According to the instructions, these reports must "aim to find any useful clues likely to help inform the armistice services about the tendencies shown by the foreign controllers, particularly on the extension of this control to domains outside of the accepted instructions, as well as on the illicit activities of commission members."[47]

It is obvious that both the mobile and the fixed personnel occupied key counterespionage positions. These officers collected precious information on the occupation forces for the military command and the directorate of the armistice services. They also took advantage of their contacts to find out what was happening on the other side of the Rhine. Thus, in their reports, they noted the morale of the German army, but also reported on things such as the euthanasia programs in Germany.[48] Liaison officers compiled a list of the commission personnel with notes on the personality of each individual and records of their movements.[49] They also tried to find out the identities of agents or informers of the commissions. A report written by a liaison officer in Pau shows clearly their role in the detection of unauthorized relations with the Germans: "The liaison officer notes that the delegate receives everyday a substantial amount of mail that currently originates mainly from French correspondents. For documentary purposes he notes that he accidentally read two of these letters."[50] The liaison officer succeeded in finding out the names of the authors of these letters he had seen "accidentally." It transpired that one sender was a woman living in the Hautes-Pyrénées who wrote to the Germans on behalf of some Belgian refugees and that the other was a war veteran who wrote looking to find employment with the Germans. The second case was considered particularly serious by French authorities because this veteran had written, "Since the French are unable, in spite of all their promises, of finding me a job, I am wondering if there is any possibility of being employed by you in the occupied zone." General Louis Koeltz, head of the French armistice services, wrote to the secretary general of veterans to request that this individual be expelled from the Veterans' Legion.[51]

Information provided by liaison officers was used in police investigations as shown by the following extract from a biweekly report by the liaison officer in Pau:

> About two weeks ago, the liaison officer's attention was drawn to the behavior of a woman of about fifty visiting the Hauptführer several times a week and chatting with him at length and with great circumspection. The municipal police tailed this woman and relayed the following information: she is a German called Bauer, Emmy, Johanna, born in Lagersdorf on 12 August 1891, married on 25 March 1938 in Pau to a Frenchman, Lauverjat, Jean, Léon, Marie, born in Pau on 30 May 1885. The municipal police were not able to ascertain whether this woman acquired French nationality through her mar-

riage. The investigation revealed several facts deserving of attention: Lauverjat is a deserter from our army; he was suspected of espionage several years ago though no categorical evidence was found but the police has a file on him. He is currently pursuing the profession of artist painter under the name Jean de Lauverjat. He lives with his spouse in Pau, 20 rue de Montpezat. It must be noted that the woman Bauer-Lauverjat has frequent contacts with a person named Viebahn, a German living in Pau since 1904, whose activities have more than once attracted the attention of the municipal police without any formal charges established against him. Attention has already been drawn to this Viebahn (see the weekly report of 18 February 1941, n° 3/RKG, addressed to Major Eberlé). The facts and actions of all these individuals will be watched and faithfully reported.[52]

In addition to police vigilance, more technical means were used for the surveillance of German organizations. In their memoirs, secret service veterans refer to planting microphones in the offices of the Axis representatives.[53] Such practices rarely leave visible traces in the archives historians consult, however, a document dated September 1942 sheds very interesting light on this topic. It contains the instructions given by the directorate of the French armistice services to its delegation based in Wiesbaden in response to the following German complaint: "the German armistice commission informed the French delegation in Wiesbaden, Germany, that the Italian and German control organizations had discovered in their offices in the Hôtel d'Angleterre in Algiers devices installed by the French on telephones that enabled the eavesdropping of all the conversations held in these offices, and they asked for a response on this subject." The directorate of the armistice services asked its Wiesbaden delegation to respond to the German commission as follows:

1. The French government was not aware of the existence of the devices in question. Instructions have been given to the French authorities to collect from the Axis control delegation in Algiers all the information necessary to investigate this affair and to find out who was responsible and that any guilty party will be held to account.
2. Any devices brought to our attention by the armistice control organizations, or that may be brought to our attention at a later date, will be immediately removed. The French government insists that it has no knowledge that any listening devices have been installed in other offices of delegations in metropolitan France or in dependent territories. Dis-

creet investigations will be undertaken to search for any clandestine installation that might exist. In this regard, French authorities would be interested in receiving information, in addition to that already given, that German and Italian authorities might possess on the nature and location of the devices that have been discovered or that might be discovered later on.

3. As is customary, the telephone installations of the Italian and German delegations in Algeria and Tunisia will be set up or modified according to the express wishes of the local control organizations.

If we believe the first part of this letter, the French authorities were offering to collaborate in the investigation of an affair of which they had no prior knowledge. However, in the last paragraph of this document, the directorate of the French armistice services offered a clarification which made clear it this was not the case:

> N.B For the personal information of the French delegation:
>
> The French delegation's attention is drawn to the fact that the German note and the Italian note pertain only to the use of ad hoc devices to eavesdrop on conversations held in the offices of the control delegations. This clarification is given by the directorate of the armistice services because, in its telegram n° 1859 C/EM of 11 September, the French delegation alludes to the tapping of telephone conversations of which there is no mention in the German note nor in the Italian note, and which thus falls outside the limited issue that should be addressed in our replies. The confusion stems from the fact that the conversations held in the offices were listened to with the help of devices installed on telephones in an unusual way.[54]

This document is interesting in several aspects. Firstly, it tends to confirm the use of the methods described in the memoirs. The late discovery of such methods (September 1942) leaves it unclear whether the Germans took a long time to discover these microphones or whether they came into use relatively late. Secondly, the directorate of the French armistice services instructed its delegation to lie and say that the French were totally ignorant of these secret listening devices. The last paragraph of the document shows not only that these armistice services were aware of the presence of bugs planted in the telephones, but also implies that a second category of devices, designed for actually tapping the telephone calls themselves, were yet to be discovered.

Another confirmation of the practice of putting microphones in German offices can be found in the diary of General Bridoux, the secretary of state for war under Premier Laval. According to Bridoux, the practice had been ordered from on high. On 5 November 1942, he noted, "They say that Geissler, head of the Gestapo in Vichy, noticed a microphone attached to his phone and also that the conversations of Krug von Nidda were tapped. Admiral Darlan had ordered these devices during his time as Vice-Premier. This makes us think that there might still be surprises in store since the actions of the admiral's general staff seem to be getting clumsier by the day." [55]

German phone communications were often listened in on, but this was not always done discretely.[56] On 8 August 1941, a Czech named François Tolpa telephoned a member of the German commission in Royat. The operator who was listening in interrupted their conversation to ask them to speak in French because she had "only a limited knowledge of German." The response was: "I am with the Royat Kommandantur and I have the right to speak in German." In her summary of the conversation for the BMA, she could only note that on the one side there was an incomprehensible monologue from Tolpa and on the other many "Ja! Ja!"[57] It is therefore not surprising that the German seemed to be aware of the tapping of their calls. Thus, Major Lorentz, of the German armistice delegation in Morocco, began a phone conversation with the naval captain Hoffmann by saying: "First of all I need to make you aware that this conversation will be listened in on."[58] In these circumstances we might wonder if tapping these conversations served any real purpose. However, there were some rare occasions when the Germans failed to take precautionary measures. For instance, on 24 March 1941, the tapping of a phone conversation between two careless members of the German commission included references to Robert Bellette, a spy of long standing, who was then tailed in Casablanca.[59]

Written communications of German services were also intercepted. France has a long tradition, dating from the sixteenth century, of intercepting private letters. Under Vichy, this was entrusted to the Postal Censor Department, known as the Contrôle Technique, though once again this task was not always carried out very discretely.[60] The German delegate for repatriation in Marseille complained about the delays in receiving his mail. Then, "after several days without any letters, he received more than fifty letters all at the same time."[61] According to the previously mentioned May 1941 report by Henri Rollin, an official in the Ministry of the Interior, this practice was not used sufficiently for counterespionage. For Rollin the difficulty was that the seized letters generally took two to three weeks to be passed between departments, which meant that they were out of date before they could be properly investigated.[62]

Despite the difficulties, the surveillance of the illicit activities of the Axis armistice commissions and diplomatic missions was actually the most straightforward part of counterespionage work. While the secret services were not always successful in keeping track of spying organized by these Axis organizations, at least the target of surveillance was readily identifiable. But we must not forget that many of the German agents sent to the nonoccupied territories had no direct contact with these diplomatic missions. Organizing counterespionage against agents operating independently from these organizations required more imagination. At least five sorts of practice were used to detect the activities of these "independent" spies: the surveillance of German organizations operating in Germany itself or in the occupied territories, the monitoring of suspect milieus, continued vigilance in sensitive locations as well as in points of transit, taking advantage of agents' mistakes and of denunciations of suspect behavior by members of the public.

Since the spies sent to the nonoccupied territories were working for German intelligence posts based in the occupied zone or in Germany, the surveillance of those posts and their infiltration by French agents could help in discovering spies. But here, as in all of Vichy's counterespionage work, staffing difficulties and shortages led to gaps in surveillance. A TR assessment of January 1942 noted that "some enemy posts are insufficiently monitored or even at times not monitored at all." Because of lack of personnel, it was usually not possible to place two double agents in each enemy post, which reduced the possibilities of cross-checking intelligence. TR's concern with professionalism excluded the possibility of increasing the number of agents too quickly: "the TR officer's role is too sensitive for us to plan on a rapid expansion of personnel." It must also be noted that the wide definition given to the word "enemy" aggravated staffing shortages. This report compiled the list of "enemy" posts where surveillance was insufficient. These included not only the German intelligence post in Nantes and the Italian intelligence post in Berne, but also the British intelligence posts in Berne and Lausanne.[63] The Germans were the main target but the surveillance of them could have been more effective if the simultaneous surveillance of Allied intelligence had not diverted resources.

Some spies were easily identified by keeping a close watch on suspicious groups such as the collaborationists, those radical groupings of Fascist sympathizers. In July 1942, the political police branch in Saint-Étienne organized the surveillance of a minor militant of Doriot's PPF after intercepting a pro-German letter she had sent to the collaborationist Dominique Sordet of the press agency Inter-France.[64] Vichy looked on collaborationist groups as rivals for power, but it also worried that information was passing in an uncontrolled manner from the collaborationists to the Germans. Police surveillance of these milieus can also be explained by the fact that some collaborationists maintained links with the underworld, as for instance in Marseille where Doriot's right hand man, Simon Sabiani, worked closely with the gangsters Spirito and Carbone.[65]

Other milieus were also suspicious, less because of their ideological position than because the secret services were aware that German agents were using them as cover in their intelligence operations or had succeeded in placing agents in their midst. "Escaped" prisoners of war were often considered suspect. One such was Édouard Frum, a Frenchman born in Charlottenburg, Germany. Frum adopted a false identity of an Edward Jean Frank, born in London, but was denounced by another individual who had escaped from the same POW camp. Information gathered convinced the SSM that "Frum must be considered an enemy agent."[66] Especially suspicious for French counterintelligence were North Africans who had "escaped" from German camps; there was a double risk: on the one hand, the Germans were promoting nationalist propaganda in North African circles against their French colonizers; on the other, Algerians, Moroccans, and Tunisians were sometimes used for espionage.[67] "Escaped" or repatriated North African POWs were interrogated very actively upon their return from Germany. Between the 13 and 19 July 1941, 140 escaped prisoners and 594 soldiers repatriated for health reasons were interrogated in Clermont-Ferrand or in the Sainte-Marthe camp in Marseille.[68] From 10 August to 23 August 1941, 237 escapees and 305 individuals freed or repatriated for health reasons were interrogated; and another 152 escapees and 510 repatriated individuals from 24 August to 30 August.[69] These interrogations revealed that the Germans were conducting major anti-French propaganda in POW camps among North African nationalists, and that some of them were recruited as spies. In response, surveillance was intensified. A "note on German propaganda aimed at North African POWs" written by the state secretary of war in January 1942 mentioned that "it is of the utmost importance that we keep a very close watch on the activities of repatriated or escaped individuals upon their return to Africa."[70]

It was not only people, but also places that were watched. The police organized the surveillance of points of transit such as border frontiers and train stations. They were on the look out for any "suspicious" behavior. This surveillance helped them identify individuals belonging to any categories targeted by the Vichy regime—Jews, Resisters, and so forth—but could obviously also serve to discover German spies. The demarcation line, the custom's barrier separating the occupied and unoccupied zones of France, represented an inevitable crossing point for German agents sent into the southern zone.[71] In April 1942, Paillole underlined that the surveillance of this line was ineffective. He gave an example to prove his point: "A recently arrested spy confessed that he had crossed the line more than twenty times in all serenity and carried compromising documents across it without being bothered by the police."[72] The protracted length of the demarcation line made things more difficult since setting up border-guard posts on all roads led to the dispersion of the personnel, making surveillance static and inefficient. Another factor was a serious lack of coordination between services responsible for preventing illicit crossing of the line. The relationship between the regular army and the gendarmerie, both which had responsibilities in this matter, was strained and did not facilitate coordination.[73]

Vigilance around sensitive sites such as military installations also helped to catch spies. Yet again Paillole was critical of this surveillance, suggesting in April 1942 that "the protection of sensitive sites is a sham" and that results were disappointing.[74] However, it did at times produce results. On 25 November 1940 Herbert Silberman and Helene Gerstl were arrested by a police captain of the political branch while they were wandering around Marseille airport and showing suspicious interest in antiaircraft weapons. A quick search revealed they were carrying compromising documents (German questionnaires, maps with penciled annotations indicating the location of factories and antiaircraft guns, etc.). Faced with proof of their wrongdoing, the two individuals had to confess.[75]

The task of counterespionage services was made easier by the poor quality of many German spies. While the Nazi secret services did have competent agents in their ranks, many were amateur as a result of a lack of selection in the recruitment process.[76] For this reason, it was often the agents' own carelessness, or even their stupidity, that led to their downfall. The basic rule of espionage is that when it comes to sending intelligence, one should be sure to send it to the right address. This is where Karl-Heinz Masson went wrong. In December 1941, he wrote a letter asking for protection against the French authorities. He meant to send it to the German armistice commission, but he mistakenly addressed it to the French delegation with this same commission.[77] Another agent, Lothar Fritz, was arrested by the French police while he was trying to pass through the demarcation line carrying a large envelope in his pocket addressed to the "Führer."[78]

Another fundamental error is to carry evidence of spying activities on one's person. German secret services tried to encourage their agents to memorize the questionnaires they gave them. It seems that this simple instruction was beyond the ability of a great number of agents, so the police easily discovered undeniable proof of their clandestine activities upon searching them.[79] For instance, a search of the clothes of an agent called Georges Bresson yielded, among other things, a large sum of money, an *Ausweis,* letters, notebooks containing intelligence, and a list of names.[80] On the back of his work permit, an Algerian agent of the Abwehr, Benabid Khier ben Mohamed, wrote the phrases of a secret code provided by his recruiting agent.[81]

Some individuals bragged about being agents for Germany. Jean-Georges Knipper in the Pyrénées-Atlantiques made no secret of his recruitment by the Nazis in a letter he sent to some acquaintances.[82] Neither was he alone in being indiscreet. In February 1941, a secretary of a French liaison delegation was invited to lunch by a delegate from the German Red Cross. During the meal, a waitress who turned out to be a German secret agent, started to give information to the German delegate without noticing the presence of a member of the French armistice commission.[83] Agents recruited too rapidly often lacked a cool head. This was the case for Émile Fillodeau, a twenty-two-year-old German agent who panicked when, at the moment he was attempting to ask for information from a passerby, the man hailed a gendarme of his acquaintance to say hello. Thinking he was discovered, Fillodeau entered into all sorts of hazy explanations that led to his arrest.[84]

The German secret services themselves were partly to blame for another aspect of carelessness that related to the agents' identification cards. The old cliché according to which spies' documents are systematically in order was not always true. Edouard Van Eynden and Marc Dreesen were both originally arrested because of the inadequacy of their identity papers.[85] Maurice Lambin's case was slightly different. On 7 November

1942, Lambin was arrested by an inspector of the ST in Limoges after crossing the demarcation line:

> Since persons coming from the occupied zone are the object of more surveillance than others, the agent checking the identity papers of this traveler noticed that he carried a pass given to him by the German authorities for three months, which is surprisingly long given that he was just a simple sales representative. Moreover, the various papers carried by Lambin listed a home address different from the one on his pass; finally, in a notebook found in his possession, there were certain notes that led, after interpretation, to suspect Lambin of belonging to the German intelligence services.[86]

These suspicions were confirmed during interrogations. Often, the problem with identity papers was that they were issued by an office known by the French police as being that of a German intelligence service. Thus, "bureau n° 35 in Strasbourg" was automatically considered suspicious.[87] Also, lists were compiled of persons having obtained their papers in suspicious circumstances: for instance, the French armistice services established a list of individuals holding passes to come into the southern zone issued without preliminary consultation with the minister of the interior. On the list dated 23 July 1941 there were several persons identified as "Gestapo agents," "Abwehr representatives," or "agents for German propaganda."[88]

The secret services also got information from the public about suspicious activities, either directly or via the intermediary of another administration. We can divide this information into two categories: "accidental" mention of pro-German activities and "intentional" denunciation of these activities.

Denunciation was common in France between 1940 and 1944. Vichy's propaganda encouraged an acute obsession with internal enemies with the result that Jews, Communists, members of the Resistance were all denounced to the authorities as enemies of the state by the regime's supporters, thus not all denunciations of "suspicious" individuals were consciously aimed at German spies. Behavior that looked suspicious to the onlooker could actually hide all sorts of activities: the circumspection shown by a Resister on a mission might actually be similar to that shown by a German spy, and so an onlooker might denounce someone thought to be a Resister but who might on closer inspection prove to be a spy.[89] Moreover, in the xenophobic climate of Vichy France, the simple fact of talking with a foreign accent was cause for suspicion. After investigation, an individual who was denounced as a foreign refugee to the authorities on the sole basis of the informer's xenophobia could also end up being uncovered as a German spy. The German agent Willy Sommann "drew attention because of his foreign accent," and it was only the ensuing police investigation that brought to light his real activity.[90] These sorts of cases were quite rare, however, as most German spies were actually French nationals.

In other cases denunciations to the police were made by a person convinced from the outset of the pro-German engagement of the suspicious individual. But we need to insist on the fact that this sort of information would only be provided by a specific segment of the population—those who thought that pro-German sympathies were reprehensible and who believed that the Vichy administration really would pursue persons suspected of such sympathies. Of course this second requisite seriously limited the population's help in the counterespionage process. In an anonymous letter to Marshal Pétain in the spring of 1941 a person who signed himself simply as "a 100% Frenchman" discussed the government's public declarations of its resolve to defend the territory against "all comers." However, this "100% Frenchman" expressed serious doubts that the Germans were included in Vichy's definition of "all comers."[91] This view of Vichy's political stance as unreservedly in the German camp was far from isolated. It was thus not very likely that those who doubted Vichy's neutrality would make the effort or take the risk of denouncing pro-German activities. There were nevertheless cases where members of the public did put their faith in the Vichy government to arrest German agents and were thus prepared to denounce them. In the spring of 1942, a doctor named Bougarel in Châteauroux informed the BMA of the activity of four men who had contacted him claiming to be agents of the British Intelligence Service. Bougarel, whose wife was British and whose sympathies were unambiguously with the Allies, was so unimpressed by the amateur approach of these four men that he was convinced that they must actually be German *agents provocateurs* since he had an excessively high opinion of the work of the British Intelligence Service. This was the only reason he denounced them to the BMA, but the twist in the tale was that they were indeed British agents. The BMA recognized this straightaway and pursued them vigorously nonetheless, taking advantage of Bougarel's good faith in the process.[92]

Conscious denunciations of German agents often originated in Alsatian milieus, as shown by a 19 March 1941 report written by inspector Hansler of the political police in Avignon. A certain Charles Fuchs, from Alsace, having expressed "clearly German feelings" in a restaurant was forcibly brought to the gendarmerie by a group of anti-German Alsatian refugees. Hansler's report, copies of which were sent to the Marseille BMA and the prefect of the Vaucluse *département,* concluded that Fuchs and two other individuals harbored "pro-German and clearly anti-French feelings." The report continued: "In my opinion, there are reasons to consider Baldensperver, Meyer and Fuchs as very dubious from the national viewpoint. If ever they come back to the free zone one day, there would be good grounds for a detailed investigation of their situation and very close surveillance of their movements and actions."[93] The secret services also could benefit from information coming from individuals contacted by spies. Thus, on 5 April 1941, Guillaume Le Cunff was denounced to the police by a soldier called Baudet from whom he was trying to extract military information.[94]

Once recruitment in the German secret services was suspected, evidence was needed to carry out an arrest. The general rule was to delay arresting suspects so as to be able to tail them to find out who their contacts were and the exact nature of their activities. This is what happened with Alfredo Castoldi, an Italian working for the Germans. Castoldi made the acquaintance of someone named Perez in a bar and tried to convince him to provide military information. Perez pretended to accept but the next day he went to tell all to the local police chief. The police did not arrest Castoldi right away but asked Perez to maintain contact with him and to earn his trust and find out the nature of his intentions and his network.[95] The evidence acquired in this way was so convincing that on 3 November 1941, at 7:30 in the morning, Castoldi was executed by a French army firing squad in Algiers.[96]

A frequent counterespionage tactic involved using *agents provocateurs.* To obtain information on an individual's activities and contacts, policemen contacted German agents and pretended to be working for the German secret services. To get confirmation of Karl-Heinz Masson's activities, a couple of police officers of Alsatian origin disguised as members of a German armistice commission showed up at his hotel in December 1941.[97] Inspector Steinard of the Lyon police made use of a similar procedure on 2 January 1942 when he paid a visit to the spy Maurice Wagner in his prison cell and made him believe that he belonged to the German Red Cross.[98] In the case of Xavier Battini, it was impossible for him to later deny his original confession because Battini had earlier confessed everything during a conversation with a police inspector who was pretending to be a German agent.[99]

Sometimes, when formal evidence was difficult to obtain, suspects were arrested under a trivial pretext to hide the real motive. The report of a liaison officer in Clermont-Ferrand referred to such a practice in the case of Jeanne Le Bart: "She was arrested and condemned for having uttered insulting remarks toward the police, but, according to the BMA, the real reason was her relationship with the Germans, and at present she is interned (that must be the reason for which the Germans are searching for her present whereabouts)."[100] According to a report by the Marseille ST, the spy Ernst Ramstetter was arrested because of his violent behavior toward women in a street of Marseille. His arrest for this crime was carried out by the ST, in other words by a police service specialized in counterespionage. We might well wonder if the presence of members of this service during his outburst of violence was a complete coincidence and thus whether this transgression might have simply provided an excuse to question him about his other activities.[101]

Confessions obtained during interrogations provided valuable assistance in the struggle against German infiltration in the nonoccupied territories because they made it possible to obtain interesting information on existing networks. The need to rapidly obtain such information before the network was alerted to the arrest partly explains the brutality of these interrogations.

Counterespionage efficiency thus depended on the cooperation of many institutions and not just on the work of the secret services. Numerous methods were used to limit leaks of information to the Germans. While many of these methods (instructions regarding counterespionage, police vigilance, etc.) could be used to thwart espionage from all quarters, other aspects (surveillance of German buildings, etc.) were solely aimed at the occupier. Nevertheless it is evident that anti-German counterespionage work was only partially successful because of limited resources, a problem made worse by the fact that resources that could have been used for this activity were instead directed against the Allies. The other major difficulty was that this counterespionage ran against diplomatic positions openly held by the government and, because of this, had to be conducted with only limited support from the public. Worse still, a segment of this public believed that Vichy's propaganda in favor of collaboration gave them the green light to give information to the Germans.

6 THE FATE OF THE SPIES

Studies in espionage and counterespionage usually say little about the fate of spies. What happened to them once they were arrested? How were they treated? What punishments did they receive? What factors affected the length of their sentence? In this chapter I will attempt to answer these questions.

First we need to be aware that French counterespionage never did entirely prevent German spies from operating in the nonoccupied territories, although it undoubtedly made the spies' task harder. Numerous secret agents succeeded in their activities in the southern zone and in the French colonies. Many were never arrested because they were never caught. Indeed, the files of arrested individuals show that most of them had carried out several missions before being apprehended. We can therefore assume that, despite the efforts of the counterespionage services, the number of agents operating freely was far greater than the number in captivity. Undoubtedly frustrated, Paillole noted the disparity in the training lecture he delivered French secret service personnel in April of 1942: "The 750 spies arrested during 1941 do not account for all the foreign intelligence agents sent here."[1]

In those cases where the authorities were not able to collect the evidence required to make an arrest they could impose more minor punishments. In a letter dated 3 March 1941, General Weygand explained to Pétain that he had taken measures to that effect:

> I ordered the authorities to immediately put out of action by legal administrative measures (exile, house arrest, expulsion, etc.) any individual engaged in sustained and suspicious relations with the armistice commissions and about whom we have acquired a simple moral proof that he serves in some capacity, as an intelligence or propaganda agent. (The possibility of acquiring sufficient evidence to initiate court proceedings is indeed extremely rare and waiting for such evidence would amount to doing nothing.)[2]

In addition to the technical difficulties in finding the necessary evidence for an arrest, there were diplomatic difficulties linked to the Germans' presence. Arrests for pro-German spying occurred only in nonoccupied territories. To arrest agents operating in the directly occupied territories, they had to be convinced to cross to the other side of the demarcation line. Thus, in Raoul Gebus's case, a beautiful young woman was used to persuade him to cross into the southern zone where he was arrested.[3] But the use of this type of procedure was extremely rare. In the absence of effective repression, secret agents benefited from almost complete freedom to collect information in the northern zone. After November 1942 and the German invasion of southern France, only a few arrests of German spies were carried out in the newly occupied territory. One of the rare documents giving an account of an arrest after that date was written on 20 January by Captain Auguste Clary of the Marseille police. The arrested individual was a German agent who had infiltrated the resistance movement Combat. In his report, Clary explicitly insisted that this individual should be imprisoned in Castres in southwestern France to put an end to his pro-German activity.[4] But that was an isolated incident.

As is the case in all historical situations, diplomatic personnel used for intelligence activity posed a problem for counterespionage services. These individuals benefited from diplomatic immunity, so it was extremely difficult to crack down on their illicit activities. The Nazis took full advantage of this by using armistice commission personnel or the staff of their consulates to organize spying networks in the nonoccupied territories with impunity. There were two methods used by Vichy and its secret services to try to put an end to these illicit activities. The first was to request that the compromised individuals be sent back home, while the second involved blackmail.

It was very rare that a request for a suspect diplomat to be sent home was accepted by the Axis powers. Paillole analyzed this problem in a secret service training session in April 1942: "I could cite many cases in which we caught official persons in the act. We couldn't pursue them before the courts because of the diplomatic immunity these individuals enjoyed. We communicated on countless occasions with the Foreign Affairs Ministry. We sent letter after letter, request after request—nothing doing. Realizing that we couldn't prevent these activities, we tried to obtain reciprocity in foreign countries."[5]

With regard to blackmail against diplomatic personnel implicated in unauthorized activities, Henri Navarre of the Deuxième Bureau in Algiers has written about this sort of incident in his memoirs. He described the case of an active member of the German commission with a penchant for young Arab boys. To blackmail him into cooling his spying zeal, the secret services recruited a young Arab and took compromising photographs.[6]

Homophobia among secret service personnel was obvious in at least one of these cases of blackmailing Axis representatives. Given the severe punishments meted out in the Third Reich for homosexuality, we can well imagine the benefit the French services could draw from incriminating Nazi representatives. The target of one such maneuver was Theodor Auer, leader of the Gestapo in Morocco and a thorn in the side of counterespionage services. Born in 1899 in Cologne (Germany), Auer studied law before becoming a diplomat.[7] In October of 1940, he was sent to Morocco to head the German economic office. In reality, he was a spy, whose efficiency deeply irritated the French authorities. In April of 1941, the BMA in Morocco expressed the wish to use Auer's homosexuality against him: "In Algiers, 'Teddy' Auer met one of his old friends, Franz Duschnitz, an Austrian Jew, a former member of the French foreign legion and a notorious homosexual. Auer boasted to his 'friend' that he was the head of the Gestapo in Morocco and could obtain transit and residence permits for him thanks to his influence with the local police in Morocco. Desiderata: exploitation of the homosexual relations between Auer and Duschnitz."[8]

In July, Vice-Premier Admiral Darlan asked the German embassy to expel Auer from Morocco because "of the sodomy that he is practicing almost publicly."[9] One month later, the TR network tried to exploit the sexual relations between Auer and an informant of its service. It hoped the informant could enter into a relationship with Auer "to satisfy the

German vice: pederasty," and making it possible for the TR to take advantage of the situation.[10]

The failure of these maneuvers against Auer became obvious when he was appointed general consul in November 1941. There were several reasons why the Germans refused to bow to pressure on this issue. Firstly, the spying network organized by Auer was very successful. It was his very efficiency that so irritated the French. Secondly, the Germans did not want to let the French influence their choice of diplomatic personnel. Finally, Auer was a member of the Gestapo whose influence was on the rise. He might have been homosexual, but one of his lovers was well connected. Auer was the "intimate friend" of vice-consul Schwarzmann, a close relative of Joachim von Ribbentrop, the foreign affairs minister of the Reich.[11] As we can see even blackmail did not always manage to put an end to illicit activities.

Though not all German spies were arrested, there were still a substantial number of arrests made. Accurate statistics are difficult to obtain since they vary according to different sources. Some sources measure only the number of German agents arrested. Others, record the number of agents arrested whilst working for the "Axis" (including Italian and/or Japanese agents, and even sometimes Spanish ones). Arrests for pro-Axis propaganda, as opposed to just espionage, are also included in some statistics. A number of sources focus purely on arrests, while others refer to the cases that actually passed before the military justice courts. We must therefore be very careful in their interpretation but we can still hazard an approximate figure for the number of arrests.

Pierre Nord, who was a member of the French secret services during the war, estimated that a total of 1,800 Axis spies were arrested between 1940 and 1942.[12] In his memoirs, Paillole claimed that the number of arrests greatly increased during the war. While the yearly average of arrests for this type of activity between 1936 and 1939 hovered around 240, he claimed that 1,250 arrests were made in 1940 (without specifying how many of these were carried out before the armistice), 601 in 1941, and 1,223 in 1942—an annual average of 900.[13] A balance sheet of the repression "of enemy espionage and propaganda (German, Italian and Japanese)" was established after Liberation on the basis of the number of cases sent to the Vichy military justice. According to that estimate, there were 2,513 cases of this nature between 1940 and 1942.[14] In a June 1941 letter sent to Vice-Premier Darlan, Secretary of State for War General Huntziger noted 258 arrests for pro-German spying between December

1940 and May 1941.[15] This same month, a balance sheet presented to the Deuxième Bureau by the TR provided a nominative list of 215 arrests for the period running from January to May.[16] In that document, as in Huntziger's letter, the number of arrests was increasing each month. The BMA monthly reports are available to historians for eleven of the sixteen months between March 1941 and June 1942. According to this source, there was a monthly average of 64 German agents arrested.[17] In a November 1942 report, the head of the Marseille branch of the ST notified his bosses in Vichy that, since January 1941, 170 Axis agents had been arrested in Marseille alone.[18] A former national leader of the ST offers another figure claiming that in 1941 and 1942, 316 Axis agents were arrested in the southern zone, and 1,800 in North Africa.[19] According to the journalists Roger Faligot and Pascal Krop, there were 316 arrests in 1941 and 1,223 in 1942.[20] In the course of this research, I consulted at least one thousand files of named individuals arrested in this type of case. Despite variations in figures, all the sources imply the number of arrests of German agents by the Vichy's secret services was somewhere between 1,500 and 2,500 during the period between the defeat and the total occupation.

Nevertheless the exact activity of individuals arrested as German spies covers a wide spectrum. There was a chasm between a Robert Bellette, a long term German spy, and a Marie-Madeleine Fuchy, who was more of a fellow traveler than anything else. On 25 July 1943, Fuchy sent a letter to the German armistice commission from her cell in Lyon's Saint-Joseph prison confirming her pro-German sentiments while pointing out how limited her actions were:

> I beg you to take an interest in my fate since I am considered by the French authorities to be a German secret agent, and that consequently I was sentenced to death on 26 June 1942 along with four other persons. Even though I am not a member of the German secret services I beg that you do something for me because I have already been in prison for thirteen months awaiting an unlikely commutation of my sentence. Here the inactivity is unbearable and my health is deteriorating whereas, if I were free, I could participate in collaboration and go to work for you in Germany.[21]

Some of those caught were complete amateurs, acting on their own initiative or recruited casually and given little or no training. Only a handful had been sent on specialist training courses such as those held in Stuttgart, Altenburg, or Angers, where they learned how to use invisible ink and radio transmitters.[22] Some of those apprehended were arrested without apparently having done very much. Jean Foufounis was sentenced to seven years forced labor by the court of appeal in Aix-en-Provence, not for his own activity but for that of some of his acquaintances that he had simply failed to denounce.[23] An individual called Potier who served as French teacher to the German delegation in Oran was arrested by French police after he was overheard casually telling members of the delegation that the port was forty meters deep, and was only released when it was realized how ridiculous the charges against him were. [24]

It was the police, generally the ST brigade, that carried out the arrests. Many documents make it clear that German spies were often badly treated by the French police. Firstly, there were numerous complaints of insults. According to the accused, expressions such as "Kraut" or "filthy turncoat" were used by the police during interrogations.[25] Karl-Heinz Masson claimed that the ST police told him that the German war effort was doomed to fail.[26] An Alsatian named Riem claimed that the police told him that he should be ashamed of collaborating with the Germans.[27] It is obviously difficult to confirm the truth of these claims. The frequency of this type of complaint gives it a certain amount of credibility, but it is probable that the accused were sometimes trying to call into question the impartiality of the prosecution of their case to raise doubts about their guilt. Skepticism was expressed by the authorities about the truth of such claims on at least one occasion. When Karl Langer claimed (with little credibility) that the policemen who were interrogating him "wanted to force him to go to England," an anonymous commentator noted in the margin of the document "What imagination!"[28]

Accusations of torture, such as those made by arrested spy Asoka Chand, were much more serious. Chand, originally from India, joined the German secret services well before the war because of his hostility toward the British. In April 1943, from his cell in Nontron prison (Dordogne), he sent a letter to the German armistice commission giving an account of his arrest by the ST of Lyon:

> I was arrested (on 18 October 1941), robbed (of the sum of 23,100 dollars) by the ST of Lyon, tortured, threatened with deportation to Africa, transferred to Montpellier (Hérault) to hide me from the German authorities searching for me in the Lyon region, finally, after twelve months in isolation, condemned to death by a military tribunal (on 6 October in Montpellier) constituted by

> order of the traitor de Lattre de Tassigny, commander of the sixteenth military district. On 17 November 1942, I was transferred from Montpellier to Mauzac (Dordogne), and on 17 December 1942, from this last place to Nontron where I am presently imprisoned and complaining of the mistreatment I suffered in Mauzac at the hands of fanatically Anglophile personnel. . . . Even though I am no longer at risk of being killed by firing squad, there is still the possibility I could be transferred from here—even turned over to dissident elements in Africa, or simply left to die from lack of medical care and from the persecutions I am suffering—a real possibility given the critical state of my health at present.[29]

Through diplomatic channels, the Germans complained numerous times of the mistreatment suffered by their agents, as we can see in the file about Francis Voelkel: "From the information received by the German embassy it appears that Voelkel, during his interrogation, which lasted more than four days, was so violently mistreated with punches and blows that he became deaf in one ear." In this same file, the German embassy also noted that the abuse meted out to Voelkel was not unusual in this sort of case: "We would stress to the French government that this is not an isolated case. The embassy has been recently informed of several other cases of mistreatment."[30] Some arrested agents pointed to physical scars resulting from their interrogations. Ernst Ramstetter claimed that scars on his wrist and head were the physical proof of the methods used by the French police.[31]

Of course, we need to be careful when interpreting these sorts of documents. The accused had a vested interest in claiming police brutality. On the one hand, just as with the insults, the "victims" of this violence could hope to throw doubt on the prosecution's impartiality. A report on Edouard Buch reads, "When he was in front of the judge, Buch retracted part of his confession. He claimed to have made certain statements only because he was threatened with a whip."[32] In the case of Watrin, a former agent of the French secret services who had become a German agent, Darlan provided the following summary to Pétain: "He claimed to have lied in his previous declaration of having been given special missions relating to machine guns and aircraft pilots at Aumnat. He claimed that he lied because the police manhandled him. Later he did not dare to retract his confession in front of the first military prosecuting judge."[33] Darlan nonetheless concluded that Watrin should be executed. Another reason for exaggerating the extent of violence suffered was that the Nazis were particularly ferocious with those confessing to their enemies. The arrested individuals often hoped that they would be shortly freed and repatriated to Germany, so it was important that they could claim that any information given to their French interrogators was given under extreme duress. As to official complaints, it is easy to imagine the diplomatic advantages the Germans hoped to draw from this sort of incident in their negotiations with Vichy.

While some doubt might be warranted on the extent of the brutality in specific cases, there is overwhelming evidence that torture was used against German agents. It was not only through diplomatic channels that the Germans complained of the violence suffered by their agents. In a much more informal context, Theodor Auer was indignant because of the brutality inflicted on his agents, which was rather ironic given the extensive practice of torture by his own organization. The following statements were attributed to Auer at the beginning of 1942 and reported to the French secret services by "a sincere and well-placed informer" who was accompanying the Gestapo chief when he heard screams coming from the ST office.

> "These sadists appear to be mistreating yet another poor devil. It's impossible to describe what those pigs are capable of. I used to think that the SS and the SA had the monopoly of acts of violence, but the French are outdoing them. I have received at least a dozen reports on these new methods. First they undress the fellows (it's a principle) and then they electrocute them up for an hour or two. I must say that our military is well informed on these matters. . . . They are collecting much useful information on these cases of mistreatment."[34]

The last sentence of this quote clearly shows that Auer was referring to the torture practiced against German agents and not against individuals working for the Allies.

Documentation on the violent treatment of Nazi spies is not limited to German sources. In an account recorded in December 1945 the Resister Jean Gemähling declared that, during his arrest by the Marseille ST in late 1941, there were many mistreated German agents among the prisoners: "Among the prisoners there were as many Gaullists as collaborators." Gemähling was in the hands of the ST and claimed "its members were much harsher towards the collaborators to whom they gladly gave a thorough beating."[35] Memoirs of former secret services members also refer to the use of torture against German agents. Paul Paillole of the TR wrote that during the arrest of someone named Silberstein by the police, it was only with the greatest of difficulty that he was able to prevent a lynching.[36] Robert Terres, Paillole's subordinate, provides the following account of police practices against spies, and in particular that of Robert Blémant of the Marseille ST:

> Not the least of his inventions was the "tickling device"—that's what he called the small electrode delicately inserted into the suspect's anus. He had even set up, between Marseille and Toulon, for the TR posts and with Paillole's blessings, a villa exclusively devoted to "intensive interrogations." To complete the effect and make the atmosphere more convincing, Blémant had put all the resources of his fertile imagination to work. He had chains and pincers suspended on the walls, spatterings of blood spread across the floor, and large pieces of rotten meat distributed here and there to reproduce with a gripping realism the smell of decomposing corpses. Thus, in the intimacy of subtle lighting based on spotlights aimed straight at the suspect's eyes he had created an ambiance conducive to confession. . . . Blémant, with his pale, soft, bland face, his empty eyes and his sleepwalker's demeanor was not exactly the type of individual one would want to meet on a deserted street at the stroke of two o'clock in the morning.[37]

Blémant's name recurs in many, but by no means all, of the accounts of torture. Blémant has developed into something of a local folklore legend in Marseille even becoming the hero of N'Guyen's novel *La Peau d'un caïd,* and figuring under the name Albert Clément in Jean Bazal's novel *Le Marseillais,* and as Robert Flamant in Loup Durand's tale *Le Caïd.*[38] His wartime heroism is recounted in most of the memoirs, as are his links with local gangsters.[39] Indeed after the war he left the police to become one of the most important figures in the local underworld before being assassinated in 1965 as part of a feud with his former associates the Guérini brothers.

All this talk of police violence calls for several comments. Firstly, the idea that the French police might have been worse than the Gestapo is obviously an exaggeration. However, it is certain that the French police did not wait for the Nazi occupation, nor the subsequent Algerian war (1954–62), as historians sometimes assume, to use interrogation techniques that approached torture. Extreme violence was a long-established tradition within the French police. According to Marc Bischoff, author of a book on forensic policing, the expression *passer à tabac* (literally, "turning someone into tobacco"), which means to "beat someone up," comes from a police practice used at the end of the nineteenth century whereby policemen would receive a bonus in the form of tobacco for each confession extracted. The "turning into tobacco" became synonymous with the methods used.[40] In the first forty years of the twentieth century, forensic practices (such as fingerprinting) facilitated prosecution, minimized the importance of confessions and thus reduced recourse to violence, at least in criminal cases. However, violent practices continued in counterespionage. Police violence was a means of rapidly obtaining information, as the speed of prosecution was essential to the dismantling of a spy ring. The interrogator's brutality was also a means of expressing disgust with the accused. Under Vichy, there was a considerable increase in police violence. It was used against Gaullists, Jews, Communists, and Axis spies. The risk of diplomatic incidents in Axis cases led the government to punish policemen accused of these practices. In March 1942, members of the Nice police force were imprisoned for their less than nice behavior toward Italians suspected of pro-Italian activities.[41]

According to the letters of arrested agents, the end of their interrogation did not mean the end of their ordeal as they then had to experience the harsh conditions of Vichy prisons. Until the end of 1942, foreign agents were incarcerated in military prisons in the nonoccupied territories. After 1942, suspects and convicts were not systematically freed as one might have expected, but were transferred to civilian prisons. Incarcerated agents sent numerous letters of complaint from these military and civilian prisons.

These complaints pertained as much to the material conditions of prison life as to the psychological and moral suffering they endured. Josef Beitelberger claimed to have lost twenty-three kilos in two months in prison.[42] Leona Schmidt reported that "the material conditions and the food in the prison are bad" and she found the "establishment filthy and the drinking water suspect."[43] Hans Goepel stated, "We have no soap to wash ourselves, no toothbrushes, no toothpaste" and complained that "the food they call soup is nothing more than water." "We are skin and bones," he concluded.[44] From the military prison in Casablanca, Wilhelm Alscher complained of having to share a three-bed cell with four other suspects.[45] But it was the inactivity and the long wait to know their fate that were the hardest to endure. On 25 July 1943, Floria Richelmi wrote from the Saint-Joseph prison in Lyon to the German authorities. Her letter, intercepted by the French authorities, reads, "As a secret agent in your intelligence service (Paris branch), I was, after several successfully completed missions, denounced and arrested in Limoges on April 13, 1942. I was transferred to Lyon and then tried and condemned to death on 26 June 1942 by court martial at the tribunal of the sixteenth military district. For the past thirteen months, my situation has remained the same. I am in solitary confinement, in a cell, in a desperate state of health and severely depressed; I am waiting in vain for a decision on my fate."[46] Medical care was also said to be inadequate. Willy Ebert, a forty-seven-year-old man from Hamburg who was arrested in December 1941 whilst spying on the shipping in the port of Marseille, was a serious diabetic and suffered badly from the absence of medical attention.[47]

French authorities were not usually receptive to complaints about poor prison conditions. When, in March 1942, the spy Friedrich Berger, threatened suicide because of poor prison conditions, the French armistice services pointed out that his German employers were treating incarcerated French individuals badly: "On the one hand, in fact, it is possible that Berger's request might be a blackmail attempt. On the other hand, to the humanitarian reasons that one could invoke on this matter, it will always be possible to oppose the German authorities' attitude toward numerous French persons sentenced to death whose executions were postponed by German authorities. Moreover, there are already at least two cases of suicide among French prisoners condemned to death whose executions had been postponed for many months by the German authorities."[48] As to Leona Schmidt's complaints mentioned above, the minister of justice gave Vice-Premier Darlan the following response. After first acknowledging the harshness of prison life, he added that she "is sharing the fate of all of her co-prisoners."[49] Thus, while spies were indeed suffering in prison, the fact remained that conditions in Vichy's prisons were bad for everyone. This was due, on the one hand, to the massive increase in the prison population as a consequence of the freedom-killing policies of the government, and on the other hand, to the increase in the repression of espionage under Vichy. This last aspect was well demonstrated in an August 1941 report by the commandant of the Algiers military prison. His report compared the average number of inmates in 1937, which remained around 35 (none accused of espionage) and the average number in the 1940s, which "reached or went beyond 400 inmates, of whom 100 were accused of spying."[50]

An interesting eyewitness account of the conditions in the prisons is provided by Michel Bloch who was interned as a Communist resister. His postwar testimony highlights the cramped conditions in Nontron prison in the Dordogne area of southwest France. In 1942 Bloch and one other Communist shared a cell with four common law prisoners and two German spies. One of these spies was a former used car salesman from Paris. The other, from Pamiers near the Spanish border, had made money before the war by dressing up in children's clothing and having sex with a similarly clad woman in front of rich voyeurs. Tensions were inevitable in a cell containing both Communist militants and agents who had worked for the Nazis. Bloch recalled that he got into a fistfight with the man from Pamiers after Bloch had called his cellmate "disgusting." At the end of 1943 Bloch was one of four Communists in a cell that also contained five German spies. That cell was divided by a table in the middle, with the Communists on one side and the Nazi agents on the other, and an unwritten rule that neither faction would cross the line marked by the table. Between these two factions communication was limited to the bare minimum necessitated by the sharing of chores such as collecting water and emptying the toilet bucket. Even in these cases communication was channelled through a spokesman for each group. The spokesman for the spies was a man named Giraudeau, sentenced for having denounced to the Germans two members of the Deuxième Bureau who were subsequently executed. Nor was it only in the cells themselves that tension was visible. The prison hairdresser, an anarcho-syndicalist imprisoned for insubordination, threatened to cut the throat of a German spy of Indian origin (presumably Chand) if the latter did not shut up about the tortures he had inflicted during the Spanish Civil war. Bloch claimed to have felt physically sick whenever he heard that some of these agents were to be handed back to the Germans, which happened with the used car salesman in July 1943 and about forty other Nazi agents on 17 March 1944.[51]

In contrast to other prisoners, spies were often, although not always, put into solitary confinement. This meant that, along with other prisoners accused of the same offense, they were locked up separately, often for several months, that their rights to receive visitors were extremely limited, and their mail was censored by the prison authorities. Hans Goepel was not the only one to complain about the consequences of this isolation: "We are strictly forbidden to talk to each other; we have been isolated."[52]

These conditions of secrecy were meant to prevent the Germans from finding out where their spies were being held and even sometimes that they had been arrested at all. However, from September 1941, Vichy agreed to notify the Germans within thirty days of the arrest of any German national, including Alsatians and Lorrainers. Subordinate administrations often refused to follow this instruction or they did so with considerable delay.[53] Francis Voelkel was arrested on 31 March 1942 but the Germans were only notified on 19 May.[54] On 22 June 1942, Oberfeldführer Arning, director of the German repatriation service in Lyon, was furious when he found out about Karl Danler's arrest, which had taken place on 4 November 1941. His rage increased a notch when he read that Danler's summons to appear before the Lyon military tribunal listed his offence as "having entertained relations with an enemy power in May and June 1941 and having corresponded with the German Red Cross in Lyon." Arning protested and noted that, at that time, Germany could not be considered "an enemy power." He promised sanctions.[55]

Obviously it was not easy to keep arrests secret. There were several possible sources of leaks. First in line were the prisoners' families. Letters sent by these families show that for security reasons they were not always informed of the place of detention nor of the motive for the indictment. Thus, André Bernard's wife sent a desperate letter to Marshal Pétain in October 1941 requesting information on her husband's situation since she had been without news for six months. She had heard a rumor that he had been jailed for Communist activities, information she felt was totally unbelievable given her husband's political past: "I don't know what the exact charges for his sentence are but I can confirm that he never belonged to the Communist Party, which was totally alien to his own ideas."[56] The summary of the tribunal's decision confirmed that it was definitely for pro-German activities that her husband was condemned to death on 13 November 1941.[57] Lax security measures sometimes let information reach families, and this threatened the secrecy of the trial. A letter sent to the German commission in Limoges from one Anna Kern of Basel, Switzerland, shows that it was possible for the Germans to be informed by prisoners' families. In this letter, intercepted by the postal censors, she tried to get the Germans to intervene on behalf of her husband: "I came to see you in Limoges during my stay from 6 to 9 October 1941 about my husband who is in the Naugeat asylum. He has been arrested again by the French as a spy and for his support of Germany, and for this reason he was sent to the concentration camp at Nexon, where he was foolish enough to attempt suicide, for which he was sent to an asylum. The doctor who is the director of the asylum, Dr. Calmette, keeps calls him names: 'filthy Kraut,' 'complete bastard,' 'fifth column,' 'fifth filth!' or else says to him,

'Hey, German spy, haven't you croaked yet?' I don't think that this is in keeping with the terms of the armistice!"[58]

But families were not the only possible source of leaks. There were poorly paid guards who carried messages between prisoners and the external world. Priests and lawyers were another source of leaks. A lawyer called Castan in Toulouse was accused of having told German authorities where his client, the German spy Van Eynden, was held. So Castan himself was accused of breaching state security, brought before the military tribunal in Clermont-Ferrand on 10 November 1941, and sentenced to eight months in prison. The Toulouse order of lawyers met in April and May 1942 to determine if a professional fault had been committed and ended up stripping Castan of his right to practice law.[59]

Some prisons were known to be more secure in keeping incarcerations secret. Thus, up to the summer of 1941, spies were usually transferred to French North Africa to put them at a distance from German searches.[60] The occupier intervened to put an end to this practice, but French authorities continued to keep certain places of internment secret. This was the case with a section of the Castres prison in southwest France. A note sent by the ministry of the interior to the directorate of the armistice services at the beginning of 1943 pertained to the case of Belgian Paul Termonia, imprisoned at Castres for breaching state security. According to this note, the Germans had asked to know what had happened to Termonia. The French armistice services replied that no response should be given to the German request because "the German authorities have never been told of the special role designated to Castres prison."[61]

To protect the secrecy of detentions better, prisoners were moved around from time to time, particularly in sensitive cases. Marc Dreesen (sometimes spelled "Dressen") was among those. His uncle was the owner of the Rheinhôtel Dreesen near Godesberg in Germany, where Adolf Hitler was a regular guest.[62] The counterespionage services were well aware that Dreesen was a personal acquaintance of Hitler's.[63] As a result Dreesen was moved four times during his five months of incarceration but even these precautions were not enough. One of the first things Gestapo official Klaus Barbie did upon his arrival in Lyon at the end of 1942 was to organize a commando of the German police to force its way into the Lyon military prison to identify inmates charged with breaching state security. The prison director's protests could not prevent Barbie from compiling a complete list of the prisoners held there, nor from immediately taking one of them away: Marc Dreesen.[64]

Paillole's memoirs describe another tactic used to keep incarcerations secret. Vichy allowed delegates of the German Red Cross the right to visit German prisoners on condition that, in cases involving spies, the visitors were accompanied by a French liaison officer. Paillole wrote that when German officials visited prisons where spies were held, those prisoners of which the Germans were unaware were moved from their cells and hidden in town until the end of the visit. Such a practice was confirmed by Edgar Milk, an agent interned first in Marseille and then in Oran, Algeria. During a German delegate's visit to the Oran prison, Milk told him that when he "was held in the Saint-Nicolas fort in Marseille along with sixteen other German detainees, they were kept hidden from the German commission members who were visiting the fort."[65]

This shows clearly the difficulties encountered in carrying out counterespionage activities in a partially occupied country. France's political and diplomatic situation was far from ideal when it came to organizing trials of German agents. The system of military justice moved at snail's pace because of staff shortages and a massive increase in workload caused by the proliferation of spying activities. In these circumstances, justice was hit and miss. The necessity of avoiding excessive publicity around these trials, in addition to communication difficulties, made it very difficult to collect all the necessary information. For instance, the report on Jean Polome stated that it had been impossible to assess Polome's moral standards because he was a resident of Belgium, and communication difficulties had made it impossible to gather the necessary information about his character.[66] Édouard Fier expressed regrets during his trial that it had been impossible to call defense witnesses due to the division of the country into zones: "Unfortunately the persons who could testify on my behalf are either in the occupied or the forbidden zones."[67] The investigation and prosecution of espionage cases were also affected by human factors. In June 1942, Paul Paillole complained that there was "a military judge in Marseille who freed detainees accused of espionage fairly easily even when their guilt was clearly established."[68] Political factors also came into play. The BMA in Limoges considered that in Louis Rolland's trial, the accused was only spared the death sentence thanks to the political leanings of the judge, "a committed member of the PPF and an ardent collaborator."[69]

Until the total occupation of the territory in November 1942, the trials of German spies were held in front of military or naval tribunals in the southern zone or in the colonies. These tribunals were made up of seven (then five) officers. Secret agents were judged on the basis of articles 75 and, following of the penal code concerning espionage, treason and breaching state security. The sentences were usually of two, five, or ten years of imprisonment or hard labor (sometimes for life). The maximum sentence for espionage had been increased in 1938 from five years in prison to the death penalty. Vichy's courts sentenced more than one hundred individuals to death for pro-German espionage.

Trials by military and naval tribunals were abandoned after November of 1942, following the Germany invasion of southern France, which led to Vichy's army being scrapped. This did not mean, however, that trials of German agents ceased. Paradoxically, from that time German agents were judged by the special sections of the courts of appeals, in other words by tribunals set up essentially to judge Communists. Thus on 10 February 1943, Jean Foufounis was tried by the Aix-en-Provence Court of Appeal for failing to denounce a network of German spies, and sentenced to seven years of forced labor.[70] On 17 July 1943, the same court found Pierre Arvaud guilty of being an agent of the German service for maritime intelligence.[71] On 20 January 1943, the appeals' court in Agen sentenced Léonie Schmid to five years of prison without parole.[72] I could add many more examples. To my knowledge, the last case was that of Maurice Lambin, tried on 21 December 1943 in Aix-en-Provence on a charge of treason. His file, and in particular the letters between the minister of justice and the state prosecutor, leaves no doubt that his sentence was a punishment for his work as secret agent for the Germans.[73] The explanation given for his arrest near the demarcation line on 7 November 1942 by an officer of the ST was as follows:

> Under interrogation, this individual claimed that in 1942, while he was in Paris, he was put into contact with certain persons who claimed to be agents of the French secret services who gave him the mission of collecting various military intelligence in the nonoccupied zone, and in particular looking for information about the organization of civil defense and antiaircraft weapons, the size of regiments and their garrisons. . . . Upon returning from his second mission, Lambin realized that the agents with whom he was in contact belonged to the German intelligence service. He confessed that he had nonetheless accepted the third mission they asked him to undertake and which he was in the process of undertaking when he was arrested.[74]

It is worth noting that, following a German inquiry, the justice minister suggested to Premier Laval that they should avoid revealing the true motives for Lambin's indictment and pretend that he had been tried under the terms of a law designed to prosecute Communists and anarchists. As the justice minister put it: "As to the German authorities' request about the nature of Lambin's offence, it seems that we could simply respond that this individual was arrested for breaching the law of 18 November 1942."[75]

As was already the case before November 1942, the sentences given after that date were not always applied completely. This was true for prison sentences and even more so for death penalties. There were several factors at play in the reduction of sentences. There were requests by the condemned to high officials of the state, decisions by governmental commissions, and the diplomatic compromises of the Vichy regime.

The condemned themselves or their families contacted senior figures of the French state. They usually addressed themselves to Marshal Pétain, more rarely to Laval, or to the Vichy ambassador in Paris, Fernand de Brinon. A certain Madame Rabis sent a desperate appeal to Pétain on 14 April 1942 to ask for his help on behalf of her husband, Roger, who was going to be tried the following month: "I am alone in Paris with my little girl. I don't know anybody. I am not brave, I have only one hope: You."[76] A similar faith in Pétain, mixed with Christian religious faith, was expressed in a tragic letter that Guillaume Le Cunff sent to a priest:

> I have to tell you that I was sentenced yesterday by a military tribunal and my confession led to a death penalty. I am disappointed in human justice. Now I will await the pardon of Marshal Pétain. I hope that you are still thinking about me in your prayers, perhaps I will have more luck with our great leader. I would like to live a little longer for my dear mother. How much we suffer on this planet earth, particularly when misfortune befalls us as it does me at present. Well, one must be brave, but I assure you that it's very hard. I will keep on hoping till the last minute. I have often prayed to the Holy Virgin and now I do two rosaries of Hail Marys. I am sure she'll come to my help in my time of misfortune.[77]

Looking at a few specific instances of letters sent on behalf of incarcerated spies to high-ranking personalities of the French state will give an idea of the tactics they used to try to obtain a reduction in their sentences. Let's begin with the case of nineteen-year-old René Prêtre. On 1 April 1942,

Prêtre was sentenced to death by the Lyon military court for pro-German espionage. His aunt sent a letter to Pétain a month later. She began by appealing to the Marshal's compassion: "I only wish to make you aware, Monsieur le Maréchal, of the unbearable pain, the immense distress of his mother and of the whole of his family in the face of the terrible sentence imposed on him." She continued by minimizing her nephew's crime and his share of responsibility in it: "He is a child, an unthinking child, who was led astray and who listened to the voice of evil and temptation. Even though he acknowledged having received money from foreigners, he always denied betraying his country, and the information he provided was not important. I thus hope, Monsieur le Maréchal, that your heart will be touched by the tears and sorrow of decent people and that you will grant a reduction of the sentence to this unfortunate individual."[78] It is difficult to know if this letter played a role in the reduction of Prêtre's sentence, but it was commuted to "forced labor for life" on 11 June.[79]

The cases involving Maurice Petit and Jacques Grandidier offer further insights on the methods of defense used. Both used the argument that their treason was someone else's fault. Before the war, they were both working for the French naval counterespionage service. During the 1940 campaign, the heads of the naval secret services fled from Paris hurriedly leaving behind them a list of the names and addresses of their agents. The individuals put at risk by this oversight were not informed of the danger they were facing. Since their identities were known, they were contacted by the Germans who ordered them to work for them or be punished for their previous anti-German activity. Once recruited, they were sent to the southern zone to collect intelligence. The two men used a defense frequent in appeals for clemency, pointing out that their intelligence gathering was not aimed at Vichy and thus was not anti-French. Grandidier wrote, "All of my actions were directed only against the British, (both British citizens and their French sympathizers), whether civilians or members of the military, whether in Toulon or in the navy leadership, who were preparing actions that could only harm the newly initiated Franco-German collaboration." Grandidier added some personal details that were intended to confirm that he was an honorable man: "I am the grandson of the explorer Alfred Grandidier, member of the French Institute, and am myself a veteran of commandant Jean Charco's missions to the Antarctic on board of his ship *Pourquoi pas?* and have never had any civil or military convictions. I was married on the eve of the war and leave a wife in Paris without support or resources." The attenuating circumstances invoked by Petit and Grandidier had already earned them a reduction of their sentences from ten to five years in prison, and consequently, their last request to Pétain was ignored.[80]

In a letter of 7 December 1943 sent from Nontron prison and addressed to Premier Laval, the arrested spy Jean Pézard offered a defense that was often used, and quite understandably so given the direction of Vichy's policies. He argued that in collaborating with the Germans he was merely following French governmental policy: "The public instructions issued by the government concerning collaboration both in the past and repeated without change since then, under Darlan as well as since your happy return to power, contained no restriction and seemed even to call for a very broad interpretation; in no sense could they make us mistrustful and lead us to doubt that the actions asked of us were perfectly legal."

Pézard did not deny informing the Germans, but he complained about the way the police had treated him. He claimed that the policemen conducting his interrogation had been intent on distorting his version of events by using techniques of insinuation and manipulation. Disoriented by their approach, he argued, he had signed a statement that painted his activity in a particularly negative light. According to Pézard, the same had happened with the military justice system because its courts favored supporters of the Resistance leader General de Gaulle. He compared his own sentence to that given to the dissidents of the Resistance: "During other hearings, memorable for their indulgence, these same tribunals showed limitless leniency toward those dissidents who were so notorious that it would have been impossible to quickly drop charges altogether. These were treacherous officers, or often even genuine British spies who, moreover, had a much easier time in prison whilst awaiting trial and who then received minimal sentences and were immediately freed—their sentences declared void through exemptions that were easily given." Pézard declared that he was ready to continue his anti-Communist work if Laval would agree to free him, and he asked for "the right to take part in the decisive struggle that has been undertaken for the salvation of the country, our civilization and simple human happiness against terrorism and communism."[81] His plea to Laval had no effect and on 25 January 1944 he was informed officially by Laval's office that there were no grounds to reduce his sentence of "forced labor for life." Nonetheless, he was eventually freed following negotiations between Laval and German ambassador Otto Abetz.[82]

The people who were charged and sentenced thus tried to minimize their offences or to blame someone else for them. They invoked attenuating circumstances such as youth, poor health, poverty, the fact that they were following government policy or were only working against the British. Often, they had to write several times to Pétain before getting an answer. At times, the intermediary they were using to contact him did not cooperate as expected. Using a priest as intermediary, Édouard Fier managed to get a letter delivered to a member of Pétain's military cabinet, canon Moncelle, asking him to plead his case with the Marshal. Moncelle had been Fier's history teacher. Unfortunately for Fier, the priest had added his own commentaries to Fier's letter: "And if I am passing this letter onto you in case Monsieur le Maréchal sees fit to revise the sentence, it is not . . . to take sides, since I do not know the facts and I do not have a clear enough memory of this former pupil to be sure that he is not capable of the actions of which he is accused. . . . I accompanied too many condemned men to the execution post during the First World War not to realize that the priest's role in such circumstances is to abstain from that which is not his business and just to keep within his mission of restoring hope for repentant souls."[83] The documents available suggest appeals to Pétain rarely met with positive results. Although most of the sentences were not actually applied in their entirety, this was due to two other factors: the decisions of governmental clemency commissions and Vichy's diplomatic compromises.

Until November 1942, it was Pétain who had the last word on clemency in serious espionage cases. His decisions were reached following the recommendations of a series of individuals or institutions: the government commissioners attached to the military tribunals, the general in charge of the military district where the trial had been held, the war department commission for clemency, the state secretary for war's office, and Admiral Darlan (first in his capacity as vice-premier, and then later as commander in chief of the armed forces). I am not aware of any case in which Pétain's decision went against the recommendations given to him, even though in theory he had the right to ignore them. After December 1942, the situation changed as Laval created a new interministerial commission dealing with appeals for clemency. By the end of 1943 this commission had reviewed the cases of four hundred German agents arrested since the armistice. It reduced sentences in 57 percent of cases of breaching state security, but only very rarely did it abolish sentences altogether.[84]

Diplomatic necessities also played an essential role in reducing sentences. For diplomatic reasons, executing German spies, particularly those "of German nationality or race," was a touchy issue. For instance, in Hans Goepel's file we find the following assessment that war minister General Huntziger sent to justice minister Joseph Barthélemy, in September of 1941:

> The person in question was effectively employed as a German secret agent, and the German armistice commission has already twice (on 31 January and 24 February 1941) requested information about the reasons for his incarceration, and has linked these requests to the prisoner's desire to be repatriated, which he made known at that time. So, in the present circumstances, my opinion is that this execution should not take place particularly because of the consequences the execution of a German citizen would have on the way the Reich authorities might respond to requests for pardons presented by the French government in favor of its own citizens condemned to death in the occupied zone.[85]

At the beginning of 1942, an interministerial meeting discussed the thorny issue of the execution of spies of German nationality. Present at the meeting were representatives of the BMA, the directorate of the armistice services, the foreign affairs ministry, the military justice service and the admiralty. The way this meeting unfolded was quite bizarre and demonstrated a spirit of compromise. It was said that no German nationals had thus far been executed for fear of reprisals against the French in the northern zone: "Until September 1941, the head of the French state had, on his own initiative and without any intervention from the German armistice commission, decided against the application of death sentences for those from Germany or considered German 'by race' who had been sentenced by French tribunals. Carrying out a death sentence could have had a negative impact on the attitude of the German authorities to the French government's requests for clemency toward its own citizens condemned to death by German tribunals." Yet, the failure of this policy was demonstrated by the numerous executions carried out by the Germans: "certain executions in the occupied zone in cases of alleged espionage (for instance in the Estienne d'Orves case), the killing of hostages in reprisals after Resistance attacks against the Germans seem to prove that the leniency of the French authorities has had no effect on the decisions of the occupying authorities."[86] This failure was followed in November 1941 by the impossibility of reaching a reciprocal Franco-German agreement regarding the nonexecution of the citizens of the other country. It is odd that, despite these diplomatic impasses, the interministerial meeting decided that, even without such a mutual agreement, there should be no execution of German citizens. The twenty-six spies of German nationality awaiting their executions at that time were spared being put to death.

Nationality played a determining role in the application of death sentences. Until the total occupation of France in November 1942, it was still possible to carry out death sentences on French citizens, and in one case, on an Italian. There were no official executions after the invasion of the southern zone. However, a series of letters dated November 1942 to April 1943 between Jacques Guérard of the general secretariat and Pétain and Laval shows that, at first, the top ranking officials, including Laval, thought they were going to be able to continue applying death sentences against those Nazi spies who were not German citizens. But this resolve quickly turned into hesitation and, Vichy being Vichy, into compromise. The issue was resolved by the following letter sent by Laval to Pétain on 17 April 1943:

> I am resending you seven files from the military courts pertaining to appeals for clemency filed in favor of the following individuals: de Gelobert, Henri; Decreton, Henri [Emile]; Fuchy, Marie; Richelmi, Jeanne [Floria]; Christin, Joseph; Vilain, René; Cole, Harold, sentenced to death for treason and pro-German espionage. When I sent you these files before I agreed to the advice put forward by the competent authorities against clemency. But my position was based on insufficient information about the specific circumstances of the cases in question and on the repercussions that would result from carrying out the sentences. Since you took the decision to reject the appeals for clemency for the seven convicted persons my attention has been drawn to these circumstances and to these repercussions. The German authorities have requested that those among them who are of foreign nationality should be made available to them; in these conditions, carrying out the death penalties would lead to serious incidents. Moreover, talks are currently being held concerning the exchange of certain convicted individuals against French persons condemned to death by the German authorities.
>
> In view of these circumstances, I request that you might reconsider the situation of the seven convicted persons in question. For my part, I am in favor of commuting their sentences to forced labor for life.[87]

In addition to reduction of sentences, some pro-German spies ended up simply being returned to the Germans. The handing over of German spies to the Nazis occurred in several stages. The terms of the 1940 armistice had clarified the position of those arrested before the defeat: "all German POWs and civilian prisoners, including those charged or condemned because of actions in favor of the German Reich, must be immediately handed over to the German troops." Most of the spies incarcerated prior to the defeat were thus handed over to the Germans as early as 1940. The situation was more complicated for arrests carried out after the armistice. Before the summer of 1941, only a few agents of German or Italian nationality were surrendered. But following the failure of the diplomatic agreements known as the Paris protocols, Admiral Darlan sought new means of getting the Germans interested in collaboration. Darlan considered the possibility of finding favor with the Germans again by immediately handing over certain prisoners to them. Thus, a large portion of those considered German citizens were handed over at the demarcation line. Another possibility was to exchange convicted spies against French citizens who had been sentenced in the northern zone (for espionage, clandestine crossing of the demarcation line, etc.). Exchanges did take place but the French got the raw end of the deal. Often the prisoners the occupants gave up were not of the same value as those handed over by the French. In return for Karl Rumboldt, a seasoned German spy, the French received the Lapeyronie brothers, two school-aged sons of a war veteran whose espionage activities were at best marginal.[88] In other instances the Germans simply refused to honor their obligations. An exchange was organized to hand over the German spy Albert Reymann in return for Pierre Gemin, a French citizen sentenced to death by the German tribunal in Bordeaux for his work for the French secret services. The French duly handed over Reymann but they were informed the following day that Pierre Gemin had already been executed eight days before.[89] Vichy Vice-Premier Darlan himself complained of the inequality of one exchange that proposed to swap Combatti and Duffaux, two agents with a long track record of spying for Germany, against Madame d'Autrevaux, the wife of the head of the police in Lyon, arrested because of her husband's co-operation with the Deuxième Bureau.[90]

The BMA expressed misgivings about the freeing of spies. They argued that these individuals would be able to give the Germans first hand information about the methods and personnel of the French secret services who had arrested them, and would be able to inform German intelligence networks of how much their French counterparts knew of their activity.[91] There was the real worry that these individuals would resume their espionage work. Counterespionage services were given rapid proof that their concerns in this respect were well founded. As soon as he was released, the thirty-year-old Belgian citizen Raymond Jamar rejoined the Lille branch of the Gestapo and attempted to renew his contacts with the milieus he frequented before his arrest.[92] The Germans arrested Robert Dumas, a writer of spy novels and French secret agent in Lille during the summer of 1942 thanks to the information given by a freed agent.[93]

The freeing of spies continued despite the opposition of counterespionage services. This was not surprising with men such as Darlan, and later, Laval, in power. More surprising is that many spies were not handed over. At the time of the invasion of the southern zone, there were forty-eight of them still held in the Marseille prison alone.[94] In January 1944, the directorate of the armistice services gave the following instructions regarding Jean Jobet, an incarcerated German agent: "Should the German police ask to visit the detainee in his prison or to look at the records relating to his case, the response should be a categorical refusal."[95] Although there were agreements to return certain agents such as Jean Pézard in May 1944, other agents were still being held in prison as late as the summer. Léonie Schmid, condemned by the special section of the Agen court in January 1943 for having denounced two supposed Gaullists to the Germans, was still in prison in July 1944, and General Debeney of the armistice services stressed his intention to refuse to hand her over to the Germans.[96] The Germans were still trying to secure the release of some of their agents on the very eve of Liberation. On 19 August 1944, the Feldgendarmerie in Paris sent a note to Nordling, the neutral Swedish consul, to ask him to act as an intermediary in obtaining the release of a certain Marcel Ricourd: "The French citizen Marcel Ricourd, born on 23 June 1921, is a German intelligence agent and was taken prisoner by the French police during a mission undertaken for his service. He wishes to place himself under the protection of the Wehrmacht. The present message confirms that Ricourd shall receive protection and help from the Wehrmacht."[97]

Also surprising perhaps is that a number of death sentences were actually put into effect. According to Paillole, there were two kinds of executions of Nazi spies: unofficial and official. In the first case, executions were organized by the secret services without recourse to the official system of justice and were carried out by gangsters. These unofficial liquidations were known by the euphemism "D measures." Paillole claims that about fifty of these D measures were carried out.[98] It is extremely difficult to find confirmation for them as this sort of action would leave little trace in the archives. I have seen only one reference to an unofficial liquidation of a Nazi spy, and it is an extremely surprising one. This is contained in a report of November 1943 written by the SD (Sicherheitsdienst), the German security police. Based on their analysis of captured Vichy secret service archives, the SD report states, "Among the captured documents was a note from Admiral Darlan in which he asked for a 'D measure' to be applied against an arrested German agent of French nationality."[99] In the absence of other evidence, it is not possible to establish the truth about Paillole's figures for the number of D measures carried out.

Regarding officially sanctioned executions, it is also difficult to ascertain the exact number of German spies sentenced by Vichy military courts who were actually executed by the firing squads of the French army. Paillole claims there were forty-two of them.[100] In research for the present study, I found formal proof of eight such executions, but Paillole's figure seems credible for two reasons. Firstly, during the postwar trial of Marshal Philippe Pétain, Ernest Lagarde, the former director of political affairs in the Foreign Affairs Ministry, claimed there were about thirty such executions in 1941, which does not exclude a total of forty-two for the years 1940–42.[101] Secondly, there is a register of Pétain's decisions concerning appeals for clemency from individuals condemned to death for activities ranging from Communism to army mutinies to espionage.[102] In espionage cases, the registry does not specify for which country a particular spy was working, but it would seem that, after cross-checking the names listed with other sources used for the present study, there were twenty-seven confirmed cases of Axis spies having their appeal for clemency refused. A further twenty-three cases in which clemency was refused also appear to involve Axis spies. Of course, in a handful of instances where the appeal for clemency was rejected, executions may still not have been carried out as a result of the invasion of the southern zone by the Germans, which brought a sudden end to official executions. This registry nevertheless adds credibility to Paillole's estimate.

The most famous of these official executions was that of Henri Devillers.[103] Several references to this execution feature in memoirs by former members of the Resistance and other books on the war period.[104] Devillers was born in November 1914 in Vincennes. He was taken prisoner during the battle of France and whilst in a POW camp learned that his wife had become a German secret agent in Paris. Devillers agreed to a similar engagement, seemingly to ensure his return from the POW camp. Once recruited by the Abwehr, Devillers made contact with various members of the Combat Resistance group, including its leaders Henri Frenay, Maurice Chevance-Bertin, and Berthie Albrecht, and gained their confidence by posing as a Gaullist. They agreed to use him to transport their mail, copies of which he passed to his bosses in the Abwehr, who organized a series of arrests within the movement. Through one of its own agents, the TR learned in November 1941 that the Abwehr post in Dijon had managed to place a double agent in Combat. Once Devillers was identified, he was arrested on 25 February 1942 in Lyon by the police captain Louis Triffe of the ST. After a quick trial, Devillers was sentenced to death on 15 April 1942. His appeal for clemency was rejected by Pétain on 12 June 1942 and he was executed the following week in the courtyard of Fort Montluc.[105] A laconic announcement in the paper *Progrès de Lyon* reported the execution without mentioning his name: "On June 19 1942 at 3.15 in the afternoon, an individual of French nationality, sentenced to death by the military tribunal of the 14th military district, was executed by firing squad."[106] This execution was known in Resistance circles—Frenay, the head of the Combat movement, claimed to have been informed of it by Paillole.[107] The shooting of Devillers infuriated the Germans and strained diplomatic relations between the French and German governments.[108] Vichy's reasoning in this sort of case will be examined in the next chapter.

Overall the fate of German spies under Vichy varied considerably. Between 1,500 and 2,500 individuals were arrested on suspicion of pro-German espionage. Some of them were subjected to violence during arrests; some of them were severely punished after arrest. Of course the majority of those informing the Germans were never arrested or punished. Either they were not found or they succeeded in avoiding the worst punishments because of lack of evidence or diplomatic immunity. Vichy's policy in this domain oscillated between severity, which was uncharacteristic of Vichy's relations with the Germans, and compromise, which was more in keeping with the usual relationship of Pétain's government with the Nazi occupier.

7 UNDERSTANDING VICHY'S POLICY

What was the attitude of Pétain's collaborating Vichy government toward the anti-German activities of its secret services? Unsurprisingly, the memoirs of secret service veterans present their own activities as a form of resistance.[1] At best, they depict the Vichy government as ambivalent toward the secret service; at worst, they describe a constant struggle between the two.[2] This last interpretation is all the more easily accepted by nonspecialists because it fits with a popular preconception whereby secret service activity is always somewhat maverick and independent of governments. It is true that the low-level daily functioning of these services was autonomous. But the idea that the main thrust of their anti-German activity was not known at governmental level or that it was in opposition to Vichy's policies does not stand up to scrutiny. Secret service activities against Germany can be squared with Vichy's policies, even though relations between Vichy and the secret services were extremely complicated.

Memoirs written by French secret service veterans usually underplay the administrative complicities necessary for any counterespionage work. During the Vichy period, counterespionage agencies within the military, the navy, and the police were assisted by other nonspecialist organizations. The postal censors, known as the Contrôle Technique, who intercepted and read the private correspondence of ordinary French citizens, passed onto them letters from individuals suspected of spying for Germany and monitored correspondence exchanged between the public and Axis armistice delegations. Prefects and the regular police sent reports on suspicious individuals to the BMA. The directorate of the armistice services did likewise with the information obtained by its liaison officers placed within German commissions. Bringing arrested agents to justice inevitably required the cooperation of military and civilian courts and prisons. If Vichy had wanted to put a stop to anti-German counterespionage, it could have given stricter instructions so as to discourage such administrative complicity in the process. Moreover, given that Vichy authorities were made fully aware of where the headquarters of the secret services themselves were and clearly knew how to summon secret service leaders when the need was felt, one might wonder why they did not simply close down these offices and arrest their staff if they were truly as hostile to them as secret service memoirs suggest.

Another factor contradicting the idea that counterespionage services enjoyed total independence is what happened to previously arrested spies at the time of the German invasion of southern France in November 1942. At that moment the secret services scuppered themselves or at least cut off all contact with Vichy and often fled the country. Had these secret services been entirely responsible for the process of counterespionage up to that point, one might have expected spies arrested before November 1942 to now simply be released from Vichy prisons as their presence was discovered. This did not happen and some Nazi spies were still held in Vichy's prisons right through to the summer of 1944.[3] This was not based on ignorance of the continued presence of these agents in prison, since in some cases the authorities actually had to make active decisions about what to do with spies previously arrested. Indeed, as discussed in the previous chapter, Premier Pierre Laval established an interministerial commission in December 1942 that reviewed the trials of 400 Axis agents arrested since the armistice. The commission, made up of Laval's representatives as well as officials from some other ministries reduced sentences in 57 percent of the cases, but only very rarely granted pardons.[4] Moreover, as I have shown, the trials of previously arrested German spies continued in the newly occupied southern zone right through to December 1943.[5] Espionage suspects were no longer tried in military courts but in civilian ones, and certain ministers were certainly aware of these trials.[6] All of this confirms that the decision to pursue and punish German agents must have gone well beyond the secret services themselves.

The final and decisive confirmation that this counterespionage was not completely at cross-purposes with the aims of government can be found in letters from ministers. It was probably true, as Colonel Rivet, head of the Cinquième Bureau, claimed, that during the summer of 1940 the government had initially hesitated to support anti-German counterespionage.[7] By the fall of that same year, however, it seems that the need for it was better recognized. From that time on, letters from ministers mentioned the necessity of actually expanding counterespionage.[8] For instance, a series of letters exchanged during the spring of 1941 between Weygand, the general delegate in North Africa, and Vice-Premier Darlan at Vichy emphasized the need to reinforce the ST.[9] The reply from Darlan's office shows that Allied espionage was not the sole target of these expansion plans: "The general delegate feels, and I agree, that, given the vastness of the task to be accomplished, we need to proceed by stages beginning with the ST police, and first of all with that of Morocco, the sensitive point in North Africa that it would seem is directly threatened by Germany."[10] The role played by ministers in the appeals for reductions of sentences should also be noted. These were sent to Pétain himself who was the one who had to decide whether to grant clemency.[11] For this, the head of state consulted individual files as well as the comments of officials from other ministries. Documents exist in which Darlan and Pétain ratified decisions by military tribunals to execute German spies. Even Pierre Laval declared himself ready to consider executions.[12]

A retrospective report on the activities of French counterintelligence written by the Sipo-SD in November 1943 after their reading of captured French secret services archives, confirmed Vichy's participation in this policy:

> It is certain that, from the political viewpoint, this secret service used against German intelligence agencies was known of and supported by the whole of the French government. When the BMA was set up, although it was a solely military organization, the minister of the interior gave his agreement on 16 November 1940. From the start, Marshal Pétain, the head of state, was informed of the existence of this secret service, as became apparent in a letter addressed to him by General Weygand on 7 December 1940.[13] Among these documents were copies of secret decrees and confidential orders signed by Pétain, Laval, Darlan. One of these involved a secret instruction by the Mar-

> shal dated 15 August 1941 through which he entrusted the various secret service posts to the vice-premier (who was also at the time the minister of the navy) and also took care of financial issues. Moreover, other decrees dated 24 August 1942 pertaining to the dissolution of the BMA and the setting up of the new organization SSM are signed by Pétain, Laval and Darlan.[14]

In fact, the government was more divided on this question than this German report implies, and certain elements of Vichy's policies weakened anti-German counterespionage. But before we look at potential weaknesses within counterespionage policy, let's examine why Vichy showed more firmness on the question of counterespionage than in the rest of its relations with Germany. In essence, explanations are to be found in a continued anti-German feeling within some quarters of the Vichy government, but more especially in the desire to preserve French sovereignty and to maintain autonomy within the framework of collaboration.

To think of the Vichy regime between the summer of 1940 and the spring of 1942 as a homogeneous block of pro-German elements would be a massive oversimplification. This in no way implies that Vichy's overall orientation was anti-German, far from it. But we should not forget that many members of this government were long-time sympathizers of the Action Française. Action Française was a movement founded in 1899 and led by the monarchist Charles Maurras. Through its newspaper it set out a nationalist agenda that identified certain categories—Jews, left-wingers, foreigners—as dangers to France. The nationalism adopted was strongly anti-German, even if Maurras himself began from the late 1930s to see Britain as the number one enemy. Action Française had influence that stretched beyond its small band of followers, and it certainly held some sway over many who would occupy positions in the Vichy government.[15] A genuine anti-German feeling persisted in the corridors of certain ministries, notably among individuals who came from the army. In a letter sent to Joachim von Ribbentrop in the spring of 1943, Fernand de Brinon, Vichy's ambassador to the occupied territories, discussed the anti-German bent of some of the ministers of the early Vichy cabinets, including General Huntziger, who was secretary of state for war from September 1940 until his death in a plane crash in November 1941. De Brinon saw Huntziger's hand behind the dismissal of Vice-Premier Laval in December 1940 and what he saw as the failure of the policy of collaboration initiated after Pétain and Hitler's meeting at Montoire: "General Huntziger was certainly an honest man; because of his temperament and his origins

[Alsatian] he was a firm adversary of Germany and left the army in the grip of his hostility to Germany, which unavoidably led to the minor coup of 13 December 1940. In these conditions, one can state that the policy initiated at Montoire failed. Your enemies held too many important positions within what was then called the new government."[16] It is significant that figures who were extremely hostile toward Germany were appointed to positions most strategically important to counterespionage. Thus, North Africa was entrusted to General Weygand and Henri Rollin was named director of the counterespionage police.

Weygand was among those who had sought an armistice in 1940, but he considered it a temporary measure that would allow France to rebuild and take up arms again.[17] In a letter he addressed to Marshal Pétain on 26 March 1941 he discussed demands put forward by the German diplomat Hemmen before adding that France was still at war with Germany: "Hemmen seems to forget that an armistice is not a peace settlement and that the Germans are still our enemies."[18] Weygand at times spoke of the Germans as "ex-enemies" but the word "enemy" featured frequently in his letters,[19] as for instance his mention of "enemy German commissions" in his 15 November 1941 letter to Darlan. Weygand was not hostile to the idea of collaboration, which he saw as a short term necessity, but he felt that German demands had to be curbed. He explained this in the same letter to Darlan: "Hitler himself has expressed the thought that too much submission on the part of the loser encourages the winner to make greater and greater demands." He concluded this letter, written on the eve of his dismissal from his post in North Africa, as follows: "By acting with firmness to keep the Germans within the limits set by the armistice agreement, I have accomplished my duty as a soldier and a Frenchman."[20] Giving Weygand the responsibility of North Africa even though it would have been easy, given his advanced years, to insist on his retirement clearly shows that the Vichy of 1940 understood that to let the Germans have carte blanche in the colonies would cause problems.[21] Of course, from a Vichy point of view, Weygand also had other "qualities" that made him an excellent candidate to govern North Africa. Though he disliked the Germans and the Italians, he was a true xenophobe who did not like the British either.[22] Weygand was also a reactionary and thus one of the most fervent supporters of the Vichy's backward-looking political program, the National Revolution, whose measures he applied zealously. His tenure as general delegate in North Africa for more than fourteen months shows that his energy in all these domains was appreciated at the highest governmental levels. This was explicitly noted in a letter from Pétain to Weygand in the spring of 1941. Replying to one of Weygand's missives on the need to remain firm against the illicit activities of the Germans in North Africa, Pétain replied, "I wish you the continuation of your success in Africa, a success that everyone has noticed."[23] Weygand's appointment to the most senior post in French North Africa was revealing of Vichy's initial desire to limit Germany's domination of France.

Can the same not also be said of Henri Rollin's appointment as assistant director of the general secretariat of police with specific responsibility for counterespionage? This appointment was made in the wake of a report written by Rollin for Darlan in May of 1941 about the reorganization of police counterespionage services. In it he made eleven explicit references to the need for measures against German espionage.[24] Several sources claim that Rollin himself had been an agent of the British Intelligence Service since 1939 but do not specify the exact nature or scope of his engagement.[25] Vice-Premier Darlan was probably not aware of this at the time he appointed him but it could not have escaped the admiral's attention that Rollin was the author of the book *L'Apocalypse de notre temps* (The apocalypse of our time) published in 1939.[26] From 1940 to 1942, this book featured on the list of publications explicitly forbidden by the occupying authorities because Rollin's text was an unambiguous condemnation of Nazi propaganda and German foreign policy. Rollin's attitude in the book was both anti-Communist and anti-German and his behavior during Vichy suggest that he had not changed his mind since his 1939 book in which he had written, "While Communist propaganda might eventually become a threat to our national cohesion, in the present circumstances, the danger posed by the propaganda representing the concepts of Hitler and of certain of his allies who are living among us is much more immediate and direct."[27] Putting him in charge of counterespionage highlights that in 1941 the German danger was taken seriously.

In the context of Vichy's overall strategy, the appointment of men such as Weygand and Rollin to key positions suggests a resolve to preserve the independence of the government, even if this government collaborated. Collaboration was accepted as at least a short-term imperative by all members of the Vichy regime, including by those who were instinctively hostile toward Germany such as Huntziger, Weygand, and Rollin. But it is very clear that even at the top of the state there was an initial concern about living in the Germans' shadow. Vichy considered itself a sovereign government independent from the Germans. The political model for Pétainists was less that of Hitler's Germany than of Franco's Spain or Salazar's Portugal, which were nationalist authoritarian regimes that had been able to stay in power without foreign occupation. Though the Vichy regime ended up becoming something of a puppet regime, this does not mean that its members started with the intention of serving the Germans unconditionally.

The defense of sovereignty was one of Vichy's main aims. According to the French historian Yves Durand, "The illusory search for sovereignty was probably the principal motivation . . . for State Collaboration, not only in Vichy, but in all the countries where a government presented itself as a partner of the Germans."[28] When it came to counterespionage, at least three kinds of sovereignties were directly involved: the state's sovereignty over the individual, administrative sovereignty, and territorial sovereignty.

For Vichy, the sovereignty of the state over the individual in the domain of collaboration was primordial. Vichy was an authoritarian regime that did not appreciate initiative on the part of its citizens. While the state had the right and even the duty to collaborate, the regime was reticent, at least until 1943, to countenance ordinary citizens' collaboration where this escaped governmental control. Henri Rollin, when discussing the reorganization of the counterespionage services wrote the following: "a note from the Inspector General of the ST underlines that 80 percent of German agents arrested by his service are French. He points out that 'most of them were recruited under the guise of collaboration,' a hook that gradually lured them to straightforward treason."[29] Rollin was one of François Darlan's protégés but his critique of the dangers of individual collaboration was echoed in a letter Laval sent to Pétain at the end of November 1942. Laval's letter pertained to the fate of seven individuals sentenced to death by military tribunals for pro-German espionage. Laval pleaded for a commutation of the death penalty into forced labor for life for the first six individuals. But when it came to the seventh, René Legras, he wrote, "Legras seems particularly guilty since he contributed to the arrest of French citizens by the German authorities, and before submitting my recommendation to you, I feel it necessary to find out what happened to our compatriots who became victims of his denunciations."[30] Given that Laval himself handed over many of his compatriots to the Germans, the only conclusion we can draw from this letter is that what shocked him in the behavior of René Legras was that he had acted on his own initiative without the agreement of the government.

For reasons of pragmatism, several ministers were undoubtedly hostile toward individual collaboration based on initiatives from below. When individuals such as Legras bypassed official channels by collaborating directly with the Germans in a way that Vichy could not control, the government was unable to barter their collaboration during Franco-German negotiations. Initially Vichy actively tried to prevent individual citizens entering into their own arrangements with the occupiers, unless it could gain some advantage from such dealings. By repressing this sort of individual initiative, Vichy was seeking to centralize collaboration. It was the task of the counterespionage services to let these individuals know that they were supposed to wait for official authorization before engaging in collaboration.[31]

Historians frequently refer to Vichy's intention of ensuring that the administration of France would remain in the hands of national institutions.[32] This administrative or institutional sovereignty ended up becoming the regime's Holy Grail. Right up till the summer of 1944, Vichy tried to maintain this fiction even when it became evident that French institutions were being used to impose Nazi orders and to do their dirty work for them. From the very start, Vichy's desire to prevent any breach of its institutional independence was evident. Only French governmental organs were supposed to have jurisdiction in the southern zone. Darlan's directives to prefects on 5 July 1941 were unequivocal on this point. He insisted on the necessity of making "the population of the free zone understand that for an individual to freely contact as a supplicant any representative of the occupying power is a reprehensible action and cannot be tolerated by the French government."[33] In this regard, one of the aims of counterespionage was to limit contacts between the population and Axis organizations. Another aspect of administrative sovereignty was also a part of the counterespionage mission: the independence of administrations had to be preserved by limiting German infiltration into them.

It was also for reasons of administrative sovereignty that Vichy stamped down on German attempts at directly infiltrating resistance movements in the nonoccupied territories. Such an infiltration threatened Vichy's monopoly in the repression of dissident activities. Several of the arrests of secret agents involve cases of German penetration of Resistance structures, even though such structures were generally also enemies for Vichy.

Paul Riff, who was arrested by French police in November 1941 in Limoges was working for the Geheime-Feld-Polizei with missions that included establishing whether an individual called Français living in Chamont was still engaged in Gaullist propaganda, and keeping an eye on a house where Freemasons were rumored to meet.[34] Leonie Schmid's arrest was linked to the fact that she had written to the German authorities to denounce a household of civil servants as Gaullist opposed to collaboration.[35] Alwin Rose was condemned to three years imprisonment in April 1941 for distribution of Gaullist tracts, even though the court was well aware that he was performing this activity as an agent provocateur for the Germans.[36] When investigating the Resistance movement Combat in January 1943, the Marseille police uncovered the activity of an individual who was working as a German agent within this movement. He was immediately sent to a prison in Castres, and the police report explicitly claimed that this would put an end to his work for the Germans.[37] Although some junior personnel in the counterespionage services might have seen arresting these agents as a form of Resistance or protection of the Resistance, this type of arrest manifested a more classic Vichy preoccupation—that of maintaining policing in French hands.

The defense of territorial sovereignty and the independence of the nonoccupied territories was an important issue in anti-German counterespionage. The government had lost a sizeable part of the country north of the demarcation line, so it tried to preserve its total power in the nonoccupied portion. As French historian Jean-Baptiste Duroselle puts it: "Maintaining a supposedly independent area in part of the national territory . . . was a guiding principle for the Marshal and Weygand."[38] The vocabulary used to describe the German forces in the nonoccupied territories shows the sensitivity of the topic. A September 1941 note from Huntziger insisted on the fact that in no circumstances should the armistice delegations be referred to as "occupying troops."[39] Even after total occupation, Vichy attempted to maintain this fiction by requiring the term "operation troops" rather than "occupation troops" to describe German units stationed in the south. Perhaps because of their army background, the idea of territorial defense appeared more important to military figures within the regime, who had been professionally conditioned to hold territory, than to those of its leaders issued from the navy or the civilian sector such as Darlan or Laval. Even before November 1942, these two men made important concessions affecting territorial sovereignty. In 1941, Darlan offered military bases in North Africa to the Germans and allowed their aircraft to use French airspace. During the summer of 1942, Laval made an enormous concession regarding the preservation of territorial sovereignty in what came to be known as the "Desloges affair," named for the French army captain involved. According to the agreements on police collaboration, Laval and his police chief Bousquet granted the Germans official protection under the direction of Captain Desloges to let them undertake limited missions in the southern zone with the aim of detecting Allied and Gaullist radio transmitters. From September to November 1942, 280 agents from the Abwehr, the Sipo-SD, and the Ordnungspolizei operated in the southern zone with Vichy's approval.[40] What mattered to Darlan and Laval was that in these cases the Axis encroachment into the free zone and colonies had been negotiated and concessions obtained—in other words the government did not intend to give up its sovereignty gratuitously. It fell to the counterespionage services to prevent any unauthorized breaches of territorial sovereignty.

The nonoccupied territories were supposed to maintain strict neutrality during the war.[41] In many respects, Vichy's neutrality was only a pretence. The Franco-Scottish historian Robert Frank uses the expression "asymmetrical neutrality" to describe it.[42] The government never facilitated Allied war efforts and even ordered its troops to fire on the Allies and the Gaullists in Syria in 1941 and in North Africa in 1942. In contrast, there were daily dialogues between Vichy and the Germans, and help was extended to the Reich on numerous occasions. Logistic facilities were offered to Rommel's Afrika Korps. During the summer of 1941, Darlan even raised the possibility of entering the war on the German side against the Allies, an option Laval had also discussed in passing in November and December 1940. Vichy thus negotiated collaboration on all levels: economic, administrative, and military.

While Vichy's neutrality was questionable, it is clear that the government sometimes wanted to take advantage of the pretence of a neutral stance.[43] As a consequence, Vichy could not entirely ignore pressures to preserve at least some semblance of visible balance. It was recognized that too widespread a German penetration in the Vichy zone might risk fueling Anglo-Gaullist propaganda that was already insisting on the extent of Vichy's subordination to the Nazis.[44] As to the Americans, they put direct pressure on the Vichy government to limit German activity in the nonoccupied territories—that was the price of the food aid offered following the Murphy-Weygand agreement of February 1941.[45] Maintaining neutrality could also affect internal policies. It was claimed that German activity in the nonoccupied territories risked both undermining government prestige and provoking disturbances. The secret services took advantage of Vichy's official neutrality in their struggle against German intelligence agencies.

If, because of its resolve to defend its sovereignty, Vichy was ready to tolerate anti-German counterespionage, how are we to explain the hostility expressed against this government in the memoirs of former secret service members? On the one hand, the authors of these memoirs were probably attempting to distance themselves from connections that had become embarrassing. On the other hand, there were indeed important differences between the counterespionage services and the government as to the way anti-German activity was conducted. Divergences stemmed from the methods used by counterespionage services as well as from the government's diplomatic compromises. We should also not lose sight of the fact that the Vichy government was not a homogeneous block and that a variety of positions were represented in it.

Vichy had good reasons to accept anti-Axis counterespionage. As Paillole explained to his subordinates in the military secret services in April 1942, "You must be aware that the free exercise of our national sovereignty depends on the effectiveness of counterespionage."[46] The government's independence was in part determined by the ability of the secret services to prevent the complete infiltration of French administrations by the Germans. Nonetheless, the government found it difficult to accept the diplomatic consequences of secret service actions. During the summer of 1941, members of the ST police force in Algiers provoked a serious incident by attempting to arrest Alsatian Friedrich Strohm, a suspected German agent, in the very building occupied by the German armistice commission. The Germans intervened and obtained a reprieve for their spy. However a few days later, Strohm was imprisoned in a French jail. A diplomatic struggle ensued that cast a shadow over the discussions Darlan had initiated to reach an agreement after the failure of the Paris protocols. German insistence for Strohm's return was finally successful, but there followed a lively debate over whether Strohm had been tortured whilst in French custody. The consequences of the incident led to the resignation of General Paul Doyen from his post as president of the French armistice delegation in Wiesbaden, and provoked Darlan's angry rebukes of the counterespionage services for their brutal methods.[47]

Laval's anger toward the counterespionage services during the summer of 1942 was mainly due to a series of diplomatic incidents that began with the execution of German agent Henri Devillers in Lyon.[48] As discussed in detail in the previous chapter, Devillers had infiltrated Henri Frenay's Resistance movement Combat while working for the Abwehr. His arrest by the ST of Lyon was followed by his execution by the armistice army two months later. The speed of this execution went against the legal norms of the time. The Devillers case was further aggravated by the fact that on 20 June, the authorized press of the free zone made reference to his execution as one for treason.[49] The personal diary of General Bridoux, the pro-German secretary of state for war, leaves no doubt as to the diplomatic tension caused by the Devillers affair: "Another sensitive case is that of Devillers, a French agent of the German secret services who rendered services to both countries by bringing to light the activities of Gaullist groups and was sentenced here and shot as a spy."[50] Indeed, in this same diary, Bridoux referred eleven times to diplomatic difficulties caused by the secret services between April and November. Bridoux stressed the consequences of their activities: "Monsieur de Brinon has sent to the head of government a report listing the German protests against the actions of the intelligence services. Their practices keep alive and deepen the Führer's suspicions of the French government."[51] Darlan and Laval had the impression that their political position was undermined by incidents provoked by the counterespionage services. Both men attempted to limit the autonomy of the secret services to control them better, and this deeply angered the members of these services.

When Vichy committed itself to a series of compromises on counterespionage, the strain between the government and the secret services reached its apex. In 1940, the governmental position was that the imprisonment of spies should be conducted in the most complete secrecy and that the Germans should have no right to visit these individuals in their prisons, nor even to know in which prisons they were held.[52] In August 1941, an agreement was reached giving representatives of the German Red Cross the right to visit incarcerated spies, subject to some conditions.[53] Disastrous consequences for counterespionage ensued because during these visits, prisoners could communicate to the German representatives the names of those who had denounced or arrested them.[54] From September of that same year, Vichy accepted the obligation of informing the Germans within thirty days of the arrest of their nationals.[55] In March 1942, Darlan surrendered yet more ground by returning a large number of arrested spies to the Germans.[56] As mentioned in the previous chapter, he also entertained the possibility of exchanging other spies for political prisoners held by the Germans. Exchanges did occur but the French got the raw end of the deal: either the prisoners returned to them were of lesser value than those the French were handing over, or the Nazis did not honor their commitments. One example was the case of the exchange of the German spy Albert Reymann for Pierre Gemin, an agent of the secret services condemned to death by the German tribunal of Bordeaux.[57] After Reymann had been handed over the French learned that Gemin had already been executed. The BMA had qualms about returning individuals accused of espionage:[58] released spies could give the Germans firsthand information on how the secret services that arrested them functioned, or that they could be re-employed to continue spying. Vichy's back-peddling accelerated with Pierre Laval's return to power in April 1942. The release of a greater number of incarcerated spies was followed by the greatest compromise that affected counterespionage: the increased freedom to run missions in the southern zones, under the aforementioned Desloges affair.

Underlying these compromises were two factors. Firstly, there was the heterogeneous nature of the government, which meant that support for the secret services varied between different ministries.[59] Then there was the central place held by the policy of collaboration and the desire not to put it at risk.

Of all the Vichy ministers the most ardent supporters of the anti-German mission of the secret services were the generals Weygand and Huntziger. Almost all the memoirs of secret service veterans agree on this point and the archives concur.[60] Weygand was one of the main supporters of the 1940 armistice, an armistice he saw as unavoidable because he felt the German victory was beyond doubt. But as soon as he was appointed secretary of state for defense, he contravened the clauses of this agreement on two questions. Firstly, he organized setting up secret weapons caches to protect military stocks.[61] Weygand's role in the organization of these caches is confirmed by several sources, including general Bridoux's diary: "The Italians, it seems, have discovered arms dumps in Gap and in Corsica. But there are others. These dumps were established in 1940 on General Weygand's orders. Since then they have been maintained. When I heard about them, I gave an account to President Laval and we agreed that he would tell the Germans about them at the first favorable occasion; he felt that would be his meeting with the Führer."[62]

Secondly, in breach of article 10 of the armistice, Weygand organized the revival of the secret services operating in part against Germany.[63] After he was dismissed from the government in the fall of 1940, he was appointed general delegate of the government in North Africa, a strategically very important position in which he demonstrated his resolve to defend the empire against all comers. He presented German propaganda in North Africa to Pétain as a "mortal danger" to French interests and explained that "he felt it indispensable to fight it by any means."[64] What distinguished Weygand from the other ministers on these issues was that he was ready to risk diplomatic incidents in order to fight against German espionage and propaganda. As he explained to Pétain in a letter of March 1941, "It is possible that the strict application of the measures I have ordered might lead to small incidents. I believe that we have to accept this risk."[65] Weygand had a lot of influence on Huntziger who was to replace him as secretary of state of war and Weygand encouraged him to support the secret services.[66] A letter from Huntziger on 25 February 1941 included a list of measures aimed at putting an end to the espionage practiced by the Axis armistice commissions. These measures included arrests: "Arrests will be carried out immediately of individuals in contact with these commissions and they will charged with espionage."[67]

It is clear that the three most prominent Vichy figures—Pétain, Darlan and Laval—held a more nuanced position on this issue. At the end of August 1940, Marshal Pétain signed documents giving a special status to secret service personnel (which made it possible to keep paying them through illicit means).[68] He also ratified death sentences passed on captured spies.[69] But, according to a document sent by Fernand de Brinon to von Ribbentrop, Pétain worried that Darlan had too much influence on the secret services.[70]

Indeed Admiral Darlan was a key character in this domain. His position varied according to the power struggles and diplomatic stakes of the moment. In order to gain a better understanding of his strategy, we need to consider three things. Firstly, because of his past as a naval officer, he still harbored hostility towards the British. For this reason, he usually tried to limit contacts between secret service members and their Allied counterparts to the minimum required for the technical functioning of the services.[71] Secondly, it should be noted that, even for Darlan, being anti-British did not automatically equate to be an unconditional supporter of Germany. He was ready to engage deeply in collaboration but strove to maintain his autonomy with regard to the occupier.[72] Acutely aware of the risk of diplomatic incident, he opposed the brutal methods of the secret services, notably during a cabinet meeting during the most intense phase of the Strohm affair in July 1941, although he never completely disowned these services.[73] The final thing to be noted about Darlan is that he was extremely opportunistic. For the admiral, the secret services represented both a difficulty and an opportunity. After the Strohm affair, he created a "Center for Governmental Information," an umbrella organization used to gain more control over the secret services and placed it under the direct control of his office.[74] Thereafter, he saw the secret services as a personal source of power. After he was removed from the vice-premiership following Laval's return in Spring 1942, Darlan, stayed on as commander-in-chief of the armed forces and therefore maintained control over these services, using them as leverage in his struggle with Laval.

Veterans of the secret services always present Laval as their pet hate in their memoirs.[75] In reality he spoke rarely on the issues related to the secret services. It is certain that he wanted to considerably reduce the number of incidents provoked by their activities. He thus started to purge these services of some of their more maverick personnel in the summer of 1942.[76] The following summer, he stated explicitly his opposition to any sort of secret reconstruction of the intelligence services that had been scrapped after total occupation.[77] However, according to General Bridoux's diary as well as Fernand de Brinon's letter to von Ribbentrop, Laval biggest crime when it came to the secret services was a lack of decisive action. On 1 December 1942, Bridoux complained of Laval's indecision as follows: "Already three months ago Darlan's power was supposed to be reduced and the intelligence services reorganized; Laval is still deferring these decisions."[78] Fernand de Brinon's account also highlighted Laval's inability to tackle this particular fief of Darlan:

> In reality, Monsieur Laval was the head of the government but at his side, sharing a mutual loathing for each other, was admiral Darlan, the head of land, naval, and air forces, who was independent from him and on whom depended the working of the army, and especially of the intelligence services. At that time, along with General Bridoux who thought exactly the same way I did and who kept me informed of military matters, I frequently had the opportunity to tell Monsieur Laval that it was absolutely necessary to limit Admiral Darlan's activities. Marshal Pétain wanted nothing more than to imple-

> ment this reform and especially to abolish the enormous funds that the commander-in-chief had at his disposal for the functioning of the intelligence service.[79]

The documents cited earlier about the individual cases of sentencing, as well as the fact that Laval did not systematically free incarcerated spies, suggest that he was not totally opposed to the imprisonment of German spies. He may have been pro-German, but he remained attached to a certain vision of sovereignty, at least in its administrative aspect. Laval was also very aware of the need to centralize collaboration. French individuals who took it upon themselves to collaborate without passing through governmental channels deprived his government of the possibility of bartering their collaboration.

Anti-German counterespionage must be seen in the broader context of collaboration. It was viewed by Weygand and Huntziger as a means of preventing the total colonization of France and of keeping the Germans within the framework set by the armistice. Huntziger also referred to counterespionage when reminding Darlan of the Germans' bad faith. In June 1941, following the failure of the Paris protocols, he wrote to the admiral about the arrest of Nazi agents as follows: "The implementation of collaboration policy involves the establishing of Franco-German relations based on mutual trust. In the present situation, we could have thus expected a reduction in the activities of the German intelligence services in nonoccupied French territory. But that is not the case. Quite the contrary, this activity has massively increased of late." And then he warned, "It is good, I think, that during your negotiations you are aware of the attitude of Germany toward us in this matter."[80] The idea of using counterespionage to preserve the government's autonomy was accompanied, from the second half of 1941, by the desire to make use of the arrest of German spies during Franco-German negotiations. At that time Darlan initiated a process of prisoner exchange. The spies themselves were to become a bargaining tool in the negotiations, and thus paradoxically, also served to reinforce the process of collaboration.

The Vichy regime might appear relatively firm on the question of counterespionage compared to other aspects of its relationship with Germany. Nonetheless this government was also keen that counterespionage should not compromise its broader policy of collaboration. This explains its concern with avoiding diplomatic incidents. Collaboration was essential in Vichy's eyes because the government was seeking a privileged status in a Europe dominated by the Germans. Another justification for collaboration from a Vichy perspective was its significant ideological similarities with the Nazi regime. Vichy's enemies— Freemasons, Jews, and Communists—were also the Reich's enemies. Economic necessity added an extra dimension to the search for collaboration as France became dependent on Germany as the only real market for its produce. But collaboration was never a true partnership. During negotiations, the Germans disposed of important means of pressure, such as prisoners of war, or the demarcation line that could be modified as they wished, or the constant threat of invasion of Vichy's free zone. With time, Vichy was caught in a spiral of collaboration, and a true defense of sovereignty was often difficult to reconcile with diplomatic choices.

It is only when we place anti-German counterespionage back into the more general context of a Vichy policy of sincere collaboration that we can begin to understand the relative moderation of the German reaction when faced with this flagrant violation of article 10 of the armistice. A more detailed examination of this reaction will help shed light on this point.

There certainly was a German reaction against counterespionage. The Germans sent numerous complaints, protesting that French counterintelligence targeted their spies much more than those of the Allies.[81] It was partly for reasons related to counterespionage that they insisted on the removal of Weygand in November 1941. They also pressured for the abolition of the BMA in August 1942 (Darlan and Laval decided to replace it secretly with the SSM).[82] Immediately after the total occupation of the country, the German police even visited the military prisons of Toulouse and Lyon to identify incarcerated German spies.[83] But it might seem surprising that their reaction was not more forceful than it was.

The operation undertaken in December of 1942 against the Lyon military prison is particularly revealing in this regard. A group of German policemen led by Klaus Barbie entered the prison by threatening the guards[84] and drew up a complete list of the prisoners.[85] It is interesting to note that, in spite the presence of several German spies, only one of them was immediately taken away. That was Marc Dreesen, alias Paul Fabre, a personal acquaintance of Adolf Hitler. Among the others identified on that day were three German agents of foreign origins: Harold Cole, Henri

Deu Gelabert, and Émile Decreton.[86] Pierre Laval wrote to Pétain a few months after this incident to explain that carrying out death sentences against these individuals was now impossible since the Germans had found them.[87] The risk of diplomatic incident would be too high. Instead, Laval negotiated the exchange of these prisoners for French nationals held by the occupiers. How should we interpret the German decision to leave in French hands individuals that were subsequently to serve as bargaining counters in Franco-German negotiations? Firstly, the German intelligence services were usually indifferent to the fate of their arrested agents when they were not German nationals. Once arrested, their cover was blown and they were thus of little further use. It was only in the spring of 1944 that the Germans began to take interest in these agents again because the likelihood of an Allied landing opened up the possibility of using these spies as a fifth column, if nothing else. But more importantly, the Germans understood that it was better not to upset the Vichy government in an area that seemed important to it: the defense of sovereignty. Behind this calculation was the unquestionable fact that, despite Vichy's desire for independence, it made a very important contribution to the occupiers' interests, notably in the two ideological domains that were growing increasingly important to the Nazis: the persecution of the Jews and the repression of Communist activities. France was also contributing massively to the German war economy—far more than any other power in Western Europe.

Of course anti-German counterespionage did irritate the Germans and added to their instinctive distrust of the French. Even Vichy did not entirely escape from this distrust. This was shown by the forbidding in the occupied zone of some of the organizations of the National Revolution, such as Vichy's veterans' legion or its youth groups, the Chantiers de la Jeunesse. It was also shown by the massive deployment of spies in the nonoccupied territories. If, despite this mistrust and the arrest of about two thousand German spies by Vichy between 1940 and 1942, the Germans kept on dealing with Pétain's government, it was simply because it was the best option available. The Nazi leaders understood how to play Vichy. By feeding French leaders' illusions, by letting them believe that their policies did preserve the country's sovereignty, they obtained a relatively straightforward collaboration. On the political scale, the sacrifice of some low level non-German spies was of course regrettable, but finally of no great import compared to what Vichy conceded to the occupier. In other words, the annoyance caused by Vichy's counterespionage was trifling when set alongside the active collaboration Vichy was offering the Nazis.

In sum, Vichy's policy in the domain of anti-German counterespionage oscillated between firmness and weakness as the government tried to reconcile the often conflicting needs of a defense of sovereignty and a promotion of collaboration. It is true that when it came to counterespionage, it showed greater resolution in monitoring the Axis than it did in other domains, and it was ready, up to a certain point, to support secret counterespionage activities that violated article 10 of the armistice. Some ministers were aware of, and, in principle, approved of the arrest of German spies in the nonoccupied territories. However, members of the secret services strongly criticized the timidity of the government. Vichy played on patriotic themes. Vichy insisted on the need to defend its sovereignty. Vichy paid lip service to neutrality. But would the government defend these ideas to their logical conclusion when its diplomatic position was so intimately linked to collaboration? Vichy's resolve was effectively weakened by its desire to avoid compromising this policy. Thus, in the event of diplomatic incidents, the government tended to compromise and often to sacrifice the work of the secret services.

CONCLUSION

The starting point for this study was my discovery in the archives of documents related to the torture that the Vichy police practiced against German spies. This was by no means the last of the surprises I found in the archives on this subject. I also learned that the French secret services had shaved the heads of women engaged in intimate relations with members of the German armistice commissions. The punishments was intended to hinder the espionage activity of these commissions and were apparently inflicted with the approval of Vichy's senior dignitary in North Africa, General Weygand. I was even more surprised to find that even after the Germans had invaded southern France in November 1942 the leading figures of the French government—Pétain and Laval—were still discussing the possibilities of continuing to execute German spies! Not only that, but astonishingly the trials of previously arrested German agents continued in this newly occupied zone right through till December 1943, despite the German presence. Surprising also was that the occupier was still trying to negotiate the release of some of their agents of French nationality as late as the summer of 1944. The history of anti-German counterespionage under Vichy was as surprising as it was complex.

German espionage in France grew spectacularly after the armistice both in terms of the number of posts working against the country as well as the number of agents used. This can be explained, in part by the rivalry between the military intelligence organization, the Abwehr, and the Sipo-SD, linked directly to the Nazi Party. Rivalry stimulated zeal in intelligence circles, just as it did in other sectors of German administration in occupied territories. The massive expansion of espionage also underlined the tensions within Franco-German relations despite Vichy's desire to collaborate. The victor distrusted the vanquished. In Germany, France remained a hereditary enemy. The Germans also had strong reasons to remain on their guard: they themselves had fresh memories of having cast off the shackles imposed by a diplomatic settlement, in their case a peace treaty, as they had rebuilt their own forces clandestinely after Versailles. They were determined that the French should not be able to do the same with regard to the armistice. This memory was particularly vivid within the German secret services, whose very existence had been forbidden by Versailles, but who rapidly rebuilt secretly.

Espionage was one component of a wider German strategy designed at exploiting, dividing, permanently weakening, and above all neutralizing France. German secret services sought intelligence about the French government by placing agents within the entourage of French leaders. They watched for breaches of the terms of the armistice, in particular any sign that the French army might be remobilizing secretly, hiding weapons or rebuilding its secret services. Questionnaires given to German spies also asked them to monitor trends in public opinion and to detect any sign of resistance. Finally, German intelligence agencies kept watch on Allied activity in the nonoccupied territories and laid the groundwork for future military campaigns. And, of course, they did not forget their economic role: secret agents participated actively in the black market in France and prepared the economic and cultural pillaging of the country by locating potential war booty.

German espionage was built on treason: 80 percent of spies were French nationals. What drew them toward espionage? As in all historic periods, money was undoubtedly the spies' primary motive. This explanation was even more central under Vichy since, after the defeat, the country faced an acute problem of unemployment, particularly among demobilized soldiers who were valuable recruits for the German secret services. The pecuniary rewards available were all the greater given that the Germans had practically unlimited funds at their disposal thanks to their economic exploitation of France. Even middle-ranking German agents could be well paid while also receiving administrative advantages such as passes enabling them to travel across the demarcation line into the free zone. Other factors, more specific to the time period, also encouraged recruitment. The interwar saw a growth of the spy genre in films and literature, which undoubtedly gave a new cachet to espionage thereby attracting individuals in search of adventure. This same period also saw the rise of extremist ideologies. Collaborationist milieus, such as the PPF, where radical extreme right wing politics encouraged ideological sympathy for Hitler's regime, were fertile breeding grounds for German spies. Besides, Vichy's propaganda in favor of collaboration seemed to offer official approval for espionage. Another factor was France's military defeat, which, by showing French vulnerability, encouraged Arab nationalism in North African countries. German intelligence flirted with this nationalism, and some nationalists responded by providing information. Finally the presence in France of German soldiers, policemen and officials led to some amorous relationships between occupiers and occupied, and at times these relationships facilitated exchanges of information.

Spies penetrated the nonoccupied territories under various covers. Diplomatic delegations, particularly German armistice commissions, were massively engaged in activities that exceeded their official mission such as propaganda, black marketeering, and of course espionage. Certain types of professionals, such as journalists, traveling salesmen, and businessmen, could use their professional mobility to justify the traveling needed for espionage work. Others took advantage of a political cover and pretended to be Gaullist in a country where most of the population was hostile toward the Germans. At times, spies pretended to be refugees from the exodus of civilians that had accompanied the military defeat of 1940, or Jews trying to escape from the Germans to justify their presence in areas of France in which they were outsiders.

In the face of these vast German networks, counterespionage was organized by several organizations. Firstly of course were the secret services per se, the specialized organs within the army (BMA, TR, Deuxième Bureau), the navy (CRM, SSD, Naval Security), and the police (ST). The military service collected the intelligence whilst the police carried out the actual arrests. But it is obvious that counterespionage went well beyond the framework of the secret services and involved prefectures, the regular police, the gendarmerie, the postal and telephone censors, the directorate of the armistice services, as well as military and civilian courts.

Counterespionage took several forms. The secret services undertook preventive work by attempting to counteract German propaganda and organizing counterintelligence training within the army. With the help of other administrations, they tried to limit leaks of information, notably by preventing direct contacts between the population and the Germans. A system of police vigilance was set up around German diplomatic missions in the nonoccupied territories. This had a dual purpose. On the one hand, French authorities were keen to assure the protection of these buildings so as to prevent Resistance attacks, and on the other, they wanted to intercept French citizens trying to contact members of the commissions. The police noted the identity of these French nationals, who were then investigated and sometimes summoned to explain themselves at the police department. Surveillance was also undertaken through secret service penetration into German structures, as well as through more technical means such as planting microphones in German offices and intercepting letters addressed to them. Lastly, counterespionage included the surveillance of suspect milieus, such as collaborationists, "escaped" POWs, and nationalist circles.

It must be pointed out that, despite the range of methods and services used in counterespionage, the system was far from perfect. It did not provide total protection. At most, the French secret services made themselves a nuisance to their German colleagues, but they did not really manage to keep them from operating in the nonoccupied territories. Several factors explain the limited effectiveness of counterespionage. Firstly, there were political explanations. The anti-German aspect of counterespionage seemed to run counter to the diplomatic positions of the Vichy government, and because of this, it had to be undertaken without the full support of the population who were most likely very confused about it. Worse still, for part of the population, Vichy's propaganda in favor of collaboration actually became an excuse to provide information to the Germans. Secondly, from a technical viewpoint, cooperation between the different organizations engaged in counterespionage (military, navy, police, etc.) was weakened by puerile rivalries. Other difficulties were simply consequences of the war itself. The occupation of part of the country forced the secret services to move their headquarters into the unoccupied southern sector. They had to reorganize, and this sort of reorganization required a period of readjustment. Finally, limited resources and shortages of staff were aggravated by the fact that some of the means at the disposal of the French secret services were diverted away from the anti-German struggle to be used against the Allies. In other words, some of the difficulties of anti-German counterespionage originated in the ambiguities of the secret services themselves, which operated both against the Germans and the Allies.

Secret service attitudes toward Allied and Gaullist agents cannot be explained solely by the instructions Vichy gave them. It is true that Pétain's government wished them to crack down on pro-Allied and Gaullist agitation but members of the secret services also had their own reasons to be ambivalent toward the Anglo-Gaullists. They criticized the lack of professionalism of the British Intelligence Service and claimed that their naivety endangered ordinary French citizens recruited by it. Attacks on the French empire perpetrated by Great Britain, as for example in Senegal, Syria, or Madagascar, were also roundly condemned, highlighting that long-term colonial rivalries had not ceased. As to the Gaullists, there were not only condescending criticisms of their lack of professionalism, but also attacks on their politization. The secret services did not appreciate the hostility of the Gaullists toward Vichy, suggesting that their own officially apolitical stance might also have had political undertones.

However, when it comes to the ambiguity of the Vichy secret services toward the Allies and the Gaullists, it is obvious that we need to keep it in proportion. It is clear that there were defensive links with certain resistance movements (that is those led by military men such as Henri Frenay or Alfred Heurteaux, whose organizations were more focused on attacking the Germans than on criticizing the Vichy regime). These movements thus received warnings about their infiltration by the German secret services. The secret services also exchanged information with the British Intelligence Service even if these exchanges were in reality fairly limited. They did not pass on intelligence about Vichy, only about the Germans, and this intelligence was not given gratuitously as Vichy's secret services tried to obtain information of equal value in return.

Although one can speak of ambiguity to describe the secret services' attitude toward the Anglo-Gaullists, it is of outright hostility that one must speak of when categorizing their attitude toward the Germans. Any thorough study based on Vichy secret service archives will inevitably come to the conclusion that their main enemy was Germany. Undoubtedly within these archives are signs of an anti-Communism that Vichy shared with the Nazis, and at times even an admiration for the organization and methods of the German intelligence agencies. However, beyond these two factors, secret service attitude toward their German counterparts was purely hostile. This can be explained primarily by the traditions of the institution: the Germans had been clearly identified as the main enemy ever since the Franco-Prussian war of 1870–71.

Up to now, historians have always considered that the activities of the secret services against the Germans were carried out independently of the government. I have strongly argued for a more nuanced view of this idea. While the day-to-day functioning of the secret services was autonomous, the repression of German espionage did not run counter to Vichy's policies. Indeed it was financed and supported by the government.[1] The secret services carried out this struggle with a tenacity born out of their instinctive hostility toward the Germans, but let's be quite clear: the arrest of Axis spies up to the end of 1942 was not in opposition to the policies conducted by Vichy.

Some apologists of the regime might be tempted to see this activity as a form of Vichyist resistance. This was not the case. It was rather a policy of defending sovereignty and of centralization of collaboration. Historians such as Robert Paxton, Marc-Olivier Baruch, and Éric Alary have recognized the importance of the idea of sovereignty for Vichy.[2] They particularly stress the notion of administrative sovereignty: Vichy claimed the monopoly of administrating the policies followed in France, even if this meant simply having German directives carried out by French civil servants. In terms of counterespionage, the desire to preserve administrative sovereignty was evident on two levels. On the first, Vichy hoped to prevent the infiltration of its administrations by German agents; its administrative independence depended on this. On the second, it sometimes attempted to thwart German infiltration of Resistance networks in the nonoccupied territories because it wanted to maintain its own monopoly of the repression of these movements.

Territorial sovereignty was also affected by counterespionage. Having lost part of its territory to the Germans, Pétain's government wanted to ensure that it at least maintained control of the nonoccupied territories and so sought to prevent the Germans from clandestine penetration of this area. It fell to the police and the counterespionage services to secure the inviolability of the borders of Pétain's kingdom. This idea of territorial sovereignty seemed dearer to military members of the regime, who were professionally conditioned to defend the territory, than it was to men such as Darlan and Laval, who were ready to compromise it for concessions in other domains.

The third form of sovereignty affected by counterespionage is the sovereignty of the state over the individual. Vichy was completely sincere in its quest for collaboration at the level of the state, but its main leaders were hostile to uncontrolled collaboration practiced by individual citizens. If individuals offered their services directly to the Germans without going through government channels, Vichy could no longer barter their collaboration in Franco-German negotiations. Counterespionage thus served to centralize collaboration.

Vichy's desire to defend its sovereignty was indeed real. For this reason, the government showed more firmness toward the Germans in this domain than in other areas of its policies. As a consequence, the government was ready to clandestinely recreate secret services that worked partly against Germany, thus breaching article 10 of the armistice convention, which stated that no part of the army should engage in any anti-German activity. Pétain and Darlan ratified the decisions of military tribunals that sentenced German spies to death. About forty individuals were executed as spies. Trials of German spies continued until December of 1943, and some cabinet members were certainly aware of this. Some spies were still in prison as late as the summer of 1944.

But this firmness, untypical of Vichy, must be juxtaposed with a spirit of conciliation and compromise, which will come as no surprise to anyone who has studied the regime. By 1941, Darlan allowed German Red Cross delegates to visit imprisoned spies of German nationality. Then, he agreed to inform the Germans of the arrests of their nationals. Finally, he released a number of imprisoned agents either gratuitously or in exchange for French citizens condemned by German tribunals in the occupied zone. Laval accelerated this collaboration from the fall of 1942 and even went as far, with the so-called Desloges affair, to offer official protection to German agents who had entered the southern zone with a mission to detect Allied radio transmitters and their operators.

The government's position thus oscillated between firmness and compromise. Firmness was explained by the desire to ensure the independence of the government from the occupier. But not all government officials favored the activity of the secret services in this respect. This was the case of Eugène Bridoux, secretary of state of defense under Laval, and of Fernand de Brinon, the general delegate of the government in the occupied territories. Only Maxime Weygand, secretary of state for war in 1940, and then the general delegate of the government in North Africa, was truly ready to risk diplomatic incidents in order to support the work of the secret services. The other ministers were more hesitant in this regard, and the incidents provoked by the brutal methods used by the counterespionage services were not appreciated by Darlan and Laval, demonstrating their desire to avoid compromising the policy of collaboration.

The defense of sovereignty sat uncomfortably with Vichy's diplomatic choices and was therefore doomed to fail over time. The government was caught in the spiral of a collaboration that could never be a genuine partnership. The Germans had important means of pressure at their disposal—POWs, control of the demarcation line, the inequality between French forces weakened by the armistice and occupation forces that could revoke the armistice convention at any time. The power balance became even more unequal as time went on. The loss of the empire in November 1942, followed by the total occupation of the country, nullified the defense of territorial sovereignty. Thereafter, it was practically impossible to prevent direct contact between the population and the occupation forces, and it thus became even more difficult to put an end to individually initiated acts of collaboration. All that remained was administrative sovereignty that became gradually reduced to Vichy administrations being used to do the Nazis' dirty work—something which of course suited the occupier perfectly. Except for a few very isolated cases, the arrest of German agents ceased abruptly in November 1942.

The study of German espionage and of French counterespionage raises interesting questions about the tension between the two countries despite Vichy's resolve to collaborate. It also challenges one of our most basic assumptions about the period. It has always been assumed that the Germans readily violated the 1940 armistice, but that its terms were systematically respected by Vichy. This was clearly not the case—by allowing its secret services to collect information about Germany and to arrest German spies, Vichy was violating article 10 of this armistice. Its counterespionage apparatus engaged in a struggle against the secret services of the Reich that was certainly intense yet unequal. German intelligence agencies had substantial means at their disposal and had no trouble recruiting French agents. The French secret services arrested about 2,000 spies working for the Germans, but subject to numerous difficulties including their own government's contradictions, they did not succeed in offering total protection. The objectives of Vichy's policy of counterespionage—defending sovereignty and centralizing collaboration—were only ever partially achieved.

NOTES

INTRODUCTION

1. See for instance J. Baynac, *Les Secrets de l'affaire Jean Moulin* (Paris: Le Seuil, 1998), 125; R. Belot, *Henri Frenay* (Paris: Le Seuil, 2003), 121–23; M. Chalet, "La DST, service français de contre-espionnage," in P. Lacoste, ed., *Approches françaises du renseignement* (Paris: FED, 1997), 59; J.-P. Cointet, *Histoire de Vichy* (Paris: France Loisirs, 1996), 155; D. Cordier, *Jean Moulin, l'inconnu du Panthéon* (Paris: J.-C. Lattès, 1993), III, 693–95; J.-L. Crémieux-Brilhac, *La France libre* (Paris: Gallimard, 1996), 233; L. Douzou and D. Peschanski, "Les premiers résistants face à l'hypothèque Vichy (1940–1942)," in L. Douzou, R. Frank, D. Peschanski, and D. Veillon, eds., *La Résistance et les Français* (Cachan: Actes du colloque, 1995), 433; F.-G. Dreyfus, *Histoire de la Résistance* (Paris: Éditions de Fallois, 1996), 44–46; A. Guérin, *Chronique de la Résistance* (Paris: Omnibus, 2000), 1455–58; H. R. Kedward, *Resistance in Vichy France* (Oxford: Oxford University Press, 1978), 40–41; S. Kitson, "L'évolution de la Résistance dans la police Marseillaise," in J.-M. Guillon and R. Mencherini, eds., *La Résistance et les Européens du Sud* (Paris: L'Harmattan, 1999), 259–60; S. Laurent, "Pour une autre histoire de l'État," *Vingtième siècle* 83 (2004): 178; R. Mencherini, "Naissance de la Résistance à Marseille," in J.-M. Guillon and P. Laborie , eds., *Mémoire et Histoire: La Résistance* (Paris: Privat, 1995), 142–43; H. Noguerès, *Histoire de la Résistance en France de 1940 à 1945* (Paris: Laffont, 1967), I, 69–72; R. O. Paxton, *Parades and Politics in Vichy* (Princeton, NJ: Princeton University Press, 1966), 303; J. F. Sweets, *Choices in Vichy France* (Oxford: Oxford University Press, 1986), 173; M. Thomas, "Signals Intelligence and Vichy

France, 1940–1944: Intelligence in Defeat," *Intelligence and National Security* 14, no. 1 (2000): 176–200.

2. R. Faligot and P. Krop, *DST: Police secrète* (Paris: Flammarion, 1999); S. Kitson, "Arresting Nazi Spies in Vichy France (1940–1942)," *Intelligence and National Security* 15, no. 1 (2000): 80–120; S. Laurent, "Le renseignement et le contre-espionnage militaires face à l'Allemagne: étude du dispositif de renseignement français," in S. Mertens and M. Vaïsse, eds., *Frankreich und Deutschland im Krieg (November 1942–Herbst 1944). Okkupation, Kollaboration, Résistance* (Bonn: Bouvier Verlag, 2000), 783–92; D. Porch, *The French Secret Services, from the Dreyfus Affair to the Gulf War* (Oxford: Oxford University Press, 1997); P. J. Stead, *Second Bureau* (London: Evans Brothers, 1959). Please see also the several internship reports written on the topic by several army officers under the direction of Olivier Forcade: F. Delalez, *Le Service des menées antinationales, 1940–1942* (Guer, Brittany: Mémoire des Écoles de Coëtquidan, 1998); T. Guillet, *Le Renseignement au Maroc,* Mémoire des Écoles de Coëtquidan, 1999; Slt Zajec, *"Travaux ruraux": Le contre-espionnage clandestin de l'armée d'armistice* (Guer, Brittany: Mémoire des Écoles de Coëtquidan, 1999).

3. P. Nord, *Mes camarades sont morts* (Geneva: de Crémille, 1970); J. Abtey and F. Unterberg-Gibhardt, *Deuxième bureau contre Abwehr* (Paris: La Table ronde, 1966); M. Garder, *La Guerre secrète des services spéciaux français* (Paris: Plon, 1967); D. Loisel, *J'étais le commandant X* (Paris: Fayard, 1970); Gilbert-Guillaume, *Mes missions face à l'Abwehr* (Paris: Plon, 1971); M. Pasquelot, *Les Dossiers secrets de la marine* (Paris: NEL, 1973); P. Paillole, *Services spéciaux, 1935–1945* (Paris: Laffont, 1975); P. Bernard, *Roger Wybot et la bataille pour la DST* (Paris: Presses de la Cité, 1975); H. Koch-Kent, *Doudot, figure légendaire du contre-espionnage français* (Paris: Casteman, 1976); R. Terres, *Double jeu pour la France* (Paris: Grasset, 1977); H. Navarre, *Le Service de renseignements, 1871–1944* (Paris: Plon, 1978); H. Navarre, *Le Temps des vérités* (Paris: Plon, 1979); J. Bézy, *Le Service de renseignements air* (Paris: France-Empire, 1979); J.-P. Vittori, *Une histoire d'honneur: La Résistance* (Paris: Ramsay, 1984), see chap. 6, 83–96, conversation with Paul Paillole; P. Paillole, *L'Homme des services secrets* (Paris: Julliard, 1995).

4. On the history of the Fonds de Moscou, see : C. Sibille, "Les archives du deuxième bureau SR-SCR récuperées de Russie," in G.-H. Soutou, J. Frémeaux, O. Forcade, eds., *L'Exploitation du renseignement en Europe et aux États-Unis des années 1930 aux années 1960* (Paris: Économica, 2001), 27–47; S. Cœuré, F. Mounier and G. Naud, "Le retour de Russie des archives françaises: Le cas du fond de la Sûreté," *Vingtième siècle* 45 (1995): 133–39; S. Cœuré, F. Mounier, "De l'ombre à la lumière: Les archives françaises de retour de Moscou (1940–2002)," in S. Laurent, ed., *Archives "secrètes," secrets d'archives? L'historien et l'archiviste face aux archives sensibles* (Paris: Éditions du CNRS, 2003), 233–48.

5. Boxes Archives Nationales (hereafter Boxes AN), 2^{AG} 521, 524, 528, 595, 596, 597, 601.

6. Boxes AN BB^{24} 2381; AN BB^{30} 1709, 1712, 1723.

7. Respectively the series AN 2^{AG}, AN F^{60} and An F^{1a}.

8. See the following trials: AN 3W 88–95, Haute Cour c/ René Bousquet; AN 3W 100–105, Haute Cour c/ général Bridoux; AN 3W 163–164, Haute Cour c/ général Delmotte; AN 3W 208–216, Haute Cour c/ Pierre Laval; AN 3W 258–266, Haute Cour c/ général Noguès; AN 3W 277–309, Haute Cour c/ maréchal Pétain; AN 3W 310–313, Haute Cour c/ Marcel Peyrouton; AN 3W 340–345, Haute Cour c/ général Weygand.

9. Notably Boxes AN AJ[41] 491–99.

10. E. Jäckel, *La France dans l'Europe de Hitler* (Paris: Fayard, 1968); R. O. Paxton, *Vichy France: Old Guard and New Order,* 1940–1944 (New York: Columbia University Press, 1972).

11. Robert Owen Paxton, *Vichy France, Old Guard and New Order* (Columbia University Press, New York, 2nd ed., 1982), p. 51.

CHAPTER 1

1. Quotations from Adolf Hitler, *Mein Kampf* (Reedy, WV: Liberty Bell Publications, 2004), pp. 355, 340, 341.

2. In addition to the cited documents, the sources for this chapter are E. Alary, *La Ligne de démarcation* (Paris: Perrin, 2003); J.-P. Azéma and O. Wieviorka, *Vichy, 1940–1944* (Paris: Perrin, 1997); P. Burrin, *La France à l'heure allemande, 1940–1944* (Paris: Le Seuil, 1995); M. and J.-P. Cointet, *Dictionnaire historique de la France sous l'Occupation* (Paris: Tallandier, 2000); J. Delarue, *Histoire de la Gestapo* (Paris: Fayard, 1962); J. Delarue, *Trafics et crimes sous l'Occupation* (Paris: Fayard, 1968); M. Garder, *La Guerre secrète des services spéciaux français* (Paris: Plon, 1967); E. Jäckel, *La France dans l'Europe de Hitler* (Paris: Fayard, 1968); J. Jackson, *France: The Dark Years* (Oxford: Oxford University Press, 2001); B. Kasten, "Gute Franzosen," *Die französische Polizei und die deutsche Besatzungsmacht in besetzten Frankreich, 1940–1945* (Sigmaringen: Thorbecke, 1993); C. Metzger, *L'Empire colonial français dans la stratégie du IIIe Reich (1936–1945),* thèse de doctorat d'État (state doctoral thesis), University of Paris IV-Sorbonne, 1988; A. Meyer, *Die deutsche Besatzung in Frankreich, 1940–1944* (Darmstadt: Wissenschaftliche Buchgesellschaft, 2000); H. Navarre, *Le Service de renseignements, 1871–1944* (Paris: Plon, 1978); L. Nester and F. Schulz, *Die faschistische Okkupationspolitik in Frankreich* (Berlin: Deutsche Verlag der Wissenschaften, 1990); P. Nord, *Mes camarades sont morts* (Geneva: de Crémille, 1970); P. Paillole, *Services spéciaux, 1935–1945* (Paris: Laffont, 1975); P. Paillole, *L'Homme des services secrets* (Paris: Julliard, 1995); O. Reile, *L'Abwehr* (Paris: France-Empire, 1970); Général Louis Rivet, "Abwehr et Gestapo en France pendant la guerre," *Revue d'histoire de la Deuxième Guerre mondiale* 1 (1950): 28–50; H. Rousso, *La Collaboration* (Paris: MA éditions, 1987): Paul Sanders, "Anatomie d'une implantation SS—Helmut Knochen et la police nazie en France, 1940–1944," *Revue de la Shoah* 165 (1999): 111–45; L. Steinberg, *Les Allemands en France, 1940–1944* (Paris: Albin Michel, 1980); R. Thalmann, *La Mise au pas* (Paris: Fayard, 1991); H. Umbreit, *Der Militärbefehlshaber in Frankreich* (Boppard am Rhein: Harald Boldt Verlag, 1968).

3. R. Thalmann, *La Mise au pas* (Paris: Fayard, 1991), 17.

4. J. Barthélemy, *Ministre de la Justice, Vichy 1941–1943* (Paris: Pygmalion, 1989), 80.

5. Boxes AN (Archives Nationales) AJ[41] 496, tribunal militaire permanent de la 16e division militaire, Montpellier, "Acte d'accusation contre Chand," 17 September 1942.

6. SHAT (Service Historique de l'Armée de Terre) Fonds de Moscou, 312/14078, note of the TR 113 (Clermont-Ferrand), n° 1, "a/s de la Gestapo et des personnes en relations avec elle à Vichy," 29 August 1942. See also AN F[7] 15279, Inspection générale des services de RG, 22 September 1941.

7. AN F[7] 15306, direction des RG, note pour le secrétaire général de police, Vichy 19 March 1943.

8. SHAT Fonds de Moscou, 934/1936, renseignement, 10 October 1941.

9. AN AJ 41 496, Note de renseignement communiquée par les Services de la Surveillance du Territoire, undated; AN AJ41 499, Note de renseignement, cabinet BMA, N° 6204/MA/B, 24 October 1941; AN AJ41 499, Direction des Services de l'Armistice, Hôtel Thermal, Vichy (signé Platon), note pour M Benoist-Mechin, secrétaire d'état auprès du chef du gouvernement, N° 16342/DSA/7, 10 July 1942.

10. SHAT 1P 200, Note n° 3945/CBST, 12 November 1941 (no indication of source but presumeably ST); AN AJ41 498, Mesures Prises en faveur des individus ayant fait l'objet de la protestation de la CAA, 8 December 1941; AN AJ41 499, Compte-rendu de l'officier de liaison sur la visite de M Klaube à Alscher et Gassner, 24 November 1941.

11. AN AJ41 499, Dossier Demoulin.

12. AN AJ41 499, le commandant Paillole, chef du SSM, note pour la Direction des Services de l'Armistice, N° 000011/SM/B, 2 September 1942; AN AJ41 499, Extrait du compte-rendu de l' officier de liaison à Lyon, N° 714/D, Lyon, le 5 December 1942.

13. AN AJ 41 496, Citation directe à comparaitre à l'audience, Parquet du Tribunal Militaire de la 16 Division Militaire séant à Montpellier, N° 2976, 26 October 1942.

14. O. Reile, *L'Abwehr* (Paris: France-Empire, 1970), 80.

15. For an example of a questionnaire, see AN F[7] 15306, Contrôle général des services de ST, Vichy, 6 March 1942; "Object: arrestation de Lacour, Paul, agent du SRA."

16. AN AJ[41] 499, secrétariat d'État à la Guerre, cabinet, BMA, note pour a DSA, n° 3690/MA/M, 17 July 1941; AD BDR (departmental archives of Bouches-du-Rhône), 5W 365, note: police renseignements, no 3694/1, "Activité de la Gestapo à Marseille," 23 May 1941; *Les Petites Ailes de France,* 8 July 1941.

17. SHAT 1P 89, le général Weygand au vice-président du Conseil, n° 9745/EM/E, 15 November 1941.

18. SHAT Fonds de Moscou, 715/166, TR, "Note sur l'activité des agents doubles et analyse des questionnaires des SR étrangers," 15 January 1942.

19. SHAT Fonds de Moscou, 933/1976, renseignement: "Les achats irréguliers allemands en zone non occupée," Lyon, 12 March 1942.

20. Paul Sanders, "Prélèvement économique: les activités allemandes de marché noir en France, 1940–1945," in O. Dard, J.-C. Daumas, and F. Marcot, eds., *L'Occupation, l'État français et les entreprises* (Paris: ADHE, 2000), 41.

21. In addition to the archives mentioned, the sources for this section are C. Levisse-Touzé, *L'Afrique du Nord dans la guerre, 1939–1945* (Paris: Albin Michel, 1998); C. Metzger, *L'Empire colonial français dans la stratégie du IIIe Reich (1936–1945),* thèse de doctorat d'État, Université de Paris IV-Sorbonne, 1998; Martin Thomas, *The French Empire at War, 1940–1945* (Manchester: Manchester University Press, 1998).

22. SHAT 1P 89, le général Weygand à M. le maréchal de France, 3 March 1941; SHAT 1P 89, le général Weygand à M. le maréchal de France, 26 March 1941

23. SHAT Fonds de Moscou, 466/327, synthèse de l'activité du SRA en France, 30 March 1941.

24. M. Ferro, *Pétain* (Paris: Hachette, 1987), 211; C. Levisse-Touzé, *L'Afrique du Nord dans la guerre, 1939–1945* (Paris: Albin Michel, 1998), 97.

25. SHAT 1P 135 Weygand à Huntziger, n° 1247/EM/2, 5 March 1941, "Object: incidents de Maison-Carrée"; AN AJ[41] 65, dossier relatif à la mutinerie de Maison-Carrée; AN 2[AG] 524, condamnation à mort des tirailleurs Djedi Salah et Besaid Ali et du caporal Manahaoui Lakhdar.

26. SHAT 1P 200, DDSA to Weygand, "Note sur la propagande germanophile en Algérie," 15 February 1941; SHAT 1P 200, l'inspecteur de police spéciale Martin à M. le commissaire spécial, 19 July 1941; SHAT 1P 200, état-major de l'armée, cinquième bureau, note de renseignements, "La propagande allemande auprès des prisoniers nord-africains," 21 July 1941; SHAT 1P 200, note de renseignements, "La propagande allemande auprès des prisoniers nord-africains,": 23 August 1941; SHAT 1P 200 section des affaires musulmanes, note de renseignements, "La propagande allemande auprès des prisonniers indigènes nord-africains," 6 September 1941.

27. This agreement was no secret. Pétain mentioned it in his radio address of March 19: "We are counting on American assistance to help with our food supplies": J.-C. Barbas, *Philippe Pétain: Discours aux Français* (Paris: Albin Michel, 1989), 117.

28. It must be noted that General Weygand's transfer from his post in November 1941 stemmed from German pressure. A part of their complaint was linked to the too friendly contacts between Weygand and the Americans with whom, the Germans pointed out, they were practically at war. See An AJ[41] 1609, procès-verbal de l'entretien du colonel Böhme et du colonel Vignol, 13 November 1941.

29. AN AJ41 491, capitaine de Bruce, officier de liaison auprès du Délégué Allemand au Rapatriement, à M l'amiral de la flotte, ministre de la défense nationale, DSA, Vichy, N° 317, Marseille, 28 February 1942; AN AJ 41 496, Note de renseignement communiquée par les Services de la Surveillance du Territoire, undated; AN AJ41 499, Direction des Services de l'Armistice, Délégation Française au Maroc, N° 2690/DIA, 9 December 1941; AN AJ41 499, Le Commissaire, chef de la Brigade de ST, Henry GODBARGE, à M le Général Commandant la Division territoriale, Casablanca, N° 3906 BST, 10 December 1941; AN AJ

41 499, Direction des Services de l'Armistice, Délégation en AFN, N° 12964/DDSA/B2, 13 December 1941; AN AJ41 499, "Note sur BEITELBERGER, Josef, Vichy le 17 décembre 1941", no indication of source.

30. SHAT Fonds de Moscou, 784/368, étude schématique sur l'organisation et l'articulation des services spéciaux allemands en AFN, 14 August 1942.

31. SHAT 5P 2, DDSA, rapport n° 47 sur l'activité des commissions italiennes et allemandes de contrôle en AFN, 23 October 1942.

32. SHAT Fonds de Moscou, 464/176, conférence Paillole: "Le CE en face de l'adversaire," 15 April 1942.

33. W. Jasper, *L'hôtel Lutetia, un exil allemand à Paris* (Paris: Michalon, 1995).

34. L. Douzou and D. Peschanski, "Les premiers résistants face à l'hypothèque Vichy (1940–1942)," in L. Douzou , R. Frank, D. Peschanski and D. Veillon, *La Résistance et les Français* (Cachan: Actes du colloque, 1995), 427–46; D. Peschanski, "La Résistance, l'occupant et Vichy," *Cahiers de l'IHTP* 37 (1997): 47–71; D. Veillon, "The Resistance and Vichy," in S. Fishman et al., *France at War* (Oxford: Berg, 2000), 161–77.

35. SHAT Fonds Paillole, 1K 545.

36. Interrogatoire du SS Hauptsturmführer Roland Nosek, 1945.

37. SHAT Fonds de Moscou, 312/14078, 113 to 6 000, n° 6271, 29 August 1942; SHAT Fonds Paillole, 1K 545 5, interrogatoire du SS Hauptsturmführer Roland Nosek, 1945; AN AJ^{41} 1644 [09–10], général de division, DSA, note for the DFA à Wiesbaden, n° 6371/DSA/7, 28 February 1941; AN 72^{AJ} 82, résumé de l'activité des services de CE militaire français de juilllet 1940 à novembre 1944, October 1946, vol. II, April 1942 to November 1942.

38. SHAT Fonds Paillole, 1K 545 5, interrogatoire du SS Hauptsturmführer Roland Nosek, 1945.

39. AN 393 MI/3/33, notice technique de CE, "Object: les services spéciaux allemands en France pendant l'Occupation," 12 March 1946.

40. A. Meyer, *Die deutsche Besatzung in Frankreich, 1940–1944* (Darmstadt: Wissenschaftliche Buchgesellschaft, 2000).

41. AN F^{60} 1682, CNI, D3195/5, 27 March 1942.

42. SHAT Fonds de Moscou, 784/368, étude schématique sur l'organisation et l'articulation des services spéciaux allemands en AFN, 14 August 1942.

43. AN F^{60} 1682, CNI, D3195/5, 27 March 1942.

44. AN F^{60} 1682, CNI D3195/5, 27 March 1942.

45. See for instance, SHAT Fonds de Moscou, 312/14086, compte rendu d'arrestation pour espionnage, n° 3715/1200/412054, 29 September 1941.

46. SHAT Fonds de Moscou, 269/47320, rapport du CST de Bourg-en-Bresse, "procès-verbal d'examen de situation d'Edouard Buch," 9 September 1942.

47. SHAT Fonds de Moscou, 466/325, synthèse de l'activité du SRA en France, 30 March 1941.

48. SHAT Fonds de Moscou, 784/368, étude schématique sur l'organisation et l'articulation des services spéciaux allemands en AFN, 14 August 1942.

49. SHAT "Fonds de Moscou, 466/327, synthèse de l'activité du SRA en France, 30 March 1941.

50. SHAT Fonds Paillole, 1K 545/10, rapport du TR, July 1941.

CHAPTER 2

1. SHAT Fonds de Moscou, 761/73, conférence du capitaine Bernard, 9 June 1942.

2. AN 72[AJ] 1911, "Note Rollin sur le fontionnement du SR de la SN," 2 May 1941.

3. P. Laborie, *L'Opinion française sous Vichy* (Paris: Seuil, 1990).

4. SHAT Fonds de Moscou, 761/73, conférence du capitaine Bernard, 9 June 1942.

5. AN AJ[41] 499, BMA, note de renseignements sur des ressortissants allemands arrêtés pour espionnage, 5 July 1941; AN AJ[41] 499, direction du contentieux de la justice militaire et de la gendarmerie, note pour la DSA, 27 November 1942; SHAT Fonds de Moscou, 761/73, conférence du capitaine Bernard, 9 June 1942.

6. M. Baudot, *Libération de la Bretagne* (Paris: Hachette, 1974); J. Sainclivier, *La Bretagne de 1939 à nos jours* (Rennes: Ouest-France, 1989).

7. AN AJ[41] 25, synthèse hebdomadaire des interceptions des contrôles téléphoniques, télégraphiques et postaux (8 to 24 Octobre 1940).

8. SHAT Fonds Paillole, 1K 545 10, rapport du TR, July 1941, "SR allemand."

9. SHAT Fonds de Moscou, 269/47321, CST, audition du nommé Marcel Jaminais, 17 September 1942; SHAT Fonds de Moscou, 667/14519, affaire Charpentier-Dreano, autonomistes bretons (October 1941–March 1942); AN BB[30] 1709, rapport sur Eugène Charpentier et Charles Daguet.

10. SHAT Fonds de Moscou, 466/327, synthèse de l'activité du SRA en France, 30 March 1941.

11. SHAT Fonds Paillole, 1K 545 10, TR, tableau nominatif des arrestations, 7 July 1941; SHAT Fonds de Moscou, 761/73, conférence du capitaine Bernard, 9 June 1942.

12. AN41 499, l'amiral de la flotte, ministre à M le ministre de la défénse nationale, Direction des Services de l'Armistice, Hôtel Thermal, Vichy, n° 1922, 30/1/42- n° 3634/DSA, 4 February 1942.

13. AN AJ 41 499, le secrétaire d'état à l'intérieur à M l'amiral de la flotte, ministre de la défense nationale, DSA, n° 1094P/Pol 9, Vichy, 31 March 1942.

14. AN AJ41 491, le chef d'escadrons de ROYERE, officier de liaison auprès du Délégué Allemand au Rapatriement à M l'amiral de la flotte, Direction des Services de l'Armistice, Hôtel Thermal, Vichy, n° 148/D, Lyon, 5 March 1942.

15. SHAT 1P 200, le général Noguès à M. l'amiral de la flotte, n° 391, 12 March 1941, "Action allemande dans les milieux indigènes marocain."

16. AN F[60] 1431, vice-présidence du Conseil, note de 22 février 1942; C. Levisse-Touzé, *L'Afrique du Nord dans la guerre, 1939–1945* (Paris: Albin Michel, 1998), 109–10.

17. SHAT 1P 89, Weygand à Pétain, n° 1175/EM/2, 3 March 1941. See also: SHAT 1P 200, note sur la propagande germanophile en Algérie," 15 February

1941; SHAT 1P 200, le ministre de la Défense à la délégation de la DSA, Alger, "note sur la propagande alemande auprès des prisonniers nord-africains," 26 January 1942.

18. SHAT Fonds de Moscou, 464/176, conférence du commandant Paillole, 15 April 1942.

19. SHAT 1P 200, le général Noguès à M. l'amiral de la flotte, n° 391, 12 March 1941, "Action allemande dans les milieux indigènes marocains."

20. SHAT Fonds de Moscou, 761/73, conférence du capitaine Bernard, 9 June 1942.

21. AN AJ[41] 499, dossier Kramer; AN AJ[41] 499, le chef d'escadron d'Americourt au ministre de la Défense nationale, 3 December 1941.

22. AN 72[AJ] 1911, "Note Rollin sur le fonctionnnement du SR de la SN," 2 May 1941.

23. SHAT Fonds de Moscou, 761/73, conférence du capitaine Bernard, 9 June 1942.

24. AN 2[AG] 596, Germaine Desseigne à M. le Maréchal, 24 June 1941.

25. AN 2[AG] 596, Suzanne-Marie Desseigne à M. le Maréchal Pétain, 16 August 1941.

26. SHAT 1P 89, Weygand à Pétain, 3 March 1941; AN 2[AG] 596, le conseiller de justice militaire Parès, commissaire du gouvernement près le tribunal militaire permanent d'Alger, à M. le général d'armée, ministre secrétaire d'État à la Guerre, 7 August 1941; AN 2[AG] 596, Germaine Desseigne à M. le Maréchal, January 1942; AN 2[AG] 596, le conseiller de justice militaire adjoint Rondreux, juge d'instruction au tribunal militaire permanent d'Alger, à M. le commissaire du gouvernement près le tribunal militaire permanent d'Alger, 3 March 1942; AN 2[AG] 596, le général chef du cabinet militaire du chef de l'État à M. le général de corps d'armée, secrétaire d'État à la Guerre, 29 May 1942; SHAT Fonds de Moscou, 1195/13814, dossier sur Suzanne Dessaigne (1941–42).

27. SHAT Fonds de Moscou, 480/1730, "liens existant entre le PPF et le SRA."

28. SHAT Fonds Paillole, 1K 545 10, rapport du TR, July 1941.

29. AN 2[AG] 597, Romain à Pétain, 2 October 1942.

30. AN F[7] 15306, Pézard à Laval, 7 December 1943.

31. AN F[7] 15279, déposition de Roland Nosek, 18 November 1947.

32. AN 2[AG] 524, tribunal militaire de Marseille, condamnation à mort du nommé André Bernard, 13 November 1941.

33. AN F[0] 1431, vice-présidence du Conseil, note du 22 février 1942; SHAT Fonds de Moscou, 466/327, synthèse de l'activité du SRA en France, 30 March 1941. *Combat* 1 (1942) gives the example of a SRA branch located on the Paraban to Lyon road and claims that "they live like princes and are not affected by the restrictions."

34. SHAT Fonds de Moscou, 466/327, synthèse de l'activité du SRA en France, 30 March 1941.

35. P. Aziz, *Tu trahiras sans vergogne* (Paris: Fayard, 1970), p. 16.

36. AN AJ 41 499, Secrétariat d'Etat à la Guerre, Cabinet-Bureau MA (signé Commandant Paillole), note pour la Direction des Services de l'Armistice, n° 005557/MA/B/45842, 19 August 1942.

37. AN AJ41 499, Dossier Demoulin.

38. E. Alary, *La Ligne de démarcation* (Paris: Perrin, 2003).

39. P. Sanders, *Histoire du marché noir, 1940–1946* (Paris: Perrin, 2001), 174–93.

40. SHAT Fonds de Moscou, 466/327, synthèse de l'activité du SRA en France, 30 March 1941.

41. Patrice Miannay, *Dictionnaire des agents doubles dans la Résistance* (Paris: Le Cherche Midi, 2005) p. 76.

42. Philip Aziz, *Au service de l'ennemi, la gestapo française en province, 1940–1944* (Paris: Fayard, 1972), pp. 109–16; Philip John Stead, *Second Bureau* (London: Evans Brothers, 1959), p. 46 also points to the immunity these individuals believed they had.

43. SHAT Fonds de Moscou, 676/15087, dossier sur Henri Lafont (August–October 1942).

44. SHAT Fonds de Moscou, 821/10655, TR 120, renseignement, n° 507, 13 May 1942.

45. AN BB[30] 1709, rapport sur Marcel Auguin.

46. AN 2[AG] 597, le ministre de la Défense nationale au directeur du cabinet civbil du chef de l'État, 19 February 1942.

47. SHAT Fonds de Moscou, 761/73, conférence du capitaine Bernard, 9 June 1942.

48. AN BB[30] 1709, rapport sur Gabriel Le Guenne.

49. O. Reile, *L'Abwehr* (Paris: France-Empire, 1970), p. 91.

50. AN BB[30] 1709, rapport sur Georges Besançon.

51. AN BB[24] 2381, secrétaire d'État à la Guerre, rapport à Pétain, 23 May 1941.

52. AN BB[30] 1709, rapport sur Rachel Galy.

53. SHAT Fonds de Moscou, 269/15162, le commissaire du gouvernement près le tribunal militaire (14e division militaire) au sercrétaire d'État à la Guerre, 11 September 1942; SHAT Fonds de Moscou, 269/15162, le commissaire de ST Baud, Bourg-en-Bresse, à l'inspecteur général de ST, Vichy, 1 September 1942.

54. SHAT COI 232, conférence du commandant Matriolet, 14 October 1942. H. R. Kedward, "Resistance: The Discourse of Personality," in K. Robertson, ed., *War, Resistance and Intelligence* (London: Leo Cooper, 1999), 140–41.

55. M. Miller, *Shanghai on the Métro: Spies, Intrigue and the French between the Wars* (Los Angeles: University of California Press, 1994), 174–238; R. Young, *France and the Origins of the Second World War* (London: Macmillan, 1996), 115.

56. Dr. Mike Gelles of the Naval Criminal Investigative Service, *Exploring the Mind of a Spy,* on website address http://rf-web.tamu.edu/security/SECGUIDE/Treason/Mind.htm.

57. AN BB[30] 1709, report au sujet de Maurice Broaurd-Villiod; AN 2[AG] 524, condamnation à mort du nommé Pierre Cherouvrier; AN 2[AG] 597, l'amiral de la

flotte à M. le directeur du cabinet civil de M. le chef de l'État, "Rapport sur les faits reprochés au nommé Roux Christian," 19 February 1942; AN 72^{AJ} 1911, "Note Rollin sur le fonctionnement du SR de la SN," 2 May 1941.

58. AN 72^{AJ} 1911, "Note Rollin sur le fonctionnement du SR de la SN," 2 May 1941.

59. AN AJ^{41} 498, note pour la délégation française d'armistice à Wiesbaden, n° 9052/DSA/7, Vichy, 23 March 1941; AN AJ^{41} 498, état des ressortissants allemands détenus dans les prisons militaires d'Algérie, 19 July 1941; AN AJ^{41} 498, le contrôleur des services extérieurs pénitentiaires et de l'éducation surveillée Malmassari à M. le directeur de la Sécurité générale, 10 March 1942; AN AJ^{41} 498, BMA, compte rendu d'arrestation, destinataire: secrétariat d'État à la Guerre, cabinet, DSA, 17 October 1940; AN AJ^{41} 498, Hans Goepel au délégué allemand au rapatriement, Algiers, n.d.

60. AN AJ41 499, Dossier 'Christin.'

61. PRO (Public Records Office), KV 2/415, dossier Harold Cole.

62. AN F^{7} 15306, rapport sur Robert Alesch, 1946.

63. AN 2^{AG} 524, condamnation à mort du nommé Pierre Cherouvrier.

64. AN AJ^{41} 491, le capitaine de Bruce, officier de liaison auprès du délégué allemand au rapatriement, Marseille, à M. l'amiral de la flotte, ministre de la défense nationale, DSA, n° 317, 28 February 1942; AN AJ^{41} 499, DSA, délégation française au Maroc, n° 2690/DIA, 9 December 1941; AN AJ^{41} 499, le commissaire, chef de la Brigade de ST, Henry Godbarge, à M. le général commandant la division territoriale, Casablanca, n° 3906 BST, 10 December 1941.

65. SHAT Fonds de Moscou, 1195/13815, renseignements sur Oscar Rohr, Charles Rumbold, Marcel Führer, Allemands consdamnés pour espionnage (1941–1942); SHAT Fonds de Moscou, 761/73, conférence du capitaine Bernard, 9 June 1942; AN AJ^{41} 1547, le capitaine de Bruce, en liaison près le délégué allemand au rapatriement, Marseille, au secrétaire d'État à la Guerre, DSA, n° 151, 18 November 1941; AN AJ^{41} 1547, DSA (signed Rivet) à la délégation française d'armistice, Wiesbaden, 20 January 1942; AN AJ^{41} 491, le lieutenant Amann, officier de liaison auprès du délégué Allemand au rapatriement, Marseille, à M. l'amiral de la flotte, ministre de la défense nationale, DSA, n° 290, 16 February 1942; AN AJ^{41} 1547, le vice-amiral Bourragué, DSA, note pour le capitaine de Bruce, en liaison près le délégué allemand au rapatriement n° 1812/DSA/7, 4 February 1943; AN AJ^{41} 1547, le capitaine de Bruce, en liaison près le délégué allemand au rapatriement, à M. le général de division directeur des services de l'armistice, n° 1039, Marseille, 28 July 1943.

66. AN BB^{30} 1709, report au sujet de Paul Ducornetz.

67. "Le réseau policier en France," *Les Petites Ailes de France,* 8 July 1941.

CHAPTER 3

1. In addition to the archival documents cited in the chapter, the sources for this section are M. Garder, *La Guerre secrète des services spéciaux français* (Paris: Plon, 1967); S. Laurent, "Le renseignement et le contre-espionnage militaires face

à l'Allemagne: étude du dispositif de renseignement français," in S. Martens and M. Vaisse, eds., *Frankreich und Deutschland im Krieg* (Bonn: Bouvier Verlag, 2000); P. Paillole, *Services spéciaux* (Paris: Laffont, 1975).

2. SHAT 3P 102, le général Lavaud, note de service, n° 1279 C / EMA, Vichy, 20 March 1941.

3. AN F[7] 15306, note d'information, 6 February 1951.

4. SHAT 3P 102, secrétariat d'État à la Guerre, cabinet, "Note au sujet du service des renseignements," Vichy, 26 July 1940.

5. SHAT Fonds de Moscou, 488 / 86, instruction sur l'organisation et le fonctionnement des BMA des divisions militaires (signed Picquendar), 20 November 1940; SHAT Fonds de Moscou, 1095 / 1415, projet d'organisation du service MA; SHAT Fonds de Moscou, 1095 / 1415, directive du général Colson, 25 August 1940; SHAT Fonds de Moscou, 1095 / 1415, compte rendu de mission du commandant d'Alès à Marseille, Montpellier et Toulouse, 8 November 1940; SHAT "fonds Paillole" 1K 545 1, journal Gérard-Dubot; SHAT "fonds Paillole" 1K 545 1, journal de marche du général Rivet; SHAT 1P 6, Conseil supérieur de la Défense nationale, "Note sur l'organisation de la résistance à l'emprise allemande en zone occupée," 6 July 1940.

6. SHAT Fonds Paillole, 1K 545 1, journal de marche du général Rivet.

7. P. Paillole, *Services spéciaux, 1935–1945* (Paris: Laffont, 1975); P. Paillole, *L'Homme des services secrets* (Paris: Julliard, 1995).

8. R. Terres, *Double jeu pour la France* (Paris: Grasset, 1977), 50–51.

9. J. Soustelle, *Envers et contre tout* (Paris, Laffont, 1970), III, 114.

10. Navarre points out the difficulties the second bureau experienced in collecting the necessary funds for its functioning: H. Navarre, *Le Temps des vérités* (Paris: Plon, 1979), 81. Rollin, from the ministry of the Interior, refers to the shortage of funds available to the police SR: AN 72[AJ] 1911, "Note Rollin sur le fonctionnement du SR de la SN," 2 May 1941.

11. SHAT Fonds Paillole, 1K 545 9, "TR a un an d'existence,:" rapport de TR, July 1941.

12. SHAT Fonds de Moscou, 510 / 1447, secrétariat d'État à la Guerre, cabinet, instruction n° 13 600 sur l'organisation des BMA des divisions militaires, 20 November 1940.

13. SHAT Fonds de Moscou, 510 / 447, note no 879 / BMA 100 / G / 1168 / AA-AI (signed d'Alès), 9 February 1942.

14. AN 3W 104, journal intime du général Bridoux, 19 August 1942.

15. AN 72[AJ] 82, résumé de l'action des services de contre-espionnage militaire français, July 1940 to November 1944; SHAT Fonds Paillole, 1K 545 4, transcription d'interview ORTF de Paillole, 1950; SHAT Fonds Paillole, 1K 545 10, Tagung der V16 Referenten in Paris am 17 / 18 July 1943; SHAT Fonds Paillole, 1K 545 16, instruction d'application du décret du 24 août 1942 portant organisation de service de contre-espionnage, n° 1269 contre-espionnage C 624 EM; SHAT 1P 200, général Mast, commandant la division territoriale d'Alger, note au sujet de la transformation du BMA en SSM, 3 September 1942.

16. SHAT Fonds Paillole, 1K 545 10, rapport de l'Einsatzkommando, SD, Strasbourg, 17 November 1943; SHAT Fonds Paillole, 1K 545 16, la DPSD: ses racines (historique succinct) de 1872 à 1984; AN F^{60} 782, Darlan à Baudoin, 26 December 1940; AN 72^{AJ} 1911, Henry Rollin, note sur le fonctionnement du SR de la SN, 2 May 1941; AN 72^{AJ} 63, note du capitaine de vaisseau Sanson, chef du deuxième bureau de l'amirauté française, 8 October 1941; AN 72^{AJ} 63, SR marine, témoignage du commandant Jonglez, 29 October 1946; AN 72^{AJ} 63, SR marine, témoignage du capitaine de vaisseau Édouard Blouet, 21 June 1948.

17. SHAT Fonds Paillole, 1K 545 1, journal de marche du général Rivet, 3 August 1940.

18. SHAT Fonds de Moscou, 1095 / 1415, note de Rivet sur les difficultés rencontrées par le BMA dans l'exécution de ses missions, 5 September 1940.

19. SHAT Fonds de Moscou, 1K 545 10, rapport de l'Einsatzkommando, SD, Strasbourg, 17 November 1943.

20. AN F^{60} 782, le gouverneur général de l'Algérie à Weygand, n° 3740 E, 20 February 1941; AN F^{60} 782, le préfet, directeur des services de sécurité, à M. l'amiral Esteva, résident général de France à Tunis, n° 9531 S / C, 12 March 1941.

21. For the discussions between Weygand, Darlan, Pétain, Esteva and Abrial on the expansion of the police and the ST between February and September 1941, see AN F^{60} 782.

22. SHAT COI 232, conférence de M. Vassaille, direction des RG, Lyon, 7 October 1942.

23. SHAT Fonds Paillole, 1K 545 / 1, journal de Paul Gérard-Dubot.

24. SHAT Fonds Paillole, 1K 545 1, journal de marche du général Rivet.

25. O. Reile, *L'Abwehr* (Paris: France-Empire, 1970), 80.

26. AN 2^{AG} 597, Maurice Petit, détenu à la maison d'arrêt de Saint-Étienne, à M. le maréchal de France, chef de l'État, 26 April 1942; AN 2^{AG} 597, Jean Grandidier, maison d'arrêt de Saint Etienne, à M. le Maréchal, chef de l'État français, 27 December 1942; AN 2^{AG} 597, le contre-amiral Auphan, secrétaire d'État à la Marine, à M. le général , chef du cabinet militaire du chef de l'État, P.M.3.JP. n° 445, Vichy, 7 May 1942; AN 2^{AG} 597, le capitaine de frégate Archambaud, note pour M. le général, chef du cabinet militaire du chef de l'État, Vichy, 23 October 1942.

27. AN F^{60} 1682, CNI, *Bulletin d'informations générales,* 19 March 1943; AN F7 15306 (SRA 54), note d'information, 6 February 1951.

28. AN 72^{AG} 82, "Résumé de l'action des services de contre-espionnage militaire français de juillet 1940 à novembre 1944," October 1946.

29. J. Abtey and F. Unterberg-Gibhardt, *Deuxième bureau contre Abwehr* (Paris: La Table ronde, 1966), 27–28.

30. SHAT Fonds de Moscou, 269 / 15143, le général Bridoux au juge d'instruction, tribunal militaire d'Oran, 28 September 1942.

31. SHAT 1P 6, CSDN, "Note sur l'organisation de la résistance à l'emprise allemande en zone occupée," 6 July 1940.

32. SHAT Fonds de Moscou, 1095/1415, compte rendu de mission du lieutenant-colonel d'Alès à Marseille, Montpellier et Toulouse, 8 November 1940.

33. SHAT Fonds Paillole, 1K 545 17, conférence Paillole, 3 June 1942 (this document is also available in the box AN 72[AJ] 82)

34. SHAT Fonds Paillole, 1K 545 17, conférence Paillole, 3 June 1942.

35. SHAT Fonds de Moscou, 269/47330, 15e division militaire, renseignement, 19 September 1942; ibid., 29 September 1942.

36. AN F[60] 782, le général Weygand à M. le maréchal de France, 7 December 1940.

37. Ibid.,

38. AN F[60] 782, Baudoin aux ministres des affaires étrangères, de la Guerre, de l'Intérieur, de la Marine et aux secrétaires d'État à l'Aviation et aux Colonies.

39. AN F[60] 782, Peyrouton à Baudoin, 9 February 1941.

40. AN F[60] 782, le secrétaire d'État à l'Aviation (unreadable signature) à Baudoin, 26 December 1940.

41. AN F[60] 782, Huntziger à Pétain, 12 February 1941.

42. AN F[60] 782, Darlan à Baudoin, 26 December 1940.

43. SHAT Fonds de Moscou, 488/81, personel du BMA.

44. SHAT Fonds de Moscou, 269/47321, renseignement recueilli le 17 September 1942.

45. AN AJ[41] 499, le commandant Paillole, chef du SSM, note pour la DSA, n° 000011/SM/B, 2 September 1942.

46. Robert Terres, *Double jeu pour la France, 1939–44,* (Paris: Grasset, 1977) p 40.

47. Pierre Nord, *Mes camarades sont morts,* (Geneva : de Crémille, 1970) Vol II, p 264.

48. Paul Paillole, *Services Spéciaux, 1935–1945,* (Paris: R.Laffont, 1975, p 256.

49. J. Britsch, *Nous n'accepterons pas la défaite (journal 1940–1945)* (Neuilly-sur-Seine: n.d.).

50. AN 3W 91, le Commissaire Principal de la Surveillance du Territoire, Marseille à M Le directeur de la Police de Sûreté, Vichy, n° 4488, 15 November 42.

51. Unpublished memoirs of Louis RIVET, p 7.

CHAPTER 4

1. R. Terres, *Double jeu pour la France* (Paris: Grasset, 1977).

2. Oral account by Paul Paillole, May 2001. See also SHAT 1K 545 20, lettre de Robert Terres au colonel Paillole, 30 April 1974.

3. J. Britsch, *Nous n'accepterons pas la défaite (journal 1940–1945)* (Neuilly-sur-Seine: n.d.), entry of 2 March 1941.

4. SHAT Fonds Paillole, 1K 545 17, conférence Paillole, 3 June 1942 (this document is also accessible in the carton AN 72[AJ] 82).

5. J. Britsch, *Nous n'accepterons pas la défaite (journal 1940–1945)* (Neuilly-sur-Seine: n.d.), entries of 1 January and 6 October 1941.

6. P. J. Stead, *Second Bureau* (London: Evans, 1959), 39.

7. P. Nord, *Mes camarades sont morts* (Geneva: De Crémille, 1970), I, 26.

8. Britsch, *Nous n'accepterons pas la défaite (journal 1940–1945)* (Neuilly-sur-Seine: n.d.), entries of 2 and 5 December 1940 and 26 June 1942.

9. SHAT 3P 102, colonel Louis Baril, "Note pour le commandement: la situation militaire à la fin de 1941, perspectives pour 1942," Vichy, 4 January 1942.

10. SHAT COI 232, conférence de M. Vassaille, direction des RG, Lyon, 7 October 1942, p. 5.

11. AN 3W 104, journal intime du général Bridoux, 14, 15 and 16 July 1942.

12. SHAT Fonds Paillole, 1K 545 10, Tagung der V16 Refereten in Paris, 17,18 July 1943. See also AN 72^{AJ} 82, n.d., réunion des chefs des sections à Paris, 17 and 18 July 1943.

13. SHAT Fonds Paillole, 1K 545 10, rapport de l'Einsatzkommando, SD, Strasbourg, 17 November 1943.

14. For articles from the collaborationist press with criticism of the secret services, see "En traversant les décombres," *Nouveaux temps,* 26 August 1942; Marius Larique, "L'attentisme, nourriture insuffisante," *Le Petit Parisien,* 25 September 1942; Marius Larique, "Voyage autour de ma source," *Le Petit Parisien,* 25 September 1942; "La Trahison," *Le Cri du peuple,* 21 November 1942; René Chateau, "Acculés à la Révolution," *La France Socialiste,* 30 November 1942; Georges Suarez, "La dalle de Mahomet," *Aujourd'hui,* 2 December 1942; Marcel Déat, "La politique de l'armée," *L'Œuvre,* 21 December 1942; Georges Suarez, "Degrés danns la trahison," *Aujourd'hui,* 5 January 1943; Marcel Déat, "Prétendants et comploteurs," *L'Œuvre,* 18 January 1943; Marcel Déat, "Le bolchevism et l'Europe," *L'Œuvre,* 5 February 1943; "Unité de la France," *Nouveaux temps,* 23 February 1943; Jean Marques-Rivière, "Les réactionnaires maçons," *L'Appel,* 15 April 1943.

15. SHAT Fonds de Moscou, 748/131, service de la justice militaire, note pour l'état-major de l'armée (SSM), 3 November 1943.

16. SHAT 3P 102, colonel Louis Baril, "Le conflit germano-russe: ses conséquences et ses incidences sur la conduite de la politique française," 27 June 1941.

17. SHAT 3P 102, colonel Louis Baril, "Note pour le commandement: la situation militaire à la fin de 1941, perspectives pour 1942," Vichy, 4 January 1942.

18. AN 3W 104, journal intime du général Bridoux, 11 April 1942: "Measures have already been taken to orient the Deuxième Bureaus, which, often, have let themselves be guided by their systematic hostility toward Germany, thus biasing the information. There is also something that needs to be done with the SR, which, in the past, was putting all of its resources against Germany and should today also work against England."

19. SHAT 3P 102, secrétariat d'État à la Guerre, Deuxième Bureau, note au sujet de la conservation des archives de campagne des deuxièmes bureaux, no 171/EMA/TS, 17 March 1942. The Secret Services try to keep informed on the weaponry used by the German army: SHAT 1P 135, BCC, synthèse de renseignements, 4 September 1941.

20. SHAT Fonds de Moscou, 761/73, conférence du capitaine Bernard, 9 June 1942.

21. SHAT Fonds de Moscou, 862/2218, BMA à CIG, "Synthèse sur l'activité des services spéciaux anglais et alliés depuis l'armistice," 11 December 1941.

22. SHAT Fonds de Moscou, 715/166, TR, "Note sur l'activité des agents doubles et analyse des questionnaires des SR étrangers," 15 January 1942.

23. SHAT Fonds de Moscou, 784/381, conférence du commandant Paillole, 6 June 1942.

24. AN AJ^{41} 496, lettre interceptée: Asoka Chand, prison militaire de Nontron, à M. l'officier commandant la délégation de la commission d'armistice, Lyon, 14 March 1943.

25. SHAT Fonds de Moscou, 686/14020, TR 115 à BMA, renseignement n° 1244, 21 May 1941, comments pencilled in the report.

26. AN F^{1a} 4539, IGSA (signed J. Carayon), rapport à M. le chef du gouvernement, 10 October 1942.

27. Ibid.

28. Ibid.

29. Ibid.

30. SHAT Fonds de Moscou, 715/166, TR, "Note sur l'activité des agents doubles et analyse des questionnaires des SR étrangers," 15 January 1942.

31. SHAT Fonds Paillole, 1K 545 9, "TR a un an d'existence," rapport de TR, July 1941.

32. SHAT Fonds de Moscou, 464/176, conférence Paillole, 15 April 1942. The monthly BMA bulletins have been studied by F. Delalez, *Le Service des menées antinationales 1940–1942* (Mémoire des écoles de Coëtquidan, 1998), 109–20.

33. R. Terres, *Double jeu pour la France* (Paris: Grasset, 1977), 55.

34. Ibid.

35. For instance, AN 3W 310, le directeur général de la Sûreté nationale (Chavin) à MM. les préfets, 12 October 1940.

36. SHAT 1P 134, le général Huntziger à M. le général commandant supérieur des troupes de Tunisie n° 12.272 C/10, 2 April 1941.

37. SHAT Fonds Paillole, 1K 545 4, déclarations du colonel Paillole, a/s activité clandestine du réseau FFC SSM/TR, transcription d'interview ORTF, 1950.

38. SHAT Fonds Paillole, 1K 545 10, rapport de l'Einsatzkommando, SD, Strasbourg, 17 November 1943.

39. On the rivlary between Vichy Secret Services and the Gaullist SR see S. Laurent, "Renseignement militaire et action politique: le BCRA et les services spéciaux de l'armée de l'armistice," in P. Lacoste, ed., *La Culture française du renseignement* (Paris: Êconomica, 1998), 79–89; S. Laurent, "The Free French Secret Services: Intelligence and the Politics of Republican Legitimacy," *Intelligence and National Security* 15, 4 (2000): 14–41.

40. Public Records Office (PRO), carton no 204/12351/106564, report by the British secret services, October 1942.

41. R. Terres, *Double jeu pour la France* (Paris: Grasset, 1977), 62–63.

42. SHAT Fonds de Moscou, 784/381, conférence du commandant Paillole, 6 June 1942.

43. The author's private archives: colonel Louis Baril, "Note pour le commandement: la situation militaire à la fin de 1941, perspectives pour 1942," Vichy, 4 January 1942. I am grateful to Henry Rousso for providing me with this document. It must be noted that, in a transcription of this same document, probably done after the war, this passage is missing. See SHAT 3P 102.

44. SHAT Fonds de Moscou, 784/381, conférence du commandant Paillole, 6 June 1942.

45. Ibid.

46. Ibid.

47. SHAT Fonds de Moscou, 761/73, conférence du capitaine Bernard, 9 June 1942.

48. Ibid.

49. *Liberté,* no 6, 30 May 1941.

50. SHAT Fonds de Moscou, 761/73, conférence du capitaine Bernard, 9 June 1942.

51. SHAT Fonds Paillole, 1K 545 16, conférence du commandant Paillole, 3 June 1942.

52. Ibid.

53. AN 72AJ 82, Général Louis Rivet, "Défense du SR français: réplique à un chapitre du volume *D'Alger à Paris,* de Monsieur Jacques Soutelle," pamphlet written in Paris in December 1951.

54. S. Laurent, "The Free French Secret Services: Intelligence and the Politics of Republican Legitimacy," *Intelligence and National Security* 15, 4 (2000): 19–41; S. Laurent, "Les services secrets gaullistes à l'épreuve de la politique (1940–1947)," *Politix. Revue des sciences sociales du politique* 14, 54 (2001): 139–53.

55. SHAT Fonds de Moscou, 761/73, conférence du capitaine Bernard, 9 June 1942.

56. H. Navarre, *Le Temps des vérités* (Paris: Plon, 1979), 116.

57. M. Garder, *La Guerre secrète des services spéciaux français* (Paris: Plon, 1967), 227.

58. SHAT Fonds Paillole, 1K 1.

59. R. Terres, *Double jeu pour la France* (Paris: Grasset, 1977), 62.

60. J. Britsch, *Nous n'accepterons pas la défaite (journal 1940–1945)* (Neuilly-sur-Seine, n.d.), entry of 24 September 1940.

61. SHAT Fonds de Moscou, 761/73, conférence du capitaine Bernard, 9 June 1942.

62. M. Garder, *La Guerre secrète des services spéciaux français* (Paris: Plon, 1967), 248.

63. J. Britsch, *Nous n'accepterons pas la défaite (journal 1940–1945)* (Neuilly-sur-Seine, n.d.), entries of 10 June and 7 September 1941.

64. AN 72[AJ] 46, témoignage d'Henry Frenay, 1948.

65. AN 72^{AJ} 1912, témoignage de Roger Warin, dit Olivier-Ronald-Wybot, 1947. P. Bernert, *Roger Wybot et la bataille pour la DST* (Paris: Presses de la Cité, 1975), 27.

66. J. Soustelle, *Envers et contre tout* (Paris: Laffont, 1970), I, 279.

67. SHAT Fonds de Moscou, 761/73, conférence du capitaine Bernard, 9 June 1942.

68. SHAT 3P 102, colonel Louis Baril, "Note pour le commandement: la situation militaire à la fin de 1941, perspectives pour 1942," Vichy, 4 January 1942.

69. SHAT Fonds de Moscou, 784/381, conférence du commandant Paillole, 6 June 1942.

70. Ibid.

71. J. Britsch, *Nous n'accepterons pas la défaite (journal 1940–1945)* (Neuilly-sur-Seine, n.d.), entry of 9 December 1941.

72. C.-L. Flavian, *Ils furent des hommes* (Paris: 1948), 103.

73. SHAT Fonds de Moscou, 761/73, conférence du capitaine Bernard, 9 June 1942.

74. M. Biney, *The Women Who Lived for Danger* (London: Hodder and Stoughton, 2002), 122.

75. SHAT Fonds de Moscou, 761/73, conférence du capitaine Bernard, 9 June 1942.

76. AN 3W 104, journal intime du général Bridoux, entry of 25 August 1942.

77. B. Sheppard, *Missions secrètes et déportation, 1939–1945* (Paris: Hemidal,1998), 246, 255–57. AN F^{60} 522, le procureur à Lyon à M. le procureur général, 20 January 1943; AN F^{60} 522, M. le ministre secrétaire d'État à la Justice à M. le chef du gouvernement, 1 February 1943.

78. AN F^{1A} 4565, IGSA (signed Jean Ginolhac), rapport à M. le secrétaire d'État à l'Intérieur, Vichy, 14 August 1942. On Fourcaud, see also AN 72^{AJ} 1912, le préfet Rollin, directeur général adjoint, au secrétaire général pour la police, n° 99 Pol. Dir. Gén. Adj., 11 December 1941.

79. M.-M. Fourcade, *L'Arche de Noé* (Paris: Plon, 1989), 264.

80. D. Caskie, *Le Chardon d'Écosse: un pasteur écossais dans la Résistance, 1940–1944* (Lausanne, 1969), 164.

81. M. Binney, *The Women Who Lived for Danger* (London: Hodder and Stoughton, 2002), 123.

82. SHAT Fonds Paillole, 1K 545 16, conférence du commandant Paillole, 3 June 1942.

83. AN 72^{AJ} 82, résumé de l'action des services de CE militaire français de juillet 1940 à novembre 1944, vol. I: juillet 1940 à avril 1942, October 1946.

84. R. Terres, *Double jeu pour la France* (Paris: Grasset, 1977), 112.

85. SHAT Fonds de Moscou, 686/14020, rapport de l'inspecteur Jean Calen, n° 157-I, 12 Ocotber 1941.

86. SHAT Fonds Paillole, 1K 545 4, déclaration du colonel Paillole, a/s activité clandestine du réseau FFC SSM/TR, transcription d'interview ORTF, 1950.

87. Colonel Passy, *Mémoires du chef des services secrets de la France libre* (Paris: Odile Jacob, 2000), 679.

88. SHAT Fonds de Moscou, 688/14394, TR 120, note pour 6 000, 14 October 1941.

89. SHAT Fonds de Moscou, 269/15137, TR, note pour SSM, n° 8 429, 2 November 1942.

90. P. Paillole, *Services spéciaux, 1935–1945* (Paris: Laffont, 1975), 234.

91. SHAT Fonds de Moscou, 784/381, conférence du commandant Paillole, 6 June 1942.

92. SHAT Fonds de Moscou, 464/176, conférence du commandant Paillole, 15 April 1942.

93. H. Navarre, *Le Temps des vérités* (Paris: Plon, 1979), 79.

94. SHAT Fonds Paillole, 1K 545 10, rapport du lieutenant-colonel Schlesser, retour de mission TR en zone occupée, 28 July 1940.

95. SHAT Fonds Paillole, 1K 545 9, "TR a un an d'existence," rapport de TR, July 1941.

96. For Pétain's speeches see: J.-C. Barbas, *Philippe Pétain: discours aux Français* (Paris: Albin Michel, 1989).

97. H. Navarre, *Le Service de renseignements, 1871–1944* (Paris: Plon, 1978), 134.

98. P. Paillole, *L'Homme des services secrets* (Paris: Julliard, 1995), 176, 189.

99. AN 72[AJ] 82, Mémoires inédits du colonel Louis Rivet, n.d.

100. SHAT Fonds de Moscou, 398/252, compte rendu, n° 6 804, 26 May 1942.

101. J. Britsch, *Nous n'accepterons pas la défaite (journal 1940–1945),* (Neuilly-sur-Seine, n.d.), entry of 9 May 1941.

102. Ibid., entry of 13 August 1941.

103. PRO FO 660 149, Office of the British Representative with French Committee of National Liberation, Algiers, 19 January 1944.

104. AN 72AJ 82, Général Louis Rivet, "Défense du SR français: réplique à un chapitre du volume *D'Alger à Paris,* de Monsieur Jacques Soutelle," pamphlet written in Paris in December 1951.

CHAPTER 5

1. SHAT Fonds Paillole, 1K 545 10, rapport du lieutenant-colonel Schlesser, retour de mission TR en zone occupée, 28 July 1940.

2. SHAT 1P 200, DDSA à Weygand, n° 1 153, 15 February 1941.

3. SHAT Fonds de Moscou, 466/327, synthèse de l'activité du SRA en France, 30 March 1941.

4. SHAT Fonds de Moscou, 464/176, conférence du commandant Paillole, 15 April 1942.

5. SHAT Fonds de Moscou, 961/1411, lieutenant-colonel d'Alès, "Formule de déclaration aux termes de laquelle les hommes de troupe reconnaissent avoir reçu l'instruction en matière de CE," 28 April 1941; SHAT Fonds de Moscou, 961/1411, chef de bureau de la 17e division militaire, 6 May 1941.

6. SHAT 3P 102, directive pour servir à l'instruction des officiers MA des régiments, 14 February 1941.

7. SHAT 1P 60, note de service du colonel Schneider, commandant la subdivision militaire de Périgueux, n° 354 A/Org, 21 October 1943.

8. SHAT Fonds de Moscou, 761/58, vice-président du Conseil, "Instruction concernant le secret des pièces, documents, correspondances et la manière d'établir et de transmettre des pièces," 22 December 1941.

9. SHAT Fonds de Moscou, 105/2169, note de service sur l'instruction MA, 11 July 1942.

10. SHAT 1P 89, le général Weygand au maréchal Pétain, n° 1175/EM/2, 3 March 1941.

11. SHAT 3P 102, Darlan aux secrétaires d'État à l'Intérieur et à la Guerre, n° 812/SG, 5 July 1941. A copy of the same letter is appended to the following letter: AN AJ^{41} 1562, le général de Saint-Vincent, gouverneur militaire de Lyon, commandant la 14e division militaire, à M. le préfet du Rhône, Lyon, 24 November 1941.

12. Supplementary instructions provided by the general Louis Koeltz, director of the armistice services, provided a reminder that this policy was also aimed at limiting contact between the population and the Axis delegations in the southern zone to prevent individuals from transmitting information and participating in the black market. Police assigned to the German or Italian delegations were charged with not only protecting them against attacks but also putting comings and goings under surveillance. The identity of individuals contacting these services was noted. They became the object of police investigation, and in some cases they were even arrested. This opened up possibilities for counterespionage agencies.

13. AN F^{1a} 4681, le général Huntziger à M. le ministre secrétaire d'État à l'Intérieur, 23 August 1941; AN F^{1a} 4680, le général Huntziger à l'amiral Darlan, 26 September 1941; AN F^{1a} 4681, le général Huntziger à M. le ministre secrétaire d'État à l'Intérieur, 2 October 1941, "Object: rapports directs entre le public français et les autorités allemandes."

14. SHAT 1P 135, le chef de bataillon Bourgeois au chef de la DDSA, Algiers, 10 February 1041.

15. SHAT 1P 89, le général Weygand à l'amiral Darlan, 15 November 1941 (appendix).

16. AN AJ^{41} 1680 [21–06], le préfet des Hautes-Alpes à M. le ministre secrétaire d'État à l'Intérieur, 9 December 1940.

17. AN AJ^{41} 750, le procureur gènèral près la cour d'appel d'Aix à M. le garde des Sceaux, 6 October 1941.

18. SHAT 1P 78, commission italienne d'armistice (présidence), Turin, 25 January 1941; AN F^{1a} 4685, l'amiral Duplat, président de la délégation française à la commission italienne d'armistice, à M. le ministre de l'Intérieur, 8 February 1941.

19. SHAT 5P 2, rapport du colonel Gross sur l'activité d'ensemble des commissions d'armistice, n° 112/A Cab, Alger, 19 April 1943.

20. SHAT 1P 89, le général Weygand à l'amiral Darlan, 15 November 1941 (appendix).

21. AN F[1C] III 1143, rapport du préfet des Bouches-du-Rhône, January 1942.

22. SHAT 3P 102, Darlan aux secrétaires d'État à l'Intérieur et à la Guerre, no 812/SG, 5 July 1941. A copy of this same letter is appended to the following letter: AN AJ[41] 1562, le général de Saint-Vincent, gouverneur militaire de Lyon, commandant la 14e division militaire à M. le préfet du Rhône, Lyon, 24 November 1941.

23. P. Nord, *Mes camarades sont morts* (Geneva: de Crémille, 1970), II, 28, 28–29.

24. AN F[la] 4681, le vice-amiral Moreau, délégué de l'amirauté à Marseille, à M. le préfet des Bouches-du-Rhône, 15 September 1941.

25. AN AJ 41 499, Commission de contrôle en Afrique, signé REICHEL, à M. le colonel Brossin de Saint Didier, chef de la délégation de la Direction des Services de l'Armistice en Afrique du Nord, Alger, 10 May 1942.

26. AN F[la] 4681, le général Studt à M. le général Koeltz (DSA), 18 August 1941.

27. Cited in R. Richard and A. de Sérigny, *La Bissectrice de la guerre* (Algiers: La Maison des Livres, 1945), 211–212.

28. See Sarah Fishman's excellent book, *We Will Wait* (New Haven, 1991).

29. AN AJ[41] 750, rapport de l'inspecteur de police spéciale Cape à M. le commissaire spécial, chef de service à Agen, 27 August 1940.

30. SHAT 1P 135, état-major des troupes du Maroc, synthèse d'ensemble pour la période du 16 juillet au 15 août 1941, Casablanca, 15 August 1941.

31. SHAT 1P 200, synthèse des faits signalés durant la semaine du 14 au 20 octobre inclus au sujet de l'activité extraconventionelle des délégations d'armistice, Tunis, 22 October 1940; SHAT 1P 200, note du chef de BMA à Oran, n° 3 MA/B, 25 January 1941; AN AJ[41] 750, rapport de l'inspecteur de police spéciale Cape à M. le commissaire spécial, chef de service à Agen, 27 August 1940; AN AJ[41] 491, L'aspirant Masurel, faisant fonction d'officier de liaison près du délégué de la Croix-Rouge allemande à Pau, à M. le chef de bataillon, chef de la délégation française de liaison, n° 3/RKG, 18 February 1941; AN AJ[41] 750, commandement militaire du département des Pyrénées-Orientales, n° 5005 S/2, "Rapport a/s d'un incident entre membres d'une commission allemande et inspecteurs de la Sûreté."

32. It would appear that Renée Blanc's incarceration was due to her liaison with a German soldier in the Lyon area: AN 2[AG] 596, Mlle Renée Blanc, Lyon, à M. le Maréchal, 13 September 1942.

33. SHAT 1P 135, note du deuxième bureau, Algiers, 26 August 1941.

34. SHAT 1P 135, le lieutenant-colonel Kientz à M. le général d'armée, résident général de France au Maroc, 4 September 1941.

35. SHAT 1P 135, le général Weygand au secrétaire d'État à la Guerre, no 5652/EM-2, July 1941.

36. SHAT 1P 89, déposition du général de brigade de Perier des troupes coloniales.

37. SHAT 1P 200, BMA, rapport sur l'activité italienne en Algérie au cours du mois d'octobre 1941, 3 November 1941.

38. H. Navarre, *Le Temps des vérités* (Paris: Plon, 1979), 99; R. Terres, *Double jeu pour la France* (Paris: Gasset,1977), 113–14. AN 72^{AJ} 82, "Résumé de l'action des services de contre-espionnage militaire français de juillet 1940 à novembre 1944," I, 17 (this document was written by Paillole in 1946).

39. SHAT 5P 2, rapport du colonel Gross sur l'activité d'ensemble des commissions d'armistice, Algiers, 19 April 1943.

40. SHAT 1P 135, analyse de l'exposé du général Schultheiss, 17 September 1941.

41. SHAT 1P 199, procès-verbal de l'entretien en date du 29 septembre 1941 entre le général Béthouart et le général Schultheiss, Casablanca, 30 September 1941.

42. The best work on the punitive shaving of women is the excellent book by Fabrice Virgili, *La France virile* (Paris: Payot, 2000).

43. SHAT 1P 200, le capitaine Chanzy, chef du détachement de liaison auprès de la section italienne de contrôle de Constantine, à M. le chef d'escadron, chef des détachements de liaison de la 19e région, Algiers, Constantine, 20 December 1941.

44. SHAT 1P 135, le général Vergez au général Weygand, 24 March 1941.

45. SHAT 1P 135, note du BMA (signed Yves), 2 December 1941.

46. SHAT 1P 135, ministère de la Défense nationale, DSA, mémento à l'usage des officiers de liaison détachés auprès des commissions allemandes et italiennes de contrôle, 5 February 1942.

47. Ibid.

48. AN AJ^{41} 491, le capitaine Seignobos, officier de liaison, Lyon, à M. le chef du gouvernement, DSA, n° 552/D, 21 September 1942; AN F^{1a} 4680, le ministre de la Guerre (DSA) à M. l'amiral de la flotte, secrétaire d'État à l'Intérieur, 25 April 1941, "Object: extrait des comptes rendus n° 224/RKG en date du 15 avril et 245 RKG en date du 21 avril de l'officier français de liaison à Pau, au sujet de l'activité de ce délégué;" AN AJ^{41} 491, sous-commission de contrôle de Pau, compte rendu hebdomadaire de l'officier de liaison, 1 July 1941; AN AJ^{41} 491, compte rendu du capitaine Berger, officier de liaison à Montpellier, 16 January 1942.

49. AN F^{1a} 4680, le ministre de la Guerre (DSA) à M. l'amiral de la flotte, secrétaire d'État à l'Intérieur, 25 April 1941, "Object: extrait des comptes rendus n° 224/RKG en date du 15 avril et 245 RKG en date du 21 avril de l'officier français de liaison auprès de la Croix-Rouge allemande de Pau, au sujet de l'activité de ce délégué."

50. AN AJ^{41} 491, compte rendu hebdomadaire officier de liaison à Pau, n° 382/RKG, 26 May 1941.

51. AN AJ^{41} 491, le général Koeltz à M. le secrétaire général aux Anciens Combattants, 27 June 1941.

52. AN AJ^{41} 491, 17e division militaire, sous-commission de contrôle de Pau, officier de liaison près du délégué au rapatriement de la commission allemande d'armistice de Pau, n° 138/RKG, Pau, 24 March 1941.

53. H. Navarre, *Le Service de renseignements, 1871–1944* (Paris: Plon, 1978), 68. AN 72[aj] 82, "Résumé de l'action de services de contre-espionnage militaire français de juillet 1940 à novembre 1944," vol. I, 1946.

54. SHAT 1P 135, DSA, note pour la délégation française à Wiesbaden, n° 3.581/DSA/6, 29 September 1942, "Object: écoutes clandestines dans les bureaus des délégations de contrôle (note allemande n° 560/42 du 8/9/42)."

55. AN 3W 104, journal intime du général Bridoux, 5 November 1942.

56. A. Lefébure, *Les Conversations secrètes des Français sous l'Occupation* (Paris: Plon, 1993), 137.

57. AN AJ[41] 499, service civil des contrôles techniques, note de service, Vichy, 14 August 1941.

58. SHAT 1P 135, état-major des troupes au Maroc, BCC, extraits d'écoutes téléphoniques du 6 octobre 1941.

59. AN 2[AG] 524, rapport au sujet de la condamnation à mort du nommé Robert Bellette.

60. R. Austin, "Surveillance and Intelligence under the Vichy Regime: The Service du contrôle technique, 1939–1945," *Intelligence and National Security* 1, 1 (1986): 123–37.

61. AN AJ[41] 491, compte rendu hebdomadaire du capitaine Bruce, officier de liaison auprès du délégué allemand au rapatriement, Marseille, 1 Sepember 1941; AN AJ[41] 491, compte rendu hebdomadaire du capitaine Bruce, officier de liaison auprès du délégué allemand au rapatriement, Marseille, 10 September 1941.

62. AN 72[AJ] 1911, "Note Rollin sure le fonctionnement du SR de la SN," 2 May 1941.

63. SHAT Fonds de Moscou, 715/166, TR, "note sur l'activité des agents doubles et analyse des questionnaires des SR érangers," 15 January 1942.

64. AN F[7] 15279, le commissaire principal de police spéciale à M. l'inspecteur général des services des RG, 21 July 1941.

65. SHAT 1P 89, synthèse mensuelle des contrôles télégraphiques, téléphoniques et postaux du 10 juillet au 10 août 1942, "Renseignements sur les activités antinationales sous toutes leurs formes;" SHAT Fonds de Moscou, 480/1730, "Liens existant entre le PPF et le SRA"; SHAT Fonds de Moscou, 1066/1729, renseignements sur le PPF et ses membres, activités du PPF en Afrique du Nord (juillet 1939–octobre 1942); SHAT Fonds de Moscou, 665/15024, dossier sur Michel Signe (PPF), chargé d'espionner pour les services allemands en zone libre (juin–juillet 1942); SHAT Fonds Paillole, 1K545 10, rapport de l'Einsatzkommando, SD, Strasbourg, 17 November 1943; AN F[7] 15279, le commandant Seignard, chef des services de police spéciale, à M. l'inspecteur général des services des RG, 28 June 1941; AN F[7] 15279, RG, "Renseignements sur le PPF," 9 January 1943.

66. SHAT Fonds de Moscou, 269/15154, SSM, renseignement, 25 September 1942.

67. SHAT 1P 200, DDSA à Weygand, "Note sur la propagande germanophile en Algérie," 15 February 1941; SHAT 1P 200, l'inspecteur de police spéciale

Martin à M. le commissaire spècial, 19 July 1941; SHAT 1P 200, état-major de l'armée, cinquième bureau, note de renseignements, "La propagande allemande auprès des prisonniers nord-africains," 21 July 1941; SHAT 1P 200, note de renseignements, "La propagande allemande auprès des prisonniers nord-africains," 23 August 1941; SHAT 1P 200, section des affaires musulmanes, note de renseignements, "La propagande allemande auprès des prisonniers indigènes nord-africains," 6 September 1941.

68. SHAT 1P 200, état-major de l'armée, note de renseignements, "La propagande allemande auprès des prisonniers nord-africains," 21 July 1941.

69. SHAT 1P 200, état-major de l'armée, note de renseignements, "La propagande allemande auprès des prisonniers nord-africains," 23 August 1941 and 6 September 1941.

70. SHAT 1P 200, ministre de la Défense à la DDSA, Algiers, 21 January 1942.

71. On the demarcation line, see Éric Alary's excellent book: *La Ligne de démarcation* (Paris: Perrin, 2003).

72. SHAT Fonds de Moscou, 464/176, conférence du commandant Paillole, 15 April 1942.

73. SHAT 3P 118, compte rendu de la mission effectuée du 20 au 24 janvier 1941 dans les 9e et 12e divisions militaires par le capitaine Mesnet et le capitaine Fouqualt de l'état-major de l'armée.

74. SHAT Fonds de Moscou, 464/176, conférence du commandant Paillole, 15 April 1942; P. Paillole, *L'Homme des services secrets* (Paris: Julliard, 1995), 88–90; O. Reile, *L'Abwehr* (Paris: France-Empire, 1970), 91.

75. AN AJ41 499, rapport de l'inspection générale des services de ST, Vichy, 2 December 1940.

76. SHAT Fonds de Moscou, 784/381, conférence du commandant Paillole, 6 June 1942.

77. AN AJ41 499, lieutenant Heyl, officier de liaison, au BMA, Bourg-en-Bresse, 6 December 1941; AN AJ41 499, commission allemande d'armistice à M. le président de la délégation française d'armistice à Wiesbaden, n° 90/42, 16 February 1942.

78. AN AJ41 499, DSA, Vichy (signed Bourget), note pour la délégation française d'armistice à Wiesbaden, n° 21778/DSA/7, 9 July 1941.

79. For a questionnaire example, see AN F7 15306, contrôle général des services de ST, Vichy, 6 March 1942, "Object: arrestation de Lacour, Paul, agent du SRA."

80. AN BB24 2381, secrétariat d'État à la Guerre, rapport pour M. le Maréchal, chef de l'État français, 2 September 1941; AN 2AG 524, condamnation à mort des nommés Georges Bresson et Alfred Chaudron.

81. AN BB24 2381, secrétariat d'État à la Guerre, rapport pour M. le Maréchal, chef de l'État français, 2 September 1941; AN 2AG 524, condamnation à mort des indigènes musulmans Belhadj Mebarek ben Seghir et Benabid Khier ben Mohamed.

82. AN AJ41 499, lettre interceptée: M. Jean-Georges Knipper à Soumoulou (BP) à M. Lutz, hôtel Régina, Toulouse, date du document intercepté: 25 avril

1942, date de l'interception: 1 mai 1942. Albert Glaesner was indiscrete in a similar manner: AN AJ[41] 499, secrétariat d'État à la Guerre, cabinet, BMA (signed d'Alès), note pour la DSA, n° 3478/MA/M, 16 May 1942.

83. AN AJ[41] 491, l'aspirant Masurel, officier de liaison, Pau, à M. le chef de la délégation française de liaison, 18 February 1941.

84. SHAT Fonds de Moscou, 761/73, conférence du capitaine Bernard, 9 June 1942.

85. AN AJ[41] 499, note de renseignements, n° MA/M/1168/1-B, 9 June 1941; AN AJ[41] 499, le commandant Paillole, chef du SSM, note pour la DSA, n° 000011/SM/B, 2 September 1942; AN AJ[41] 499, extrait du compte rendu de l'officier de liaison à Lyon, n° 714/D, Lyon, 5 December 1942.

86. AN AJ[41] 499, le procureur général, Limoges à M. le garde des Sceaux, 1 February 1943.

87. AN AJ[41] 499, le capitaine de Bruce, en liaison près le délégué allemand au rapatriement, Marseille, à M. le général, secrétaire d'État à la Guerre, DSA, 17 May 1942.

88. AN AJ[41] 499, DSA, Vichy, n° 23.346/DSA/11, 23 July 1941.

89. M. Binney, *The Women Who Lived for Danger* (London: Hodder and Stoughton, 2002), 121–22.

90. AN AJ[41] 499, secrétariat d'État à la Guerre, cabinet, BMA, note pour la DSA, n° 7042/MA/M, 28 November 1941. For more information on Sommann, see SHAT Fonds de Moscou, 667/14513, dossier Sommann.

91. AN 2[AG] 618, lettre anonyme envoyée au maréchal Pétain par un "Français 100%" de Marseille, April 1941.

92. AN 72AJ 1912, Note de la Direction Générale de la Sûreté Nationale (signé J. Bernhardt), Châteauroux, 19 May 1942.

93. AN F[la] 4682, l'inspecteur principal de police spéciale Hansler à M. le commissaire spécial, Avignon, n° 1327, 19 March 1941.

94. SHAT Fonds de Moscou, 1249/13922, dossier sur Guillaume Le Cunff arrêté et condamné pour espionnage au profit de l'Allemagne (April–May 1941); AN 2[AG] 524, Guillaume Le Cunff à frère Paul Aune, Marseille, 28 August 1941; AN 2[AG] 524, condamnation à mort du nommé Le Cunff.

95. AN 2[AG] 524, condamnation à mort du nommé Alfredo Castoldi; BB[24] 2381, secrétariat d'État à la Guerre, rapport à M. le maréchal, 20 October 1941; SHAT Fonds de Moscou, 1195/13835, dossier sur Alfredo Castoldi, condamné à Meknès pour espionnage (1941).

96. SHAT 1P 134, la délégation générale du gouvernement en Afrique française (troupes Maroc) à M. le général délégué général en Afrique française, télégramme, n° 300 J/IS, 3 November 1941.

97. For all the diplomatic repercussions of the Masson affair, see the Masson file in the carton AN AJ[41] 1677b. See also: AN AJ[41] 499, commission allemande d'armistice à M. le président de la délégation française d'armistice à Wiesbaden, n° 90/42, 16 February 1942; AN AJ[41] 499, le lieutenant Heyl, officier de liaison, au

BMA, Bourg-en-Bresse, 6 December 1941; SHAT Fonds de Moscou, 1319/1665, dossier Masson.

98. AN AJ^{41} 496, renseignements sur sept détenus allemands, considérés comme ne devant pas être remis, transmis le 14 août à l'amiral Bourragué pour communication à l'amiral Darlan; AN AJ^{41} 499, de Royere, officier de liaison Lyon, à M. l'amiral de la flotte, ministre de la Défense nationale, DSA, n° 21/D, 8 January 1942; AN AJ^{41} 499, général Vogt, président de la CAA, à M. le général Beynet, président de la délégation française auprès de la CAA, n° VAA/R/1236, Wiesbaden, 2 February 1942, See also the Wagner file in the carton AN AJ^{41} 1677b.

99. AN BB^{30} 1709, rapport sur la condamnation de Xavier Battini.

100. AN AJ^{41} 491, rapport hebdomadaire n° 64 du chef d'escadron d'Amecourt, officier de liaison, Clermont-Ferrand, 30 March 1942.

101. AN AJ^{41} 499, rapport du commissaire principal de la ST, Marseille, 28 August 1942; AN AJ^{41} 499, commissaire Robert Blémant à la ST, n° 145, 9 September 1941; SHAT Fonds de Moscou, 666/14244, poursuites contre le ressortissant allemand Ramstetter (November 1940–March 1942).

CHAPTER 6

1. SHAT Fonds de Moscou, 464/176, conférence du commandant Paillole, 15 April 1942.

2. SHAT 1P 89, Weygand à Pétain, n° 1175/EM/2, 3 March 1941.

3. AN AJ^{41} 499, le capitaine Amann, officier de liaison à Royat, à M. le vice-amiral, DSA, 22 August 1942; SHAT Fonds de Moscou, 691/10355, dossier concernant Gebus, espion à la solde de l'Allemagne (August 1936–March 1942).

4. AD BDR (archives départementales des Bouches-du-Rhône) M^6 10988, le commissaire de police de sûreté, note au sujet du chef du service des affaires indigènes à Marseille, Pol. Sûr. 7/R, 20 January 1943.

5. SHAT Fonds de Moscou, 464/176, conférence du commandant Paillole, 15 April 1942.

6. H. Navarre, *Le Temps des vérités* (Paris: Plon, 1979), 95–96.

7. T. Guillet, *Le Renseignement français au Maroc, 1940–1942* (mémoire, Saint-Cyr, 1998).

8. SHAT Fonds de Moscou, 821/10655, renseignement du BMA 19, 10 April 1941.

9. H. Coutrau-Bégarie and C. Huan, *Lettres et notes de l'amiral Darlan* (Paris: Économica, 1992), 388, letter of 24 July 1941.

10. SHAT Fonds de Moscou, 821/10655, TR 120, renseignements: "conversations de militaires de la CAA," n° 629, 18 August 1941.

11. SHAT Fonds de Moscou, 821/10655, le préfet de police à M. le ministre de la Guerre, "au sujet du nommé Auer, secrétaire à l'ambassade d'Allemagne," 17 April 1935; SHAT Fonds de Moscou, 821/10655, SCR, renseignement, 21 October 1937; SHAT Fonds de Moscou, 821/10655, MA 30, renseignement, 21 December 1940; SHAT Fonds de Moscou, 821/10655, renseignment du BMA, 15,

16 June 1941; SHAT Fonds de Moscou, 821/10655, TR 120, renseignement, n° 1015, 6 November 1941; SHAT Fonds de Moscou, 821/10655, TR 120, renseignement, "Opinion d'Auer sur la situation," n° 1068, 20 November 1941; SHAT Fonds de Moscou, 821/10655, TR 119, renseignement, n° 826, "Objet: vice-consul allemand Schwarzmann," 28 February 1942.

12. P. Nord, *Mes camarades sont morts* (Geneva: de Crémille, 1970), I, 40.

13. P. Paillole, *Services spéciaux,* 1935–1945 (Pairs: Laffont, 1975), 579 (appendix).

14. SHAT Fonds Paillole, 1K 545 10, le chef et liquidateur national—réseau FFC SSM/TR, bilan des affaires d'espionnage et de propagande ennemis (allemands, italiens, japonais) soumises par le contre-espionage à la justice militaire de 1940 à 1942.

15. AN F[60] 393, Huntziger à Darlan, 10 June 1941, "Object: activité de services de renseignements allemands."

16. SHAT Fonds Paillole, 1K 545 10, TR, rapport pour le deuxième bureau de l'état-major: Tableau nominatif des arrestations.

17. Numbers provided by F. Delalez, *Le Service des menées antinationales 1940–1942* (mémoires des écoles de Coëtquidan, 1988), 78–89. Delalez compiled his figures on the basis of the BMA monthly bulletins in the cartons SHAT Fonds de Moscou, 441/118 and 504/1462.

18. AN 3W 91, le commissaire principal de la ST, Marseille, à M. le directeur de la police de sûreté, n° 4488, 15 November 1942. Flavian, a former member of the Resistance, estimates that the Toulon police arrested fifty German spies during this period: C.-L. Flavian, *Ils furent des hommes* (Paris: NEL, 1948), 103.

19. M. Chalet, "La DST, service français de contre-espionnage," in P. Lacoste, ed., *Approches françaises du renseignement* (Paris: FED, 1997), 59.

20. R. Faligot and P. Krop, *DST: police secrète* (Paris: Flammarion, 1999), 65.

21. AN AJ[41] 499, lettre interceptée: Madeleine Fuchy, prison Saint-Joseph, Lyon, à M. le président de la commission allemande d'armistice, 25 July 1943.

22. Philip John Stead, *Second Bureau* (London: Evans Brothers 1959), 46.

23. AN AJ 41 499, Le garde des Sceaux, Ministre secrétaire d'état à la justice à M. le chef du gouvernement Direction des Services de l'Armistice, Hôtel Thermal, Vichy, n° SS. Aix, 10 June 1943.

24. AN AJ41 498, Le Colonel Gross à M. le Ministre de la Défense Nationale, n° 12473/DDSA/B, 4 December 1941.

25. AN AJ[41] 499, le capitaine de Bruce, en liaison près le délégué allemand au rapatriement, à M. le général de l'armée, ministre secrétaire d'État à la Guerre, DSA, n° 92, Marseille, 9 October 1941, "Objet: visite du délégué à la prison Présentine;" AD BDR M[6] 10990, plainte de Fernand de Brinon concernant Pierre Hervaud.

26. AN AJ[41] 499, commission allemande d'armistice à M. le président de la délégation française d'armistice à Wiesbaden, n° 90/42, 16 February 1942.

27. AN AJ[41] 491, le délégué allemand (Lutz) à M. le capitaine Pouraill, chef du détachement auprès de la Croix-Rouge allemande à Toulouse, n° 421/42,

19 March 1942: "Objet: mauvais traitement et arrestation des personnes qui viennent me rendre visite."

28. SHAT Fonds de Moscou, 398/252, renseignements recueillis au cours des entretiens de M. von Kirschten avec les Allemands du Reich et de race détenus pour espionnage dans les prisons civile et militaire d'Alger, 16 September 1941.

29. AN AJ[41] 496, lettre interceptée: Chand, prison militaire de Nontron, Dordogne, à M. L'officier commandant la délégation de la commission d'armistice à Royat, 1 April 1943.

30. AN AJ[41] 499, traduction d'une note de l'ambassade d'Allemagne Rück 3616, 13 June 1942.

31. AN AJ41 491, capitaine de Bruce, officier de liaison auprès du Délégué Allemand au Rapatriement, à M. l'amiral de la flotte, ministre de la défense nationale, DSA, Vichy, n° 317, Marseille, 28 February 1942.

32. AN BB[30] 1709, rapport sur Edouard Buch.

33. AN BB[24] 2381, Darlan à Pétain, 20 November 1941.

34. SHAT Fonds de Moscou, 821/10655, TR 120, n° 198, renseignement, confidences du Dr Auer, 26 February 1942.

35. AN 72[AJ] 46 ("Combat"), témoignage de J. Gemähling recueilli par Mlle Patrimonio, December 1945.

36. P. Paillole, *Services spéciaux, 1935–1945* (Paris: Laffont, 1975), 243.

37. R. Terres, *Double jeu pour la France* (Paris: Grasset, 1977), 115–17.

38. Georges N'guyen Van Loc, *La peau d'un caïd* (Paris: Presses de la cite, 1994); Jean Bazal, *Le Marseillais* (Paris: Hermé, 1991); Loup Durand, *Le Caïd* (Paris: Denoel, 1976).

39. At Liberation, Blémant left the police to become an important figure in the local underworld. He was shot dead in 1967 on the orders of his one time associate Antoine Guérini, one of the most famous gangsters of the postwar period. Pascale Froment, *René Bousquet* (Paris: Stock, 1994), 312–13; Philippe Bernert, *Roger Wybot et la bataille pour la DST* (Paris: Presses de la Cité, 1975), 27–36.

40. M. Bischoff, *La Police scientifique* (Paris: Payoy, 1938), 4.

41. AN BB[18] 3326, procureur général, cour d'Aix, à M. le garde des Sceaux, 9 March 1942.

42. AN AJ 41 491, capitaine de Bruce, officier de liaison auprès du Délégué Allemand au Rapatriement, à M. l'amiral de la flotte, ministre de la défense nationale, DSA, Vichy, n° 317, Marseille, 28 February1942.

43. AN AJ[41] 499, le garde des Sceaux à M. l'amiral de la flotte, ministre de la défence nationale, n° 2005/G/3/A2A, 3 January 1942.

44. AN AJ 41 498, Hans Goepel au Délégué Allemand au Rapatriement, Alger, n.d.

45. AN AJ[41] 499, compte rendu de l'officier de liaison sur la visite de M. Klaube à Alscher et Gassner, 24 November 1941.

46. AN AJ[41] 499, lettre interceptée: Floria Richelmi, prison Saint-Joseph, Lyon, à M. le président de la commission allemande d'armistice, 25 July 1943.

47. AN AJ41 491, capitaine de Bruce, officier de liaison auprès du Délégué Allemand au Rapatriement, à M. l'amiral de la flotte, ministre de la défense nationale, DSA, Vichy, n° 317, Marseille, 28 February 1942.

48. AN AJ[41] 499, note DSA à M. le secrétaire d'État à la Guerre, état-major de l'armée section armistice, 7 April 1942.

49. AN AJ[41] 499, le garde des Sceaux à l'amiral de la flotte, 3 January 1942.

50. SHAT Fonds de Moscou, 398/252, le commandant de la prison d'Alger à M. le général commandant la région, 4 August 1941. Complaints about prison overcrowding under Vichy were frequent. It must be noted that the overall prison population grew from 18,000 in 1939 to 59,000 in 1944, see Pierre Pedron, *La Prison sous Vichy* (Paris: Éditions de l'Atelier, 1993), 63–64.

51. The testimony of Michel Bloch can be consulted at the following website: http://laurent.bloch.1.free.fr/spip.php?article 36. I should like to thank his widow, Colette, for drawing my attention to this fascinating source.

52. AN AJ[41] 498, Hans Goepel au délégué allemand au rapatriement, Algiers, n.d. Secret detention was also applied to pro-Allied prisoners, see AN 72[AJ] 1912, lettre du Dr A. Guenon à M. Stanislas Mangin, n.d.

53. AN AJ[41] 499, l'amiral de la flotte, ministre de la défense nationale, à M. le secrétaire d'État à la Guerre, 23 November 1941.

54. AN AJ[41] 499, rapport du commissaire principal de la ST, Marseille, 28 August 1942; AN AJ[41] 499, le capitaine de Bruce, officier de liaison, à M. le secrétaire d'État à la Guerre, DSA, Marseille, 17 May 1942; AN AJ[41] 499, le lieutenant-colonel d'Alès, BMA, note pour la DSA, n° 002686/MA./B, 14 April 1942; AN AJ[41] 499, DSA (signed Pettier), à M. Benoist-Méchin, secrétaire d'État à la présidence du Conseil, n° 769M/DSA/7, 4 May 1942; AN AJ[41] 499, le chef du gouvernement, DSA (signd Pettier), à M. Benoist-Méchin, n° 19506/DSA/7, 23 August 1942; AN AJ[41] 499, DSA à M. Benoist-Méchin, no 1436M/DSA/7, 26 August 1942; AN AJ[41] 499, le secrétaire d'État à la vice-présidence du Conseil à M. le général Bridoux, secrétaire d'État à la Guerre, 18 June 1942; AN AJ[41] 499, traduction d'une note de l'ambassade d'Allemagne Rück 3616, 13 June 1942; AN AJ[41] 499, traduction d'une note de l'ambassade d'Allemagne Rück 3616, 5 August 1942.

55. AN AJ[41] 499, le chef d'escadron de Royere, officier de liaison, Lyon, à M. le général, secrétaire d'État à la Guerre, n° 366/D, 23 June 1942.

56. AN 2[AG] 524, Mme Bernard à M. le maréchal Pétain, Paris, 10 October 1941.

57. AN 2[AG] 524, condamnation à mort du nommé André Bernard, 13 November 1941, tribunal militaire de Marseille.

58. AN AJ[41] 502, Anna Kern, Basel, Switzerland, à M. Hauptman, commission allemande de contrôle, hôtel Jourdan, place Jourdan, Limoges, 13 November 1941.

59. Délibération du conseil de l'ordre de Toulouse. I would like to thank Liora Israël for giving me this document.

60. SHAT Fonds de Moscou, 312/14086, le commissaire du gouvernement, Périgneux, à M. le ministre à la Guerre, n° 6480, 30 Septembre 1941.

61. AN AJ[41] 502, correspondance échangée entre le ministère de l'Intérieur et la DSA, Januray 1943.

62. C. de Acevedo, *À notre corps défendant, impressions et vicissitudes d'un diplomate en France, 1939–1944* (Paris: Paul Dupont, 1945), 173.

63. AN AJ[41] 499, extrait du compte rendu de l'officier de liaison à Lyon, n°714/D, Lyon, 5 December 1942.

64. AN AJ[41] 509, l'agent principal Bartholome, commandant la prison militaire de Lyon, à M. le secrétaire d'État à la Guerre, n° 3604, 2 December 1942; AN AJ[41] 509, liste des individus recensés par la police allemande, 1 December 1942; AN AJ[41] 509, DSA (signed Bourragué), à M. l'ambassadeur de France, délégué général du gouvernement français dans les territoires occupés, n° 25961/DSA/7, "Objet: visite de la police allemande dans les prisons françaises," 4 December 1942; AN AJ[41] 509, DSA, note pour l'officier de liaison près du délégué allemand au rapatriement à Lyon, "Objet: visite de la police allemande dans les prisons françaises," n° 25960/DSA/7, 5 December 1942; AN AJ[41] 499, extrait du compte rendu de l'officier de liaison à Lyon, n°714/D, Lyon, 5 December 1942.

65. AN AJ[41] 499, rapport sur la visite de M. Von Kirschten aux détenus allemands pour atteinte à la sûreté extérieure de l'État dans les prisons militaires et civiles d'Oran, 19–20 Septembre 1941.

66. AN BB[30] 1709, rapport au sujet de Jean Polome.

67. AN 2[AG] 595, Édouard Fier à M. Moncelle, chanoine, Meknes, 22 January 1942.

68. SHAT Fonds de Moscou, 761/73, intervention de Paillole dans la conférence du capitaine Bernard, 9 June 1942.

69. SHAT Fonds de Moscou, 312/14086, compte rendu d'audience: affaire Roland, 3515 A/MA.12, 24 June 1942.

70. AN AJ[41] 499, le garde des Sceaux, ministre secrétaire d'État à la Justice, à M. le chef du gouvernement, n° SS, Aix, 10 June 1943.

71. AN AJ[41] 499, note de la DSA, 1 October 1943, "sur les détenus Oppenhauser et Arvaud."

72. AN AJ[41] 499, dossier Léonie Schmid.

73. AN AJ[41] 499, dossier Lambin.

74. AN AJ[41] 499, le procureur général, Limoges, à M. le garde des Sceaux, 1 February 1943.

75. AN AJ[41] 499, le garde des Sceaux à M. le chef du gouvernement, 10 June 1943.

76. AN 2[AG] 596, Mme Rabis à M. le Maréchal, Lyon, 14 April 1942. For the file on Rabis's activities, see AN BB[30] 1709, rapport sur Roger Rabis.

77. AN 2[AG] 524, Guillaume Le Cunff, prison militaire, Constantine, à frère Paul Aune, Marseille.

78. AN 2[AG] 597, Françoise Subirana (?) à M. le Maréchal, chef de l'État français, Brive, 12 May 1942.

79. AN 2[AG] 524, compte rendu de décisions concernant les peines.

80. AN 2[AG] 597, Maurice Petit, détenu à la maison d'arrêt de Saint-Étienne, à M. le maréchal de France, chef de l'État, 26 April 1942; AN 2[AG] 597, Jean Grandi-

dier, maison d'arrêt de Saint-Étienne, à M. le maréchal de France, chef de l'État français, 27 December 1942; AN 2^{AG} 597, le contre-amiral Auphan, secrétaire d'État à la Marine, à M. le général, chef du cabinet militaire du chef de l'État, P.M.3.JP. n° 445, Vichy, 7 May 1942; AN 2^{AG} 597, le capitaine de frégate Archambeaud, note pour M. le général, chef du cabinet militaire du chef de l'État, Vichy, 23 October 1942.

81. AN F^7 15306, Jean Pézard, détenu à la prison militaire de Nontron, Dordogne, à Pierre Laval, 7 December 1943.

82. AN F^7 15306, direction des RG, note a/s de Pézard, Jean René, agent SRA et SD, 1 June 1946.

83. AN 2^{AG} 597, père J.-J. Rageys, Rabat, Morocco, à M. le chanoine, 29 January 1942.

84. AN BB^{30} 1709.

85. AN AJ^{41} 498, le général Huntziger, secrétaire d'État à la Guerre, au garde des Sceaux, n° 21929, 10 September 1941.

86. AN AJ^{41} 499, procès-verbal de la réunion interministérielle, 16 January 1942.

87. AN F^{60} 522, le chef du gouvernement à M. le maréchal de France, n° 1691/SG, 17 April 1943 (this same document can also be found in carton AN BB^{30} 1709).

88. AN AJ^{41} 499, secrétariat d'État à la Guerre, cabinet, BMA, "Note pour la DSA," n° 5909/MA/M, 22 September 1941; AN AJ^{41} 499, secrétariat d'État à la Guerre, cabinet, BMA, "Note pour la DSA," n° 002109/MA/B/46492, 25 March 1942.

89. AN AJ^{41} 499, secrétariat d'État à la Guerre, cabinet, BMA (signed Rivet), "Note pour la DSA," n° 002109/MA/B/46492, 25 March 1942. On Gemin's death, see also René Terrisse, *Face aux pelotons nazis, Souge, le mont Valérien du Bordelais* (Aubérons, 2000), 118–19.

90. AN AJ^{41} 496, l'amiral Darlan à M. l'amiral Platon, secrétaire d'État auprès du chef du gouvernement, 12 September 1942.

91. AN AJ^{41} 499, secrétariat d'État à la Guerre, cabinet, BMA (signed Rivet), "Note pour la DSA," n° 002109/MA/B/46492, 25 March 1942; AN AJ^{41} 496, section PGE, PR/7/BI, 24 June 1942; AN AJ^{41} 496, renseignements sur sept détenus allemands, considérés comme ne devant pas être remis, transmis à l'amiral Bourragué pour communication à l'amiral Darlan, 14 August 1942; AN AJ^{41} 499, secrétariat d'État à la Guerre, cabinet, BMA, "Note pour la DSA," n° 002109/MA/B/46492, 25 March 1942.

92. SHAT Fonds de Moscou, 680/14335, dossiers sur les agents doubles belges Jamar et Jacobs travaillant pour le SRA et français à Montpellier (November 1941–June 1942); AN AJ^{41} 496, secrétariat d'État à la Guerre, cabinet, BMA (signed Rivet), "Compte rendu au sujet de la remise aux autorités allemandes de Jamar," no 004510/MA/G/46.379, 1 July 1942; AN AJ^{41} 496, section PGE, "Note au sujet des engagements pris par l'ambassade d'Allemagne à l'occasion des remises de détenus pour atteinte à la sûreté de l'État," 18 August 1942; AN F^{60} 1749, renseignement, "Agents nazis relachés," 27 August 1942.

93. AN AJ^{41} 496, section PGE, "Note au suget des engagements pris par l'ambassade d'Allemagne à l'occasion des remises de détenus pour atteinte à la sûreté de l'État," 18 August 1942. On Dumas's work for the French secret services, see M. Garder, *La Guerre secrète des services spéciaux français* (Paris: Plon, 1967), 179.

94. AN AJ^{41} 499, secrétariat d'État à la Guerre, télégramme n° 3381/JC de la 15e division militaire (14 November 1942, 18 h30) au cabinet de la guerre et à la justice militaire.

95. AN AJ^{41} 499, le secrétaire général auprès du chef du gouvernement, DSA, à M. le secrétaire d'État à la Défense, n° 2281/DSA/7, 25 February 1944. Jobet's membership in the German intelligence service is explicitly confirmed in another letter: AN AJ^{41} 492, services de l'armistice, détachement français de liaison auprès de la commission allemande chargée du rapatriement, Marseille, compte rendu hebdomadaire, n° 1331/44, 2 January 1944.

96. AN AJ^{41} 499, le général Debeney, DSA, à M. le chef du gouvernement, ministre de l'Intérieur, Direction de l'administration de la police, quatorzième bureau, n° 6990/DSA/7, 6 July 1944.

97. AN F^{7} 15306, Feldgendarmerietrupp an das Schwedische Konsulat, Paris, 19 August 1944.

98. Paul Paillole's oral account, May 2001. On the setting up of the D measures see P. Paillole, *Services spéciaux, 1935–1945* (Paris: Laffont, 1975), 244.

99. SHAT Fonds Paillole, 1K 545 10, rapport de l'Einsatzkommando, SD, Strasbourg, 17 November 1943.

100. Paul Paillole, *Services spéciaux, 1935–1945* (Paris: Laffont, 1975), appendix.

101. Haute cour de Justice, *Procès du maréchal Pétain* (Paris: Imprimerie des Journaux officiels, 1945), 302.

102. AN 2^{AG} 524, registre des grâces.

103. SHAT Fonds de Moscou, 678/14661, dossier sur Henri Devillers; SHAT Fonds de Moscou, 761/73, conférence du capitaine Bernard, 9 June 1942; SHAT Fonds de Moscou, 1250/13800, affaire Grangier-Devillers (December 1940–February 1942); SHAT Fonds Paillole, 1K 545 4, déclarations du colonel Paillole, a/s activité clandestine du réseau FFC SSM/TR, transcription d'interview ORTF, 1950; AN 72^{AJ} 82, "Résumé de l'action des services de contre-espionnage militaire français de juillet 1940 à novembre 1944," vol. I, 1946.

104. C. Bourdet, *L'Aventure incertaine* (Paris: Félin, 1998), 118; M. Granet, *Les Jeunes dans la résistance* (Paris: France-Empire, 1996), 149–50; G. de Benouville, *Le Sacrifice du matin* (Geneva: de Crémille, 1970), I, 241–43; H. Navarre, *Le Service de renseignements, 1871–1944* (Paris: Plon, 1978), 136; M. Granet and H. Michel, *Combat, histoire d'un mouvement de Résistance* (Paris: Presses Universitaires de France, 1957); P. J. Stead, *Second Bureau* (London: Evans, 1959), 43; Patrice Miannay, *Dictionnaire des agents doubles dans la Resistance,* (Paris: Cherche Midi, 2005), 104–5.

105. AN 2AG 524, registre des grâces.

106. *Progrès de Lyon,* 20 June 1942; SHAT Fonds Paillole, 1K 545 4, déclarations du colonel Paillole, a/s activité clandestine du réseau FFC SSM/TR, transcription d'interview ORTF, 1950.

107. H. Frenay, *La nuit finira* (Paris: Laffont, 1973), 167.

108. For the diplomatic tensions caused by this incident see AN 3 W 104, journal intime du général Bridoux, 14, 15, 16 July 1942.

CHAPTER 7

1. P. Nord, *Mes camarades sont morts* (Geneva: de Crémille, 1970); J. Abtey and F. Unterberg-Gibhardt, *Deuxième bureau contre Abwehr* (Paris: La Table Ronde, 1966); M. Garder, *La Guerre secrète des services spéciaux français* (Paris: Plon, 1967); D. Loisel, *J'étais le commandant X* (Paris: Fayard, 1970); Gilbert-Guillaume, *Mes missions face à l'Abwehr* (Paris: Plone, 1971); M. Pasquelot, *Les Dossiers secrets de la marine* (Paris: NEL, 1973); P. Paillole, *Services spéciaux, 1935–1945* (Paris: Laffont, 1975); P. Bernert, *Roger Wybot et la bataille pour la DST* (Paris: Presses de la Cité, 1975); H. Koch-Kent, *Doudot, figure légendaire du contre-espionnage français* (Paris: Casterman, 1976); R. Terres, *Double jeu pour la France* (Paris: Grasset, 1977); H. Navarre, *Le Service de renseignements, 1871–1944* (Paris: Plon, 1978); H. Navarre, *Le Temps des vérités* (Paris: Plon, 1979); J. Bézy, *Le Service de renseignements air* (Paris: France-Empire, 1979); J.-P. Vittori, *Une histoire d'honneur: la Résistance* (Paris: Ramsay, 1984), chap. 6, 83–96 (conversation with Paul Paillole); P. Paillole, *L'Homme des services secrets* (Paris: Julliard, 1995).

2. H. Navarre, *Le Service de renseignements, 1871–1944* (Paris: Plon, 1978), 134; P. Nord, *Mes camarades sont morts* (Geneva: de Crémille, 1970), I, 27; P. Paillole, *Services spéciaux, 1935–1945* (Paris: Laffont, 1975), 231. AN 72^{AJ} 82, Mémoires inédits du colonel Louis Rivet, 11–12. See also his comments on Vichy in the document SHAT Fonds Paillole, 1K 545 18, Rivet: mémoire pour servir à une reconstitution du SR français, July 1944.

3. AN F7 15306, Feldgendarmerietrupp an das Schwedische Konsulat, Paris, 19 August 1944; AN AJ^{41} 492, services de l'armistice, détachement français de liaison auprès de la commission allemande chargée du rapatriement, Marseille, compte rendu hebdomadaire, n° 1331/44, 2 January 1944; AN AJ^{41} 499, le secrétaire général auprès du chef du gouvernement (DSA) à M. le général, secrétaire d'État à la Défense, n° 2281/DSA/7, 25 February 1944; AN AJ^{41} 499, le général Debeney, DSA, à M. le chef du gouvernement, ministre de l'Intérieur, Direction de l'administration de la police, quatorzième bureau, n° 6990/DSA/7, 6 July 1944.

4. AN BB^{30} 1709.

5. AN AJ^{41} 499, le garde des Sceaux à M. le chef du gouvernement, n° SS. Aix, 10 June 1943; AN AJ^{41} 499, note de la DSA, Vichy, 1 October 1943, "sur les détenus Oppenhauser et Arvaud"; AN AJ^{41} 499, dossier Lambin; AN AJ^{41} 499, dossier Léonie Schmid.

6. AN AJ^{41} 499, le procureur général, Limoges, à M. le garde des Sceaux, 1 February 1943; AN AJ^{41} 499, le garde des Sceaux à M. le chef du gouvernement, 10 June 1943.

7. On the government's support for the secret reconstitution of the secret services, Rivet wrote on 7 August 1940: "Overall, in spite of the government half-

hearted velleities at action. . . . not the hoped for support:" SHAT Fonds Paillole, 1K 545 1, journal de marche du général Rivet.

8. SHAT 1P 89, le général Weygand à M. le maréchal de France, no 146 / cab, Algiers, 10 November 1940. The carton AN F^{60} 782 contains numerous letters between different ministers (Weygand, Huntziger, Darlan, Pétain, etc.) on this issue.

9. AN F^{60} 782, Darlan à Weygand, n°1108 / SG, 24 March 1941; AN F^{60} 782, Weygand à Darlan, n° 1760 / SGP, 15 April 1941; AN F^{60} 782, Weygand à Darlan, n° 2579 / SGP, 23 May 1941.

10. AN F^{60} 782, M. l'amiral de la flotte, vice-président du Conseil (signed Tracou), à M. le ministre secrétaire d'État à l'Intérieur, 23 April 1941.

11. See for instance AN 2^{AG} 524.

12. For Pétain's and Darlan's roles in death sentences, see AN 2^{AG} 524. For letters in which Laval clarifies his position, see: AN F^{60} 522, rapport du chef du gouvernement au Maréchal, chef de l'État français, Vichy, 26 November 1942; AN F^{60} 522, le chef du gouvernement à M. le maréchal de France, n° 1691 / SG, 17 April 1943 (this same document is also included in carton AN BB^{30} 1709).

13. For the original of this document, see AN F^{60} 782, le général Weygand à M. le maréchal de France, 7 December 1940.

14. SHAT Fonds Paillole, 1K 545 10, rapport de l'Einsatzkommando, SD, Strasbourg, 17 November 1943.

15. Even though by the end of the 1930s *Action Française* leader Maurras had changed direction and began to see England as the main enemy: H. R. Kedward, "Charles Maurras and the True France," in R. Bullen, H. Pogge and A. Polonsky, eds., *Ideas into Politics* (London: Croom Helm, 1984), 119; H. R. Kedward, "The Vichy of the other Philippe," in G. Girshfeild and P. Marsh, eds., *Collaboration in France* (Oxford: Berg, 1989), 37; H. R. Kedward, *Naissance de la Résistance dans la France de Vichy* (Paris: Champ-Vallon, 1989), 85.

16. SHAT Fonds Paillole, 1K 545 19, Fernand de Brinon à von Ribbentrop, 17 May 1943. About the anti-Germanism of military milieus in general, see R. O. Paxton, *Parades and Politics in Vichy, The French Officer Corps under Marshal Pétain* (Princeton, N.J.: Princeton University Press, 1966), 94–101.

17. J.-P. Azéma and O. Wieviorka, *Vichy, 1940–1944* (Paris: Perrin, 1997), 58.

18. SHAT 1P 89, Weygand à Pétain, 26 March 1941.

19. SHAT 1P 200, Weygand à M. l'amiral, gouverneur général de l'Algérie, 28 February 1941.

20. SHAT 1P 89, Weygand à Darlan, 15 November 1941.

21. One should not draw the same conclusions as apologist texts such as that of Jacques Le Groignec, *Pétain, gloire et sacrifice* (Paris: NEL, 1991), 190–91. In reality it wasn't an attempt at resistance as Le Groignec claims but rather simply an attempt at preserving sovereignty.

22. On Weygand's hostility toward the British, see SHAT 1P 89, Weygand à Pétain, 10 November 1940.

23. AN F^{60} 393, Pétain à Weygand, 25 April 1941.

24. AN 72[AJ] 1911, "Note Rollin sure le fonctionnement du SR de la SN," 2 May 1941.

25. R. Bargeton, *Dictionnaire biographique des préfets, septembre 1870–mai 1982* (Paris, 1994), 481; H. Couteau-Begarie and C. Huan, *Darlan* (Paris: Fayard, 1989), 482; R. Faligot and P. Krop, *DST: police secrète* (Paris: Flammarion, 1999). Centre d'archives contemporaines (CAC) Fontainebleau, 920231/14; AN F[1b] 837; AN 72[AJ] 82, entretiens avec Paul Paillole, April–May 1948; AN 72[AJ] 35, attestation de M. Joseph Rivalland, 5 July 1947; AN 72[AJ] 35, attestation d'Henri Rollin, 5 January 1949; SHAT Fonds Paillole, 1K 545 10, rapport de Jean Osvald, commissaire central à Marseille de 1940 à 1944.

26. H. Rollin, *L'Apocalypse de notre temps, les dessous de la propagande allemande d'après les documents inédits* (Paris: Gallimard, 1939). A new edition was published by Allia in 1991.

27. H. Rollin, *L'Apocalypse de notre temps* (Paris: Allia, 1991, new edition), 715.

28. Yves Durand, "Collaboration, French Style" in Sarah Fishman, et al., *France at War: Vichy and the Historians* (Oxford: Berg, 2000), 69.

29. AN 72[AJ] 1911, "Note Rollin sure le fonctionnement du SR de la SN," 2 May 1941.

30. AN F[60] 522, rapport du chef du gouvernement au Maréchal, chef d l'État français, Vichy, 26 November 1942. For more information on Legras, see SHAT Fonds de Moscou, 676/15100, dossier sur René Legras, condamné pour atteinte à la sûreté extérieure de l'État français (August–September 1942).

31. Courts sometimes explicitly mentioned the notion that individuals must wait for governmental authorization before engaging in collaboration. For instance, in his letter to Pétain, Renée Blanc explains the motives for her condemnation as follows: "On 7 October, the military tribunal of Lyon (XIVth region) sentenced me to two years in prison and five years of banishment for having exchanged letters with a German without the government's authorization," AN 2[AG] 596, Mlle Renée Blanc, Lyon, à M. le Maréchal, 13 September 1942.

32. See for instance M.-O. Baruch, *Servir l'État français* (Paris: Fayard, 1997), 65–97; É. Alary, *La Ligne de démarcation* (Paris: Perrin, 2003), 219–20.

33. SHAT 3P 102, Darlan aux secrétaires d'État à l'Intérieur et à la Guerre, n° 812/SG, 5 July 1941. A copy of this same letter is attached as an appendix to the following letter: AN AJ[41] 1562, le général de Saint-Vincent, gouverneur militaire de Lyon, commandant la 14e division militaire, à M. le préfet du Rhône, Lyon, 24 November 1941.

34. AN AJ 41 491, Le Capitaine POURAILLY, Chef du détachement de liaison auprès du délégué de la Commission Allemande d'Armistice à M le Chef du Gouvernement, Direction des Services de l'Armistice, Hôtel Thermal, Vichy, n° 8158, Toulouse, 19 August 1942; AN AJ41 499, Dossier Riff.

35. AN AJ41 499, Secrétariat d'Etat à la Guerre, Cabinet, Bureau MA, Note pour Direction des Services de l'Armistice (signed Paillole), n° 005852/MA/M, 29 August 1942.

36. AN AJ41 499, Secrétariat d'Etat à la Guerre, Cabinet, Bureau MA, Note pour Direction des Services de l'Armistice, n° 3690/MA/M, 17 July 1941. On German provocation in the form of Gaullist action see: AD BDR 5W 365, Note: police renseignements, n° 3694/1, *"Activité de la Gestapo à Marseille"*, 23 May 1941; a similar complaint is made on 2 April 1941 by General Orly (Commandant le 1er groupe de division militaire) in a correspondence (n°161/2) to the secrétaire d'Etat à la Guerre in Vichy (AN AJ 41 46).

37. AD BDR M6 10988, Le Commissaire de Police de Sûreté, "note au sujet du chef du service des affaires indigènes à Marseille," Pol. Sûr. 7/R, 20 January 1943. This type of operation regarding *agents provocateurs* who were infiltrating Gaullist movements had already been the subject of AN F1a 3690–32, le Directeur Adjoint du Cabinet à M. le Secrétaire Général pour la Police, AC/MG, 14 April 1942.

38. J.-B. Duroselle, *L'Abîme, 1939–1944* (Paris: Points Seuil), 268.

39. AN F1a 4685, le général Huntziger, secrétaire d'État à la Guerre, à M. le secrétaire d'État à l'Intérieur, 5 September 1941.

40. AN 3W 91, le commandant Berge à M. le président Mitton, SN/RG 2e SN, 1947 (n.d.); AN 3W 91, déposition de Helmut Knochen, 30 April 1947; AN 3W 91, déposition de Rémy Desloges, 28 March 1946; AN 3W 91, le secrétaire général à la Police à M. le préfet des Bouches-du-Rhône, n° 1311/SCC, 1 September 1942; AN 3W 91, déposition de Rolf Mühler, 29 May 1947; AN 3W 91, le secrétaire général à la Police à M. le préfet des Bouches-du-Rhône, n° 687 299, 17 September 1942; AN 3W 91, 8e note concernant la mission spéciale de détection des postes clandestines, n.d. O. Reile, *L'Abwehr* (Paris: France-Empire, 1970), 177–85; J. Delarue, *Histoire de la Gestapo* (Paris: Fayard, 1962), 384; P. Nord, *Mes camarades sont morts* (Geneva: de Crémille, 1970), II, 266–67; F. Kupferman, *Laval, 1883–1945* (Paris: Flammarion, 1988), 344–45; P.-J. Stead, *Second Bureau* (London: Evans Brothers, 1959), 96.

41. J.-P. Azéma and O. Wieviorka, *Vichy, 1940–1944* (Paris: Perrin, 1997), 52.

42. R. Frank, "Pétain, Laval, Darlan," in J.-P. Azéma and F. Bedarida, eds., *La France des années noires* (Paris: Points Seuil, 2000), I, 307–48.

43. SHAT 1P 200, l'amiral Ollive, commandant en chef des forces maritimes du Sud, à M. le délégué général dy gouvernement en Afrique française, 4 May 1941.

44. For instance there were Resistance periodicals critical of the penetration of German spies in the southern zone. *Combat* (no. 1, January 1942) gave the example of a suboffice of the SRA located on the chemin de Paraban in Lyon and claimed that its members "were living in a princely manner and did not suffer from restrictions [shortages]."

45. J.-P. Azéma and O. Wieviorka, *Vichy, 1940–1944* (Paris: Perrin, 1997), 52.

46. SHAT Fonds de Moscou, 464/176, conférence du commandant Paillole, 15 April 1942.

47. A very large file on the diplomatic ramifications of the Strohm affair can be found in the carton AN AJ41 1577b. For more information, see AN F1a 4683, DSA (signed Koeltz), note pour la DDSA à Alger, 14 June 1941; SHAT 1P 200,

renseignements recueillis, le juillet 1941, au cours de l'entretien du capitaine Simonin avec M. von Kirschten; SHAT 1P 89, Weygand à Darlan, 15 November 1941; SHAT Fonds de Moscou, 686/14031, dossier Strohm.

48. SHAT Fonds de Moscou, 678/14661, dossier sur Henri Devillers; SHAT Fonds de Moscou, 761/73, conférence du capitaine Bernard, 9 June 1942; SHAT Fonds de Moscou, 1250/13800, affaire Grangier-Devillers (December 40–February 42). H. Frenay, *La nuit finira* (Paris: Laffont, 1973), 167; C. Bourdet, *L'Aventure incertaine* (Paris: Félin, 1998), 118; M. Granet, *Les Jeunes dans la Résistance* (Paris: France-Empire, 1996), 149–50; G. de Benouville, *Le Sacrifice du matin* (Geneva: de Crémille, 1970), I, 241–43; H. Navarre, *Le Service de renseignements, 1871–1944* (Paris: Plon, 1978), 136; M. Granet and H. Michel, *Combat, histoire d'un mouvement de Résistance* (Paris: PUF, 1957); P. J. Stead, *Second Bureau* (London: Evans, 1959), 43.

49. SHAT Fonds Paillole, 1K 545 4, déclaration du colonel Paillole, a/s activité clandestine du réseau FFC SSM/TR, transcription d'interview ORTF, 1950; *Progrès de Lyon,* 20 June 1942.

50. AN 3W 104, journal intime du général Bridoux, 14, 15, 16 July 1942.

51. Ibid, 22 July 1942.

52. AN AJ^{41} 497, le général d'armée (signed Lachenaud) à MM. les généraux commandant les 7e, 9e, 12e à 17e divisions militaires, 11 August 1941; AN AJ^{41} 499, le général Huntziger au ministre de la Défense nationale, DSA, no 818/PG, 19 July 1940; AN AJ^{41} 499, le ministre de la Défense nationale, DSA (singed Koeltz) à M. le garde des Sceaux, n° 2218/DSA, Vichy, 3 August 1940; AN AJ^{41} 491, DSA, note pour la DDSA à Alger, n° 13912/DSA/7, 4 May 1941.

53. AN AJ^{41} 499, note de la DSA (signed Coudrin), 14 January 1942; AN AJ^{41} 499, note pour la DSA (signed Coudrin), n° 1535/DSA/7, 16 January 1942.

54. SHAT 1P 135, note (signed Zacharie), 15 October 1941; AN AJ^{41} 499, le chef du gouvernement, DSA, à M. Benoist-Méchin, secrétaire d'État auprès du chef du gouvernement, n° 21251/DSA/7, 16 Septembre 1942; AN AJ^{41} 499, le capitaine Amann, officier de liaison à Royat, à M. le vice-amiral, DSA, 22 August 1942.

55. AN AJ^{41} 499, l'amiral de la flotte, ministre de la Défense nationale à M. le secrétaire d'État à la Guerre, 23 November 1941; AN AJ^{41} 499, rapport du commissaire principal de police de la ST, Marseille, 28 August 1942; AN AJ^{41} 499, le capitaine de Bruce, officier de liaison Marseille, à M. le secrétaire d'État à la Guerre, 17 May 1942; AN AJ^{41} 499, le lieutenenant-colonel d'Alès, BMA, note pour la DSA, n° 002686/MA/B. 14 April 1942; AN AJ^{41} 499, DSA à M. Benoist-Méchin, secrétaire d'État à la présidence du Conseil, n° 769M/DSA/7, 4 May 1942; AN AJ^{41} 499, le chef du gouvernement, DSA, à M. Benoist-Méchin, n°19506/DSA/7, 23 August 1942; AN AJ^{41} 499, DSA à M. Benoist-Méchin, n° 1436M/DSA/7, 26 August 1942; AN AJ^{41} 499, le secrétaire d'État à la vice-présidence du Conseil au général Bridoux, 18 June 1942; AN AJ^{41} 499, traduction d'une note de l'ambassade d'Allemagne Rück 3616, 13 June 1942; AN AJ^{41} 499, traduction d'une note de l'ambassade d'Allemagne Rück 3615, 5 August 1942; AN AJ^{41} 499, de Royere, officier de liaison, Lyon, au secrétaire d'État à la Guerre, n° 366/D, 23 June 1942.

56. AN AJ[41] 496, ambassade d'Allemagne, Paris, note pour le gouvernement français, n° 442/3/42, 3 March 1942; AN AJ[41] 496, note de la DSA, Vichy, n.d. (the inscription "seen 31 March 1942" is written in pencil in the margin).

57. See above chap. 6.

58. AN AJ[41] 499, secrétariat d'État à la Guerre, cabinet, BMA (signed Rivet), "Note pour la DSA," n° 002109/MA/B/46492, 25 March 1942; AN AJ[41] 496, section PGE, PR/7/BI, 24 June 1942; AN AJ[41] 496, resnseignements sur sept détenus allemands, considérés comme ne devant pas être remis, transmis à l'amiral Bourragué pour communication à l'amiral Darlan, 14 August 1942; AN AJ[41] 499, AN AJ[41] 499 secrétariat d'État à la Guerre, cabinet, BMA, "Note pour la DSA," n° 002109/MA/B/46492, 25 March 1942.

59. On the heterogeneity of the government, see for instance: D. Peschanski, "Le régime de Vichy a existé. Gouvernants et gouvernés dans la France de Vichy: juillet 1940–avril 1942" in D. Peschanski, ed., *Vichy 1940–1944* (Paris: Editions du CNRS, 1986), 3–50; J.-M. Guillon, "La philosophie politique de la Révolution nationale," in J.-P. Azéma and F. Bédarida, eds., *Vichy et les Français* (Paris: Fayard, 1992), 167–83.

60. M. Garder, *La Guerre secrète des services spéciaux* (Paris: Plon, 1967), 225; H. Navarre, *Le Service de renseignements, 1871–1944* (Paris: Plon, 1978), 134; P. Paillole, *Services spéciaux, 1935–1945* (Paris: Laffont, 1975), 320. See also B. Destremau, *Weygand* (Paris: Perrin, 1989), 620.

61. SHAT Fonds de Moscou, 962/1985, dossier sur les dépôts clandestins de matériel de guerre (October 1940–August 1941). On the protection of the secret weapons caches by the secret services, see SHAT Fonds de Moscou, 934/1936, note pour 1 500 (signed Yves), 15 June 1941; AN 72[AJ] 63, témoignage du capitaine de vaisseau Blouet, 21 June 1948; SHAT Fonds Paillole, 1K 545 4, déclarations du colonel Paillole, a/s activité clandestine du réseau FFC SSM/TR, transcription d'interview ORTF, 1950. For cases of denunciations of secret depots to the Axis, see SHAT 1P 60, compte rendu sur l'activité du détachement de liaison près de la CAA, n° 2, Pau, 31 December 1942; AN AJ[41] 496, note de renseignements communiquée par les services de la ST, n.d.; AN AJ[41] 499, note de renseignements, cabinet, BMA, no 6204/MA/B, 24 October 1941; AN AJ[41] 492, le chef d'escadron d'Amecourt, officier de liaison à Royat, à M. le chef du gouvernement, DSA, n° 1 855/PA, Royat, 27 February 1943; AN AJ[41] 1814, le général doyen, président de la délégation française auprès de la CAA, à M. le ministre secrétaire d'État à la Guerre, n° 14150/EM, 24 February 1941; AN AJ[41] 499, commandement supérieur des troupes du Maroc, état-major, note de renseignements n° 216, 19 April 1941.

62. AN 3W 104, journal intime du général Bridoux, 15 December 1942. See also SHAT 1P 89, déposition du général de brigade de Perier des troupes coloniales; SHAT 5P 2, rapport du colonel Gross sur l'activité d'ensemble des commissions d'armistice, Algiers, 19 April 1943. It is certain that it was Vichy that was organizing these arms caches, otherwise it would be hard to understand how Laval could have drawn such an exhaustive list of them at the beginning of 1943.

63. In a letter he addressed to Pétain, it is clear that he was aware that this activity was contrary to the spirit of the armistice because he mentions that one

should avoid " compromising the officially eliminated war SR with the Italian and Germans armistice commissions": AN F^{60} 782, le général Weygand à M. le maréchal de France, 7 December 1940.

64. SHAT 1P 89, Weygand à Pétain, 3 March 1941. In his 25 October letter to Darlan, Weygand even foresees an armed intervention of the Axis in North Africa: SHAT 1P 135, Weygand à Darlan, n° 8924/EM/2, 25 October 1941.

65. SHAT 1P 89, Weygand à Pétain, 3 March 1941.

66. SHAT 1P 135, Weygand à Huntziger, n° 2304/EM/2, 17 April 1941; AN F^{60} 782, Huntziger à Pétain, 12 February 1941.

67. SHAT 1P 200, le général Huntziger à MM. les généraux commandant les régions, 25 February 1941.

68. This is confirmed by SHAT Fonds Paillole, 1K 545 1, journal de marche du général Rivet. There are documents preparing this special status in SHAT 3P 102, particularly a "Note au sujet du service de renseignements" du secrétariat d'État à la Guerre, 26 July 1940.

69. AN 2^{AG} 524.

70. SHAT Fonds Paillole, 1K 545 19, Fernand de Brinon à von Ribbentrop, 17 May 1943.

71. AN 72^{AJ} 82, l'amiral Darlan à M. le secrétaire d'État à la Guerre, 6 October 1941.

72. M.-O. Baruch, *Servir l'État français* (Paris: Fayard, 1997), 78.

73. In a 1948 account, Paul Paillole reports on a conversation he had with the admiral in November of 1942, on the eve of the latter's departure for North Africa. The commandant asked his superior to frankly tell him what he thought of the work accomplished by the secret services. He reports Darlan gave him the following answer: "It is certain that on several occasions the Germans complained of the inconvenience caused by your services and your relationships with the Allies, and they gave me instructions for it to stop. You do know that I never followed them": AN 72^{AJ} 82, CHDGM, entretiens avec Paul Paillole, April and May 1948. This quote contradicts the image Paillole gives of Darlan in 1975: P. Paillole, *Services spéciaux, 1935–1945* (Paris: Laffont, 1975), 225.

74. SHAT Fonds de Moscou, 668/14779, dossier sur le centre d'information gouvernemental; SHAT Fonds Paillole, 1K 545 10, rapport de l'Einsatzkommando, SD, Strasbourg, 17 November 1943.

75. H. Navarre, *Le Service de renseignements, 1871–1944* (Paris: Plon, 1978), 136; P. Nord, *Mes camarades sont morts* (Geneva: de Crémille, 1970), II, 44–45; P. Paillole, *Services spécaiux, 1935–1945* (Paris: Laffont, 1975), 225.

76. AN 3W 104, journal intime du général Bridoux, 19 July 1942; AN 72^{AJ} 82, résumé de l'action des services de CE militaire français, from July 1940 to November 1944, written by Paillole in 1946.

77. AN F^{60} 393, le chef du gouvernement (signed by Laval) à M. le secrétaire d'État à la Défense, 1 July 1943. P. Nord, *Mes camarades sont morts* (Geneva: de Crémille, 1970), I, 191.

78. AN 3W 104, journal intime du général Bridoux, 1 December 1942.

79. SHAT Fonds Paillole, 1K 545 19, Fernand de Brinon à von Ribbentrop, 17 May 1943.

80. AN F[60] 393, Huntziger à Darlan, 10 June 1941.

81. SHAT 1P 200, file, "Activités anglo-gaullistes en AFN"; SHAT 5P, rapport du colonel Gross sur l'activité d'ensemble des commissions d'armistice, Algiers, 19 April 1943; SHAT 1P 89, Weygand à Darlan, 15 November 1941; AN AJ[41] 491, le délégué allemand (Lutz) à M. le capitaine Pourailly, chef de détachement auprès de la Croix-Rouge allemande à Toulouse, n° 421/42, 19 March 1942, "Objet: Mauvais traitement et arrestation des personnes qui viennent me rendre visite." A. Lefebure, *Les Conversations secrètes des français sous l'Occupation* (Paris: 1993), 156–57.

82. AN 3W 104, journal intime du général Bridoux, 19 August 1942; SHAT Fonds Paillole, 1K 545 10, rapport de l'Einsatzkommando, SD, Strasbourg, 17 November 1943.

83. AN AJ[41] 509, section PGE, "visites de la police allemande dans les prisons militaires," 11 December 1942.

84. AN AJ[41] 509, l'agent principal Bartholome, commandant la prison militaire de Lyon, à M. le secrétaire d'État à la Guerre, n° 3604, 2 December 1942; AN AJ[41] 509, liste des individus recensés par la police allemande, 1 December 1942; AN AJ[41] 509, DSA (signed Bourragué), à M. l'ambassadeur de France, délégué général du gouvernement français dans les territoires occupés, no 25961/DSA/7, "Objet: visite de la police allemande dans les prisons française," 4 December 1942; AN AJ[41] 509, DSA, note pour l'officier de liaison près du délégué allemand au rapatriement à Lyon, "Objet: visite de la police allemande dans les prisons françaises," n° 25960/DSA/7, 5 December 1942; AN AJ[41] 499, extrait du compte rendu de l'officier de liaison à Lyon, n° 714/D, Lyon, 5 December 1942.

85. Including the pro-Allied: AN 72[AJ] 1912, lettre du Dr. A. Guenon à M. Stanislas Mangin, n.d.

86. AN BB[30] 1709, secrétaire d'État à la Guerre à M. le chef du gouvernement n° 1615 JM/S, Vichy, 4 January 1943.

87. AN F[60] 522, le chef du gouvernement à M. le maréchal de France, n° 1691/SG, 17 April 1943 (this same document is also included in carton AN BB[30] 1709).

CONCLUSION

1. L. Douzou and D. Peschanski, "Les premiers résistants face à l'hypothèque Vichy (1940–1942)," in L. Douzou, R. Frank, D. Peschanski and D. Veillon, eds., *La résistance et les Français* (Actes du colloque, Cachan, 1995), 433.

2. R. O. Paxton, *Vichy France, Old Guard and New Order, 1940–1944* (New York: Columbia University Press, 1972); M.-O. Baruch, *Servir l'État français* (Paris: Fayard, 1997), 65–97; É. Alary, *La ligne de démarcation* (Paris: Perrin, 2003), 219–20.

BIBLIOGRAPHY

Abtey, Jacques and Fritz Unterber-Gebhardt. *Deuxième bureau contre Abwehr.* Paris: La Table Ronde, 1966.

Austin, Roger. "Surveillance and Intelligence under the Vichy Regime: The Service du Contrôle Technique, 1939–1945." *Intelligence and National Security* 1, no.1 (1986): 123–37.

Aziz, Philippe. *Au service de l'ennemi, la Gestapo française en province, 1940–1944.* Paris: Fayard, 1972.

Bernert, Philippe. *Roger Wybot et la bataille pour la DST.* Paris: Presses de la Cité, 1975.

Bézy, Jean. *Le Service de renseignements air.* Paris: France-Empire, 1979.

Chalet, Marcel. "La DST, service français de contre-espionnage." In *Approches françaises du renseignement.* Edited by Pierre Lacoste. Paris: FED, 1997.

Cornick, Martyn and Peter Morris. *The French Secret Services.* London: Transaction Publishers, 1993.

Delalez, François. Le Service des menées antinationales 1940–1942. Treatise for the *Ecole de Coëtquidan,* written under the direction of Olivier Forcade, 1998.

Delarue, Jacques. *Histoire de la Gestapo.* Paris: Fayard, 1962.

Faligot, Roger and Pascal Krop. *DST: Police secrète.* Paris: Flammarion, 1999.

Forcade, Olivier. "L'exploitation du renseignement stratégique français en 1936–1938." In *L'Exploitation du renseignement en Europe et aux États-Unis des années 1930 aux années 1960,* edited by Georges-

Henri Soutou, Jacques Frémeaux, and Olivier Forcade, 83–98. Paris: Économica, 2001.

———. "Histoire militaire et renseignement: Etat des lieux." In *La Culture française du renseignement,* edited by Pierre Lacoste, 49–78. Paris: Économica, 1998.

———. "Quelques réflections sur l'exploitation du renseignement stratégique français à la fin des années 1930." *Les Cahiers de Mars,* no. 162 (1999): 52–60.

———. "Le renseignement face à l'Allemagne au printemps 1940 et au début de la campagne de France," in *La Campagne de 1940,* edited by Christine Levisse-Touzé, 126–55. Paris: Tallandier, 2001.

Garder, Michel. *La Guerre secrète des services spéciaux français, 1935–1945.* Paris: Plon, 1967.

Gilbert-Guillaume. *Mes missions face à l'Abwehr (contre-espionnage 1938–1945).* Paris: Plon, 1971.

Hohne, Heinz. *Canaris, Hitler's Master Spy.* New York: Cooper Square Press, 1979.

Jackson, Peter. *France and the Nazi Menace.* Oxford: Oxford University Press, 2001.

Kahn, David. *Hitler's Spies.* New York: Da Capo Press, 2000.

Kitson, Simon. *Vichy et la chasse aux espions nazis,* Paris: Autrement, 2005.

———. "Arresting Nazi Spies in Vichy France (1940–42)." *Intelligence and National Security* 15, no. 1 (2000): 80–120.

Koch-Kent, Henri. *Doudot, figure légendaire du contre-espionnage français.* Paris: Casterman, 1976.

Lacoste, Pierre, ed. *Approches françaises du renseignement: Y a-t-il une "culture" nationale?* Paris: FED, 1997.

Laurent, Sébastien. "Faire l'histoire du renseignement." In *Archives "secrètes," secrets d'archives? Le travail de l'historien et de l'archiviste sur les archives sensibles,* edited by Sébastien Laurent, 211–20. Paris: Éditions du CNRS, 2003.

———. "The Free French Secret Services: Intelligence and the Politics of Republican Legitimacy." *Intelligence and National Security* 15, no. 4 (2000): 19–41.

———. "Le renseignement de 1860 à nos jours: Etat des sources militaires." *Revue historique des armées,* no. 4 (2000): 97–110.

———. "Le renseignement et le contre-espionnage militaires face à l'Allemagne: Etude du dispositif de renseignement français." In *Frankreich und Deutschland im Krieg (November 1942–Herbst 1944): Okkupation, Kollaboration, Resistance,* edited by Stefan Mertens and Maurice Vaïsse, 783–792. Bonn: Bouvier Verlag, 2000.

———. "Renseignement militaire et action politique: le BCRA et les services spéciaux de l'armée d'armistice," in *La Culture française du renseignement,* edited by Pierre Lacoste, 79–99. Paris: Économica, 1998.

———. "Les services secrets." In *Dictionnaire critique de la République,* edited by Vincent Duclert and Christophe Prochasson, 793–98 and 1029–32. Paris: Flammarion, 2002.

———. "Le Service secret de l'État (1870–1945): La part des militaires." In *Serviteurs de l'État: Une Histoire politique de l'administration française 1875–1945*, edited by Marc-Olivier Baruch and Vincent Duclert, 279–95. Paris: La Découverte, 2000.

———. "Les services spéciaux de la France libre: politique et légitimité républicaine." In *L'exploitation du renseignement en Europe et aux États-Unis des années 1930 aux années 1960*, edited by Georges-Henri Soutou, Jacques Frémaux, and Olivier Forcade, 133–60. Paris: Économica, 2001.

———. "Les services spéciaux gaullistes à l'épreuve de la politique (1940–1947)." *Politix: Revue des sciences sociales du politique* 14, no. 54 (2001): 139–53.

Loisel, Dominique. *J'étais le commandant X, souvenirs d'un agent secret.* Paris: Fayard, 1970.

Miannay, Patrice. *Dictionnaire des agents doubles dans la Résistance.* Paris: Le Cherche Midi, 2005.

Miller, Michael. *Shanghai on the Métro: Spies, Intrigue and the French between the Wars.* Los Angeles: University of California Press, 1994.

Navarre, Henri. *Le Service de renseignements, 1871–1944.* Paris: Plon, 1978.

———. *Le Temps des vérités.* Paris: Plon, 1979.

Nord, Pierre. *Cas de conscience de l'agent secret.* Paris: Fleurus, 1960.

———. *Mes camarades sont morts.* 3 vols. Geneva: de Crémille, 1970.

Paillole, Paul. *L'Homme des services secrets (entretiens avec Alain-Gilles Minella).* Paris: Julliard, 1995.

———. *Services spéciaux, 1935–1945.* Paris: Laffont, 1975.

Pasquelot, Maurice. *Les Dossiers secrets de la marine, Londres-Vichy, 1940–1944.* Paris: NEL, 1973.

Passy (Colonel). *Mémoires du chef des services secrets de la France libre.* Paris: Odile Jacob, 2000.

Porch, Douglas. *The French Secret Services, from the Dreyfus Affair to the Gulf War.* Oxford: Oxford University Press, 1997.

Reile, Oscar. *L'Abwehr: Le contre-espionnage allemand en France de 1935 à 1945.* Paris: France-Empire, 1970.

Rivet, Louis (Colonel). "Abwehr et Gestapo en France pendant la guerre." *Revue d'histoire de la Deuxième Guerre mondiale,* no. 1 (1950): 28–50.

Sanders, Paul. "Anatomie d'une implantation SS – Helmut Knochen et la police nazie en France, 1940–1944." *Revue de la Shoah,* no.165 (1999): 111–45.

Soutou, Georges-Henri, Jacques Frémaux, and Olivier Forcade, eds. *L'Exploitation du renseignement en Europe et aux États-Unis des années 1930 aux années 1960.* Paris: Économica, 2001.

Stead, Philip John. *Second Bureau.* London: Evans Brothers, 1959.

Terres, Robert. *Double jeu pour la France, 1939–1944.* Paris: Grasset, 1977.

Thomas, Martin. "Signals Intelligence and Vichy France, 1940–1944: Intelligence in Defeat." *Intelligence and National Security* 14, no. 1 (1999): 176–200.

Vittori, Jean-Pierre. *Une histoire d'honneur: La Résistance.* Paris: Ramsay, 1984.

Young, Robert J. "French Military Intelligence and Nazi Germany, 1938–1939." In *Knowing One's Enemies,* edited by Ernest R. May. Princeton, N.J.: Princeton University Press, 1984.

Zajec (Second Lieutenant). *"Travaux ruraux": Le contre-espionnage clandestin de l'armée d'armistice.* Mémoire des écoles de Coëtquidan under the direction of Olivier Forcade, 1999.

INDEX